the evolution
of the wooden ship

Basil Greenhill

the evolution
of the wooden ship

illustrations by Sam Manning

Facts On File
New York • Oxford

Text by Basil Greenhill 1988
Line drawings by Sam Manning 1988

    Facts On File, Inc.
    460 Park Avenue South
    New York, New York 10016

Greenhill, Basil.
  The evolution of the wooden ship.

  Includes Index,
  1. Ships, Wooden – History. 2. Shipbuilding – History.
3. Ship-building – History – Pictorial works. I. Manning,
Samuel F. II. Title.
VM144.C74 1989   623.8′207   88-31107
ISBN 0-8160-2121 X

First published in the U.K. in 1988 by B.T. Batsford Ltd.

Printed in Great Britain

contents

acknowledgements

This book, which has been many years in gestation, really began with a series of discussions in Appledore, North Devon in 1945 and '46 with the late Mr Fred Harris, then Managing Director of P.K. Harris & Sons Ltd, the local shipbuilders. Fred Harris had spent his whole life in wood shipbuilding and repair and it was his idea that a book like this should be written, but the book assumed its final form as a result of discussions in the early 1960s between the author and the illustrator, and later with Tom Perkins, a Master Shipwright of the old school, who rebuilt the ketch *Shamrock* at Cotehele on the Tamar in Cornwall, England, between 1975 and 1980.

We are most grateful to a number of people who have kindly read and commented upon the typescript of this book, or on parts of it within their special expertise, in the present or earlier versions. These include Professor Seán McGrail of Oxford University, who has done more than any other man in Britain to further the study of the archaeology of ships and boats; the late Captain W.J. Slade, a close friend for 30 years; Alan Hinks, Chairman of J. Hinks and Co. Ltd, of Appledore, Devon, the shipbuilders who specialize in wooden construction today; that most experienced seaman, Peter Allington, Master of the ketch *Shamrock*; Alan Viner, whose extensive contributions and suggestions were most valuable; Captain W.J. Lewis Parker, U.S.C.G. (retd.), of Camden, Maine; Mr Richard B. Gardner, of Lincolnville Beach, Maine; and Mr Nathan Lipfert, Curator, The Maine Maritime Museum at Bath, Maine. We would also like to thank the Hon. Angus McLean, formerly Premier of the Canadian Province of Prince Edward Island, who opened the door to the study of shipbuilding in Atlantic Canada; and the late Edgar Erikson and Captain Karl Kåhre, who performed a similar function in the Åland Islands of Finland. We also thank Aled Eames who has guided us in the study of the ways of the shipbuilders of North Wales; Captain Francis E. Bowker, Mystic Seaport Museum, for helpful oversight of the *Bertha L. Downs* drawings; and Mr William S. Howard, the late Josephine P. Howard, Susan Howard Manning and Ann Giffard for their assistance.

To all these, and to the dozens of other informants who made the writing of this book possible, we are most grateful. Its qualities come from their contributions, its faults are ours.

Basil Greenhill, Boetheric, Cornwall
Sam Manning, Camden, Maine

part one

---

the BACKGROUND

1 explanation

The world of the wooden sailing vessel is, of course, a world we have now completely lost. The same applies to many other specialized 'worlds' of the earlier stages of our technical and industrial development. Remembering the hardship, the squalor, the poverty, the overwork, ill health and misery often associated with them, in many ways this loss is not regrettable. But the wooden sailing ship played a great role in man's history. It developed around it special crafts and skills, so that the communities dependent on it acquired marked characteristics of their own. These simple products of men and women were capable of most remarkable achievements. It is therefore worth looking at some of the skills, ideas and practices involved in their making.

In this book Sam Manning and I, with the aid of Tom Perkins, a Master Shipwright who spent years working on wooden vessels and knew many older men who had built wooden ships, will look at some aspects of this subject in our different ways, both visually and by the written word. Wood shipbuilding is a complex subject, not only because the processes themselves were complicated, but also because there were endless variations in the details of the techniques involved, from country to country, from region to region in the same country, and even between neighbouring communities. Also, of course, practices changed over the years. There are some processes in wood shipbuilding, like that of shaping the planks to go round the outside of the hull, which cannot really be described in words. I have not tried to do this, but Sam Manning has drawn the planking process in detail and made it very understandable. This book is a little unusual in that the drawings do not always simply illustrate the text. Rather they are complementary to it, and the story is told partly in words, partly in drawings, partly in both.

To make the subject more readily comprehensible in the chapters which follow we have described the processes involved in building a small and relatively simple vessel as they were described to me by a number of men with whom I talked over a period of forty years or more. All came from the far south-west of England, and all had been involved in wood shipbuilding in the later years of the industry. Some men to whom I talked in the 1940s had been born in the 1860s and they had worked on the construction of some of the most famous sailing vessels built in the south-west of England in the 1870s. The genesis of this book therefore goes back a long way, and its particular difference from most other books on the subject is that it is based almost entirely on the oral accounts of the men who actually built wooden ships.

In this way the present study differs from those books about the building

Ship's boat for Master's schooner —

With hull planking progressing upward on the framed schooner in the River Tamar shipyard, the master builder slips into the shed for a quiet moment of experienced work at building the schooner's boat in the old way: by shaping and fastening her planks together, edge to edge, without internal moulds or pre-set framing.

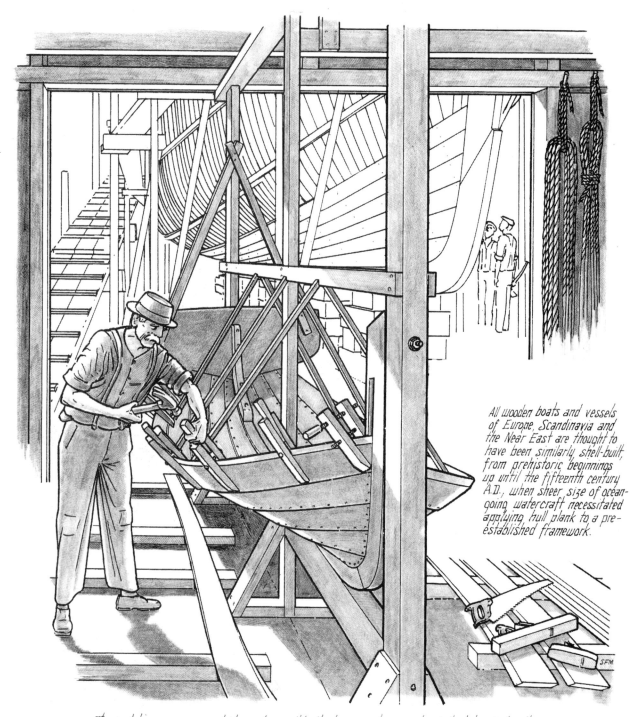

All wooden boats and vessels of Europe, Scandinavia and the Near East are thought to have been similarly shell-built, from prehistoric beginnings up until the fifteenth century A.D., when sheer size of ocean-going watercraft necessitated applying hull plank to a pre-established framework.

The evolutionary process which made possible the huge wooden vessels of the late nineteenth century (Chapters 3 through 7) is exhibited step by step in Chapter 2.

Master's schooner—

A sailing bricker and
general cargo coaster,
built on verbal contract
by a handful of men in
a small, family-operated
shipyard. River Tamar,
Cornwall, late 1880's.

Hand tools only.
Modelled by the master
builder.

Shown offloading bricks on an open beach.

of wooden ships which have tended to rely on contemporary accounts, usually written not by shipbuilders who took pen in hand and passed on knowledge of their profession but by more formally educated men – academics and bureaucrats – whose real contact with the working world of the shipbuilder was limited. Such studies can be very valuable, especially when they deal with the more academic aspects of ship design and history, but, in the words of Carl Olaf Cederlund in his splendid marine archaeological study *The Old Wrecks of the Baltic Sea*, published in Oxford in 1983:

> Today, for the ship archaeological researcher to make use of written sources of information, he must apply widely accepted critical historical analyses incorporating well developed principles. In the subject at hand intimate knowledge of the conditions and details of shipbuilding and ships is essential for proper application of critical analyses and evaluation of the information supplied by written sources.

So, on first-hand information from men who earned their livings doing the job, and not on written accounts by scholars, we have based the account in the following chapters of the building of a simple wooden ship–a small schooner–at a not quite imaginary yard in south-western England. To give an indication of the nature of the multitudinous variety of the techniques which existed we have also described in outline the building of other vessels: in North Wales, in Finland, in Canada and in the United States. In these latter cases we have described actual vessels. The schooner built in 'Master's' yard can be easily identified with a little professional detective work, but, because we cannot be sure that exactly what is described took place at every stage in the building of one particular vessel, we have not identified her.

We have tried to avoid the use of the bewildering jargon into which some writers who have endeavoured to describe wood shipbuilding in the past have only too readily retreated. We have, however, used as far as possible (and in the numerous quotations of Tom Perkins entirely) the words which were used by the men describing the essence of their lifelong skills. On the other hand, not to have used the classic terms of the sea, as we have in describing the parts of a ship, would have been as wrong as to refer to the torque-converter of a car as 'the thing that changes the gears'.

There is a second good reason for choosing to describe the building of a relatively small vessel, built in a small yard, and this is that most ships in history *were* small and were built in simple conditions. The vessels people associate with major historical events – Drake's *Golden Hind*, the *Mayflower*, all the vessels used by Captain James Cook in his voyages of the late eighteenth century which opened up the world – were small and built in what we would nowadays consider very primitive conditions. Moreover, as long as the wooden sailing ship was the normal vehicle by which the world's trade was conducted, that is, until 1865 or so, the great majority of ships were small. To give one known example, only 18 of the vessels registered at the port of Bristol in the first four decades of the nineteenth century were of 500 tons register or more. Our little vessel is therefore more typical of wooden ships throughout their history than one of the large wooden vessels developed in the mid-nineteenth century or an eighteenth-century East Indiaman. But later in the book we take a look, for the purposes of comparison, at the building of much larger vessels.

The processes of wood shipbuilding are only intelligible if the social and economic circumstances in which the vessels were produced are also described and accounted for, at least briefly. It is useless, for example, to describe the laborious methods by which rough timber from the woods was converted into shaped wooden pieces, and by which these same heavy pieces were painfully and arduousy moved into position in the growing structure of the ship, if the reader merely asks himself why capital was not invested in labour-saving machinery to speed up the work. We hope that the descriptions of the background against which the vessel was built, of the sort of men who built her, and of how they lived, will help to make intelligible something of the art and method of wood shipbuilding as it was practised in Britain, and in other countries, for about four and a half centuries before the great divide of the First World War. We do this because there is now some danger that the knowledge of how wooden ships were built will be lost. There are few full accounts of the process written in terms readily comprehensible to the ordinary interested reader. The building processes have rarely been described in a detailed, consecutive narrative, beginning with the setting up of the building place and the procurement of the timber, and ending with the launch of the completed vessel. In the second part of this book we shall attempt to do this, using terms which we hope will make this ancient and important achievement readily understandable.

M.A. James (1900) — a three-masted general cargo schooner modelled, drafted and built by a contract shipyard at Porthmadog, Wales, for the Newfoundland fish trade.

Hand tools.

Shown discharging coal by hand in a village tidal berth.

A wooden ship, even a small one, if she was to remain sound and reasonably trouble free, required the almost daily attention of one or more men. She needed all of the ceaseless care demanded by a team of draught horses – the heavy horses that once pulled wagons or field machinery – or by a herd of milking cows. To neglect her, even for a very short time, was to invite disaster. This meant that, as with a farming community, the whole pattern of life of the men connected with wooden ships, and that of their families, was shaped by the things they had to look after and by means of which they made their livings. Such communities acquired an individual flavour which transcended even national boundaries. For all the many and great differences in detail that there were between ships, shipbuilding methods, business practices and types of seafaring, the places all over the world where people depended for their livelihood on the building and operation of wooden sailing ships all had something of the same feeling about them and their people had similar approaches to their basic problems. Such people were sometimes closer to one another, even despite barriers of language, than they were with neighbouring groups whose ways of life had nothing to do with ships.

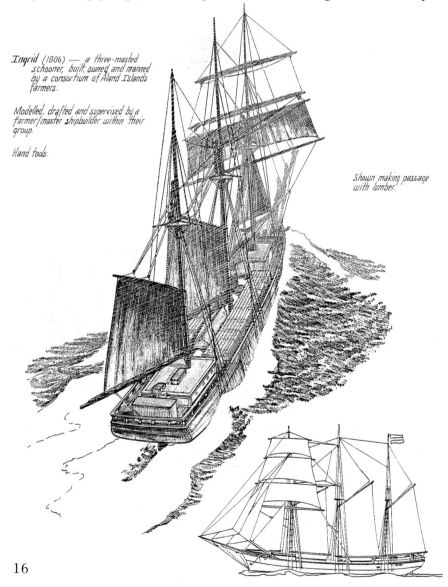

Ingrid (1906) — a three-masted schooner, built, owned and manned by a consortium of Åland Islands farmers.

Modelled, drafted and supervised by a farmer/master shipbuilder within their group.

Hand tools.

Shown making passage with lumber.

16

Shipbuilding and ship-managing communities in the era of wooden vessels, like their own seafarers but to a lesser extent, became trapped in the isolation imposed upon them by their demanding and specialized way of life. All the evidence suggests that whatever else he has been, the seafarer – and to a degree anyone associated with ships – was a man apart. Generally speaking, people, as groups or as individuals, took to the sea only when they could not live on the land. Historically, those individuals and groups who were forced off the edge of society, and became seafarers, have often been lowly regarded by their contemporaries, and these people include those who built and managed ships and lived by them as well as those who manned them. Only when societies had no real alternative to the sea for their principal source of wealth did seafaring become rationalized into a prestigious occupation. This happened in the days of the Vikings and more than once in subsequent Scandinavian history; it also hapened from time to time in some areas of Britain, New England and Atlantic Canada, as well as elsewhere in the world.

Victoria — a three-masted barque, 1872. Built of local softwoods on the beach at Prince Edward Island by farmer/shipwrights working off debt to the merchant and shipyard owner.

Hand tools only.

Shown loading timber, salt fish, and Island produce in a roadstead berth.

17

*Bertha L. Downs, Maine, 1908
— a New England coal schooner.*

It is perhaps for these reasons that knowledge of the history of seafaring and of ships is seldom part of the cultural awareness of the ordinary educated person today. The seaman's world was not merely remote from the landsman, it was positively alien to him unless the landsman made a very serious study

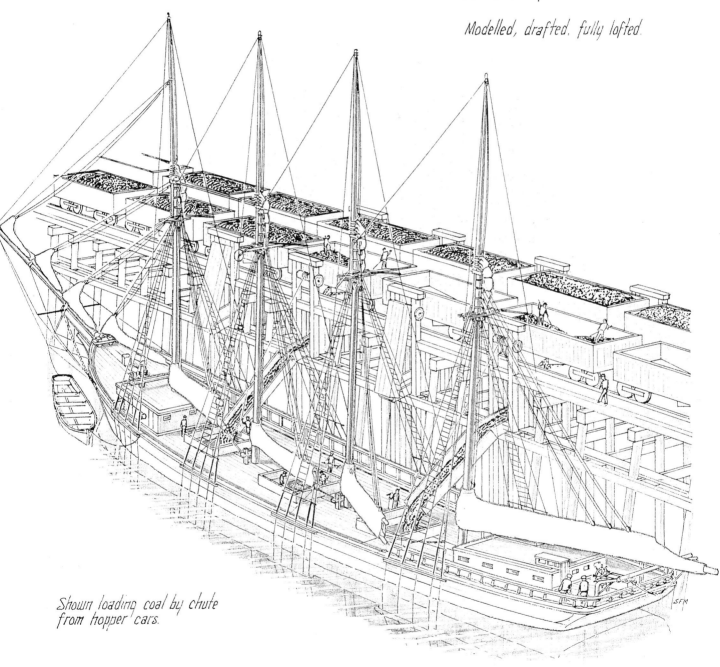

Built with shipyard machinery, from imported timber, in a series of sub-contracted operations.

Modelled, drafted, fully lofted.

Shown loading coal by chute from hopper cars.

of it. For a complex of reasons, of which the isolation and alienation of the seafarer and of those who lived in the necessary 'shore support culture' is one of the most significant, the maritime aspects of history, vastly important as they are, have been seriously neglected.

Even in the late nineteenth century there were dozens of communities all around the coastlines of Europe and North Eastern America the whole living of which was centred around the building and operation of wooden sailing ships. This was the period of the high flowering of the crafts of wood and hemp, and of the building, managing and handling of wooden sailing ships and boats. It was a period when the particular skills of individual shipwrights, seamen and ship managers were probably at their most highly developed stage. But by the end of the 1870s, except in North America, where the great development of multi-masted wooden schooners still had a long way to go, the wooden sailing ship was in decline. She was made obsolete by three associated developments: the compound and the triple expansion marine steam engine; iron-, and later steel-, shipbuilding made possible by the production of cheap iron and steel plates in the quantities (and of the minimum quality) necessary; and changes in the scale and methods of industry and finance. But the wooden sailing ship was in fact an unconscionable long time a – dying. Small wooden sailing ships survived in Britain and Northern Europe until the middle of the twentieth century, when road transport delivered the *coup de grâce*.

Wooden sailing ships could be built and maintained entirely within the resources of a local community, whether rural or urban. As in the sixteenth century so in the early twentieth there was nothing in their structure which could not be made of wood by ships' carpenters, out of iron by the local foundry and the local blacksmith, or out of natural fibre and textiles in the ropewalk and in the sail loft. The vessels could be maintained, except where major structural repairs were needed, by their own crews, who acquired the necessary skills by precept and example while they were still boys and young men.

We begin with a brief account of the history of the wooden ship from classical antiquity to the invention of the sailing ship in the 1400s, dealing in some detail with the technical changes and developments which gave rise, in the later 1500s, to the evolution of the wooden ship in the form in which it was known in the years of its ascendancy – that is, until well into the second half of the last century.

2 the evolution of the wooden ship

The vessels of classical antiquity

The history of the wooden ship stretches back at least 30,000 years. Though no identified archaeological remains of such early craft have so far been discovered, pre-historians know now that by this period men had the skills necessary to build rafts of logs, and some kind of boat or raft must have been used to take men to Australia even before then. Ten thousand years ago, cargo boats made of skin stretched on frames and boats of various kinds made by hollowing out logs with fire and with stone tools were well within European man's technical capabilities.

The hollowed-out log was the invention of the greatest significance. Soften the hollowed out log by charring it or soaking it in water heated by the immersion of red-hot stones and then force its sides apart to produce a broader cross-section – giving greater stability to the finished craft – and the ends rise to give the 'sheer', the sweeping curve we have come to associate with almost all boats and ships until about the middle of the twentieth century. By adding planks of timber to the sides it was possible to extend the log-boat almost indefinitely – even into a seagoing ship. Though there is no archaeological evidence, it is possible that the earliest seaborne trade so far positively identified, the carrying of obsidian from the Island of Melos to the mainland of Greece, 10 to 12,000 years ago, was conducted in log-boats of some kind.

By 3000 B.C. sophisticated wooden ships were trading, and fighting, all over the eastern Mediterranean – from Cairo to Syria and the Levant and right through the Aegean. These vessels appear to have been of two principal kinds, and classical scholars have categorized them as 'long ships' and 'round ships'. Generally speaking, the long ships were vessels of war, and round ships were merchantmen. This categorization of vessels by their proportions holds good for more than 3000 years, from the beginning of the Bronze Age in the Mediterranean area to the end of the Roman Empire. There are intervals during this long period of seafaring activity when, relatively, we know a great deal about the ships which were being used.

The oldest surviving ship in the world dates from c.2650 B.C. She is so-called 'Cheops Ship', a huge Egyptian river-boat, 43.4 metres long and almost six broad, found in a pit by the side of a pyramid. Contemporary models, found in tombs, and numerous wall drawings and reliefs, make it possible to follow the history of the ships and boats of the Egyptians for 2000 or more years. We know, for instance, that the Egyptians had developed rowing, as distinct from paddling, as a method of propulsion as early as 2400 B.C.

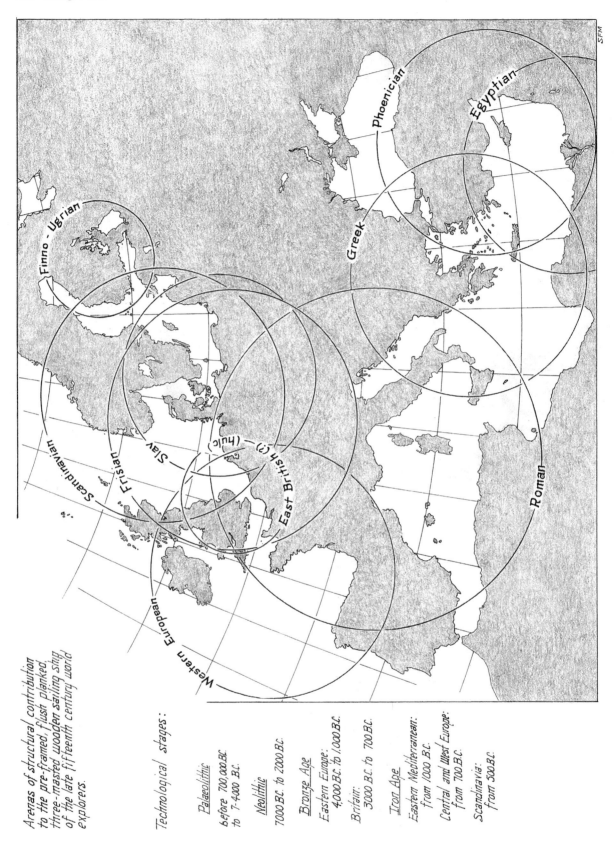

Areas of structural contribution to the pre-framed, flush planked, three-masted wooden sailing ship of the late fifteenth century world explorers.

Technological stages:

Palaeolithic
before 700,000 B.C. to 7-4000 B.C.

Neolithic
7000 B.C. to 2000 B.C.

Bronze Age
Eastern Europe:
4,000 B.C. to 1,000 B.C.
Britain:
3000 B.C. to 700 B.C.

Iron Age
Eastern Mediterranean:
from 1000 B.C.
Central and West Europe:
from 700 B.C.
Scandinavia:
from 500 B.C.

Beginnings — (Palaeolithic period) —

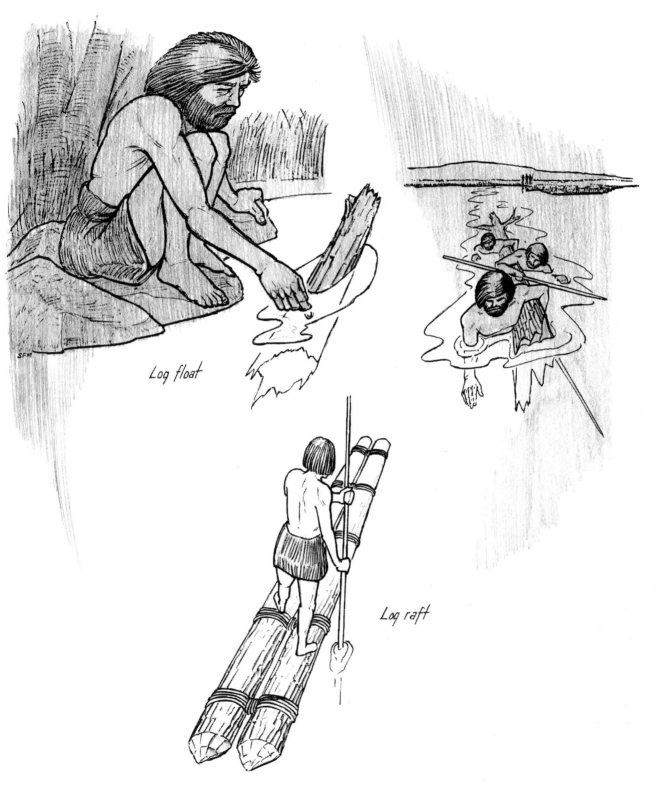

Log float

Log raft

Hollowed-out log — (Neolithic period) —

Systems historically employed to deepen or widen the dug out trunk of a tree to achieve a faster boat or a more seakindly carrier.

Logboat split and widened

Logboat extended with plank

Logboat

Logboat hollowed for expanding

Softened and spread

Expanded logboat

There is no archaeological evidence for prehistoric improvement of the basic logboat as pictured here. There is strong evidence, however, that splitting, extending and expanding of logboats was widespread in prehistoric times.

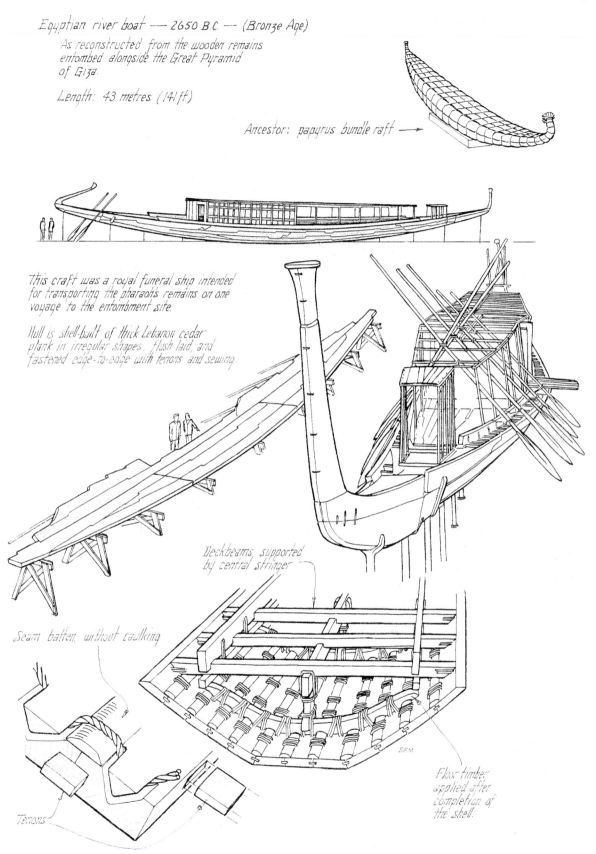

Egyptian river boat — 2650 B.C. — (Bronze Age)

As reconstructed from the wooden remains entombed alongside the Great Pyramid of Giza.

Length: 43 metres (141 ft.)

Ancestor: papyrus bundle raft →

This craft was a royal funeral ship intended for transporting the pharoah's remains on one voyage to the entombment site.

Hull is shell-built of thick Lebanon cedar plank in irregular shapes, flush laid, and fastened edge-to-edge with tenons and sewing.

Deckbeams, supported by central stringer

Seam batten, without caulking

Tenons

Floor timber applied after completion of the shell.

SFM

25

Round ships and long ships ——(Bronze Age)——

Three-dimensional interpretation of the round and long ships shown in plane silhouette on an Attic black-figure cup in the British Museum.

Greek merchantman fifth century B.C.

Greek triakontor (30 oars) fifth century B.C.)

floor timber (spike-trunnelled, through planking only)

passive frame (spike-trunnelled)

lead sheathing

draw-tenon

copper spike driven through pine trunnel, with point double-bent or "clenched"

Backbone section, fourth century B.C. Kyrenia Ship, as ascertained from a photo of the reconstructed midsection, and from description of the recovered wreck by Michael L. Katzev.

The ships of Mycenaean Greece, of the period described in the account of the siege and fall of Troy, were light long ships for transporting troops, meant to be put ashore each night. There was no conception of fighting at sea at this time. These were great, open boats, rowed by fifty oarsmen. The *Iliad*, the account of the fall of Troy, is now believed to be a compilation of memories of many events, spread over the several hundred years preceding its composition in the eighth century B.C., at which time two tiers of oars were being introduced. Contemporary illustrative material, usually in the form of drawings on vases, reveals a great deal about the Mediterranean vessels of this period. One of the finest illustrations, on the so-called 'Francois vase' dating from *c*.600–500 B.C., gives an excellent impression of what the smaller eastern Mediterranean vessels looked like at this time.

In a relief of the latter part of the seventh century B.C. found in Nineveh there is unequivocal evidence of the existence of ships with two tiers of oars, one above the other, and such vessels, together with 'round ships', almost certainly merchantmen, are very finely illustrated on a black-figured cup in the British Museum dating from this period. Almost at once, it appears, two tiers of oars led on to three and thus was born the trireme, beloved of nautically-minded classical scholars and classically-minded amateur ship historians alike as a subject of apparently inexhaustible controversy. This invention was probably made at Corinth, perhaps even as early as 700 B.C., and it emerged from the necessity to suppress the endemic piracy faced by a great trading nation. There followed what John Morrison, the leading authority in the world on this subject, and one of the principals behind the construction of a replica of the trireme, has called 'The Age of the Trireme'.

The age of the trireme

Triremes were large and expensive vessels. Their use developed as the economies of the Greek Mediterranean societies evolved and more resources, money, manpower and materials became available to meet the real threats at sea from Persia and Carthage. The trireme, with her necessarily enormous crew and her vulnerability, was not an economic proposition, but many important weapons of war, essential for the maintenance of the appearance of power and of international prestige, have been equally unrelated to the facts of real value for money, and the trireme ruled the seas in the Athenian fleet for almost 150 years, from the early fifth century to the second half of the fourth century B.C. It was with massed triremes, used as missiles, their warheads being the rams at the bows, that the Athenians defeated the combined Phoenician, Ionian Greek and Egyptian fleets at Salamis in 480 B.C. in a battle which determined that the eastern Mediterranean world would remain predominantly a Greek area of influence for several more centuries.

The prolonged arguments about the trireme centre on the way in which the oars and oarsmen were arranged. We shall not go into the complex evidence available here; the proper appreciation of it requires an understanding of ancient Greek rare in the modern world, combined with a practical approach to the problems involved. At the National Maritime Museum in London a symposium was held in the spring of 1983 at which the participants

Greek trireme — fifth century B.C. — (Bronze Age)

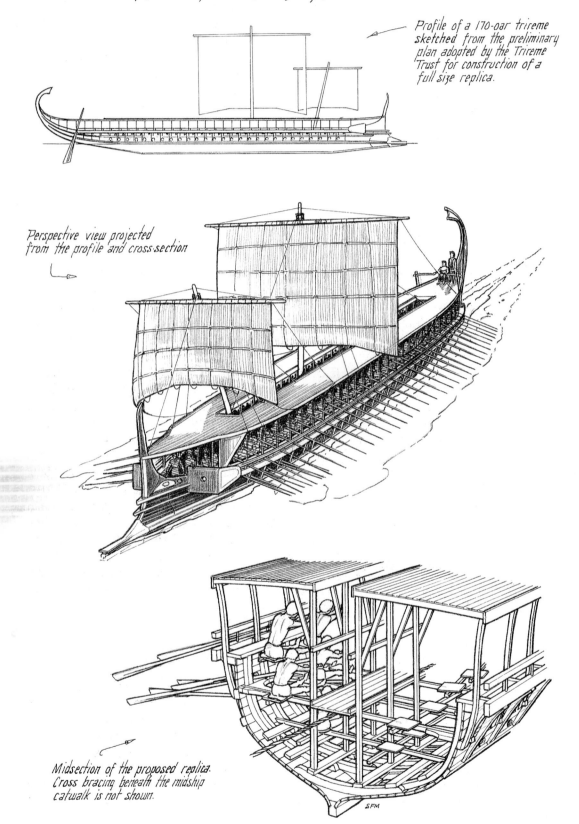

Profile of a 170-oar trireme sketched from the preliminary plan adopted by the Trireme Trust for construction of a full size replica.

Perspective view projected from the profile and cross-section.

Midsection of the proposed replica. Cross bracing beneath the midship catwalk is not shown.

varied from Greek scholars of distinction to equally distinguished naval architects. The resultant hypothetical solutions to the problem of reconstructing a trireme from the available (mostly literary) evidence indicated in the drawing, are unlikely to be improved upon in the near future, though the subject will without doubt continue to be argued, probably indefinitely.

The trireme was followed by even more complex vessels. The problem of applying the power generated by three tiers of oarsmen had been solved by the use of the outrigger. The power was increased by putting two men on each oar of one of the three tiers of oars on each side. In due course two men were put on each oar on two of the three tiers of a trireme to make what was called a quinquereme.

Merchant vessels

These fighting vessels were not by any stretch of imagination economically viable as merchantmen. Though the 50-oared single-bank rowing vessel had room for cargo and passengers the merchant activity which went on in the eastern Mediterranean for a thousand years, interrupted only by periods of intensive piracy or of war, and which provided wealth for the power politics of the nations involved, was conducted in 'round' ships. These vessels appear to have changed little in the course of the centuries, though they grew in size.

As almost always in history, those who wrote the records were interested more in political and military power than in the trade which was the basis of that power, but with the merchant vessels we have at least some archaeological evidence to work with. In the twelfth century B.C. Phoenicians from the coasts of what are now Syria, the Lebanon and Israel traded all over the Mediterranean and beyond Gibraltar. Later, the Greeks competed with them and in due course established a trading area reaching from the Black Sea to the eastern coasts of Spain. Their wooden round ships, about 50 feet long and able to carry 100 to 150 metric tons of cargo, brought the grain on which Athens was dependent for her food supplies from the Black Sea, and moved also all the luxuries of the Mediterranean to which Athenians became accustomed during a great era of prosperity. The eventual ascendency of Rome and her dependence on grain imported from Egypt, a seasonal trade, led to the building of bigger and bigger round ships which may in the end have carried as much as 450 tons of cargo.

The construction of the vessels of classical antiquity

All the planked vessels referred to so far in this text, covering more than 3000 years in less than that number of words, had one thing in common. They were constructed by building a shell of planks joined together at the edges, usually with wooden dowels, or with a mortice and tenon fastening, and into this shell, at an advanced stage of its construction were inserted strengthening frames shaped to fit the shell. The boat was conceived and designed within the shell. This 'edge-fastened shell construction', one small possible hint from Herodotus apart, was the sole method of building vessels

Roman merchantman, first century A.D. — (Iron Age)

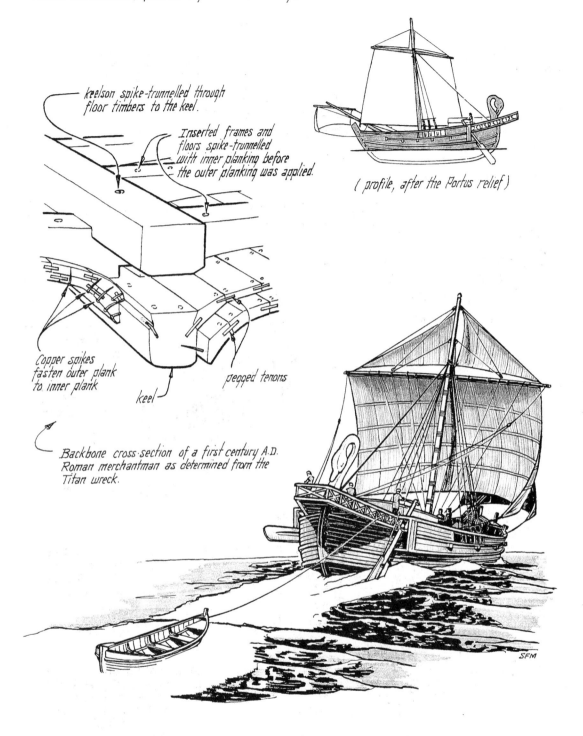

keelson spike-trunnelled through
floor timbers to the keel.

Inserted frames and
floors spike-trunnelled
with inner planking before
the outer planking was applied.

(profile, after the Portus relief)

Copper spikes
fasten outer plank
to inner plank

keel

pegged tenons

Backbone cross-section of a first century A.D.
Roman merchantman as determined from the
Titan wreck.

SFM

30

"Shell" construction —

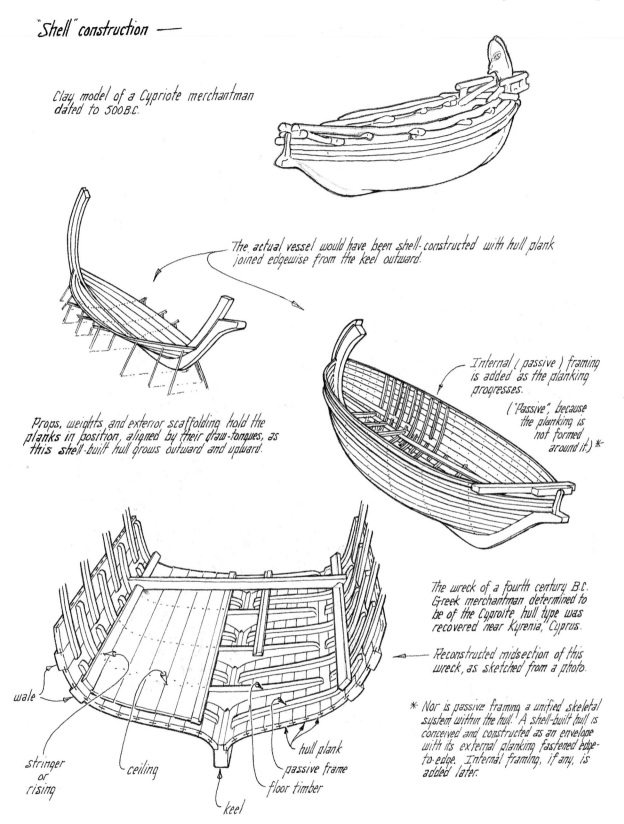

Clay model of a Cypriote merchantman dated to 500 B.C.

The actual vessel would have been shell-constructed with hull plank joined edgewise from the keel outward.

Props, weights and exterior scaffolding hold the planks in position, aligned by their draw-tongues, as this shell-built hull grows outward and upward.

Internal (passive) framing is added as the planking progresses.

("Passive", because the planking is not formed around it.) *

The wreck of a fourth century B.C. Greek merchantman determined to be of the Cyproite hull type was recovered near Kyrenia, Cyprus.

— Reconstructed midsection of this wreck, as sketched from a photo.

* Nor is passive framing a unified skeletal system within the hull. A shell-built hull is conceived and constructed as an envelope with its external planking fastened edge-to-edge. Internal framing, if any, is added later.

wale

stringer or rising

ceiling

keel

floor timber

passive frame

hull plank

throughout the classical period in the Mediterranean, and indeed it appears from available archaeological evidence that it persisted as the sole method of shipbuilding for centuries after the fall of Rome.

One fact is essential to understanding the history of the wooden ship – that is, the history of almost all shipping until the 1860s when cheap iron plates in dimensions suitable for shipbuilding became readily available for the first time. To put it very simply, in the last five centuries there have been two great classes of boat and ship in the world. There were boats and ships built of planks fastened edge-to-edge and also usually, but not always, joined to strengthening frames, and boats and ships built of planks which were not joined edge-to-edge, but only to the supporting framework inside the boat. This is a fundamental distinction of the greatest importance.

The first of these categories was, it appears, predominant the world over until the development of the second, which took place on a large scale, it seems, somewhere in western Europe as late as the 1300s and 1400s, though there had been earlier indications of gropings towards intermediate forms of construction as early as the seventh century and even before. Over a great deal of the world shell construction remained predominant as long as boats and ships were built of wood. The great majority of plank-built boats and ships in the history of man have been conceived and constructed as shells of planks joined together at their edges, their building an act which has been described as akin to that of sculpture.

There were many variations in the ways in which the building was actually done. But the fundamental fact is that the evidence presently available indicates that the builders of almost all boats and ships until the fifteenth century A.D., and the builders of a great many of the world's ships and almost all its boats for five centuries more, constructed them as continuous watertight envelopes of planks, perhaps built up on the base provided by the sides of a log-boat. They were shaped so that the submerged parts would pass through the water as easily as possible in relation to what was required of the boat; in its ability to carry goods and people, to be seaworthy in the waters in which she was built to operate, to meet local requirements for operation, and to be built cheaply and easily from readily available local materials.

At some late stage in the construction of most of these boats some internal strengthening was added, to keep the boats permanently in shape and to strengthen them against the stresses a vessel has to undergo from the workings of the sea, from heavy cargo, and from the strains imposed by beaching, etc. This strengthening usually took the form of a frame, resembling a ribcage. These 'shell-built' boats and ships all had one characteristic in common: the 'strakes', the long runs of joined-up planking that made up their sides, were fastened together edge-to-edge, in one way or another, and a great deal of the strength of the finished vessel was derived from this form of fastening.

The edge-to-edge fastening of boats and ships of classical antiquity may have made a smaller contribution to the total strength of the vessel than that of some later, north European, traditions. A large part of the general strength here may have come from the 'wales', heavy strakes built relatively high up within the structure. The vessels were nevertheless conceived and constructed as shells into which frames, shaped to fit the shell, were inserted.

32

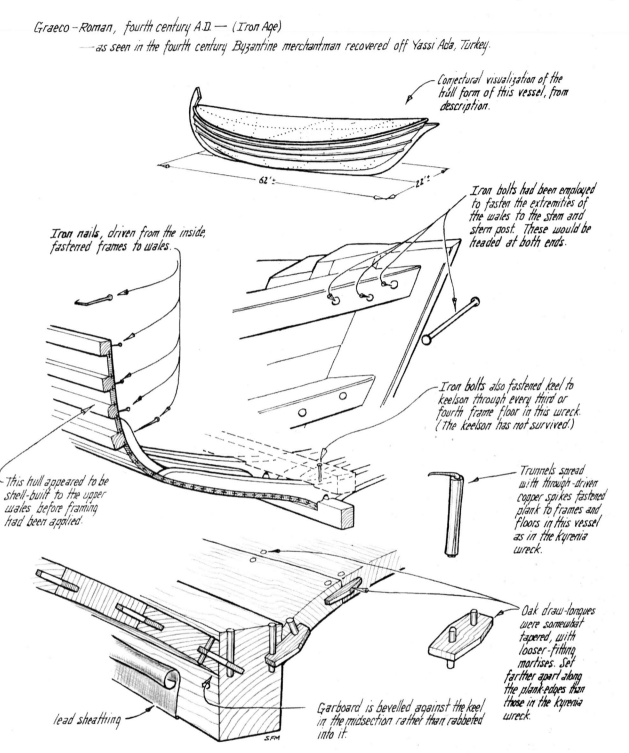

Graeco-Roman, fourth century A.D. — (Iron Age)
— *as seen in the fourth century Byzantine merchantman recovered off Yassi Ada, Turkey.*

Conjectural visualization of the hull form of this vessel, from description.

62'±

22'±

Iron bolts had been employed to fasten the extremities of the wales to the stem and stern post. These would be headed at both ends.

Iron nails, driven from the inside, fastened frames to wales.

Iron bolts also fastened keel to keelson through every third or fourth frame floor in this wreck. (The keelson has not survived.)

This hull appeared to be shell-built to the upper wales before framing had been applied.

Trunnels spread with through-driven copper spikes fastened plank to frames and floors in this vessel as in the Kyrenia wreck.

Oak draw-tongues were somewhat tapered, with looser-fitting mortises. Set farther apart along the plank-edges than those in the Kyrenia wreck.

lead sheathing

Garboard is bevelled against the keel in the midsection rather than rabbeted into it.

S.F.M.

33

Hull structure of a seventh century A.D. Greek/Byzantine merchantman — Iron Age — as ascertained from photos and description of the seventh century A.D. Yassi Ada wreck.

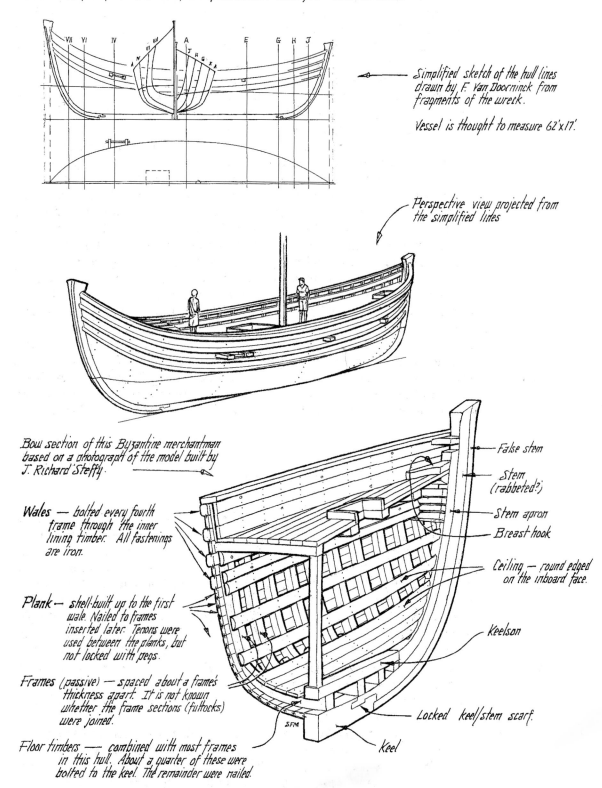

— Simplified sketch of the hull lines drawn by F. Van Doorninck from fragments of the wreck.

Vessel is thought to measure 62'x17'.

Perspective view projected from the simplified lines

Bow section of this Byzantine merchantman based on a photograph of the model built by J. Richard Steffy.

Wales — bolted every fourth frame through the inner lining timber. All fastenings are iron.

Plank — shell-built up to the first wale. Nailed to frames inserted later. Tenons were used between the planks, but not locked with pegs.

Frames (passive) — spaced about a frame's thickness apart. It is not known whether the frame sections (futtocks) were joined.

Floor timbers — combined with most frames in this hull. About a quarter of these were bolted to the keel. The remainder were nailed.

— False stem

— Stem (rabbeted?)

— Stem apron

— Breast-hook

— Ceiling — round edged on the inboard face.

— Keelson

— Locked keel/stem scarf.

— Keel

SFM

The ships and boats of southern Europe until A.D. 1300

In this brief account of the history of the wooden ship I am covering several thousands of years in a few thousand words and with the aid of Sam Manning's detailed drawings. It is necessary, therefore, to pick the important main trends of development out of a very complex story. Fortunately, the main themes are fairly readily apparent, and become clearer as the centuries go by. The development of wooden boats and ships was slow, but there were periods of rapid change when economic and social circumstance brought technical changes in vessel construction, and with them the ascendancy of a particular building tradition.

After the fall of Rome, the Mediterranean traditions of the long ship and the round ship continued. Archaeological evidence of the construction of ships in the medieval period in the Mediterranean area is available, from two finds in particular. These comprise the wrecks of a fourth-century vessel excavated at Yassi Adda in Turkey and of a seventh-century vessel found nearby. The first is in the Graeco-Roman tradition; the second, together with a wreck found in Sicily in 1964, also dated to the seventh century, may give some indication of the beginnings of a new building technique in which a vessel's main strength depends less on the edge fastenings of the planking and more on the internal framing. The frames are more massive than in earlier vessels and, more importantly, the fastenings which join the strakes together are as much as 9 cm apart in the hull below the waterline, giving little strength to the structure. Above the waterline the strakes are not edge-fastened, but joined only to the frames. It can be inferred from this that the shape of the lower part of the hull was conceived and created in the shell, but that the strength of the whole, and the form of the upper parts, where the shape of the hull is relatively simple, were derived from the frames.

The boats and ships of the north until the end of the Roman Empire

By the time of the Bronze Age in northern Europe (2500–1000 B.C.) men were technically capable of building sophisticated plank-built boats. Some Scandinavian rock carvings from the Bronze Age are believed by a number of scholars to represent plank-built boats, but the earliest actual structures of this kind found anywhere in the world outside Egypt were discovered in England, on the north bank of the River Humber, in 1937. A great deal of work on this find was done in the 1970s and early 1980s by E. V. Wright in association with the, now sadly disbanded, Archaeological Research Centre of the National Maritime Museum, headed by Professor Seán McGrail. Three boats have been located – to date – on a site which may well represent a landing place of a type familiar in many eastern countries even today, where use over many years results in a beach littered with old boats, parts of boats and general maritime debris.

Dating from the middle of the second millenium B.C., contemporary with the second stage of Stonehenge, these boats were almost flat-bottomed with two side-strakes, the ends closed with transoms. Built with prodigious use of wood – it has been calculated that the log from which the keel plank of one

Lateen rig

Settee rig

Sprit rig

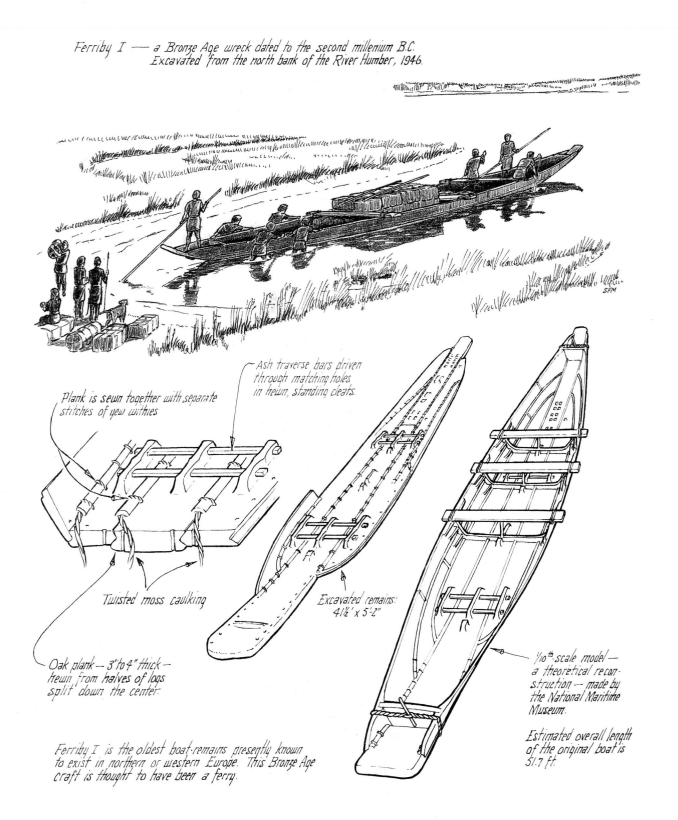

Ferriby I — a Bronze Age wreck dated to the second millenium B.C.
Excavated from the north bank of the River Humber, 1946.

Ash traverse bars driven through matching holes in hewn, standing cleats.

Plank is sewn together with separate stitches of yew withies

Twisted moss caulking

Excavated remains: 41½' x 5'-2"

¹⁄₁₀ᵗʰ scale model — a theoretical reconstruction — made by the National Maritime Museum.

Estimated overall length of the original boat is 51.7 ft.

Oak plank — 3" to 4" thick — hewn from halves of logs split down the center.

Ferriby I is the oldest boat-remains presently known to exist in northern or western Europe. This Bronze Age craft is thought to have been a ferry.

37

Brigg "raft" — 600 B.C. — (Iron Age)

Built in the same pre-Roman British tradition as Ferriby I, but a thousand years later. Probably this was a scow-type boat for river transport.

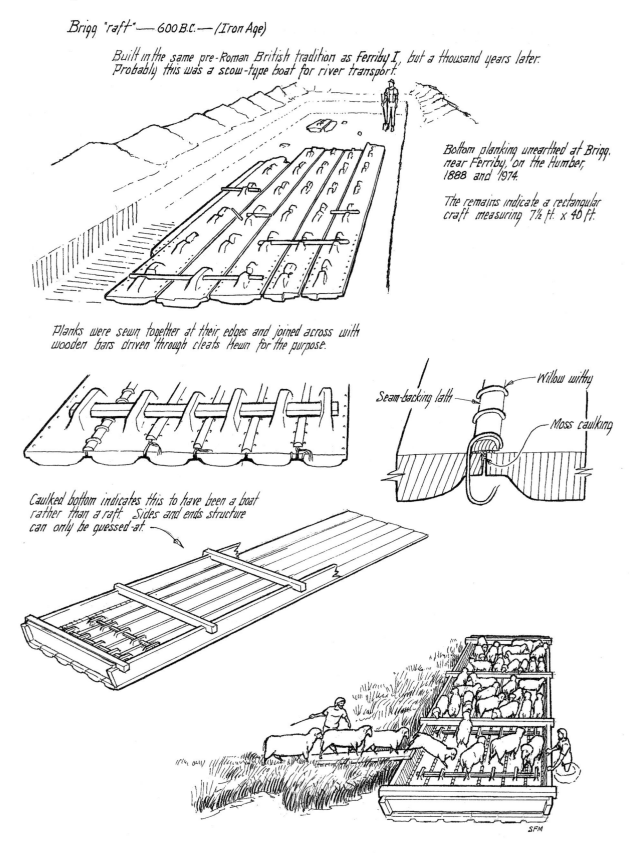

Bottom planking unearthed at Brigg, near Ferriby, on the Humber, 1888 and 1974.

The remains indicate a rectangular craft measuring 7½ ft. x 46 ft.

Planks were sewn together at their edges and joined across with wooden bars driven through cleats hewn for the purpose.

Willow withy

Seam-backing lath

Moss caulking

Caulked bottom indicates this to have been a boat rather than a raft. Sides and ends structure can only be guessed-at.

SFM

Principal groupings of hull structure — 500 B.C. to 500 A.D. — as suggested by archaeological boat-finds in northern Europe.

Pre-Roman Britain (Humber estuary) —

Flat bottom, stiffened by transverse bars, backed seams.
Flush plank joined at the edges by sewing.
Shell-built
Sheltered water.

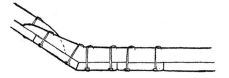

Roman Britain, west Europe —

Flat bottomed, no keel.
Bottom and first side plank spiked to floor timbers.
Topside planking spiked to independent side timbers.
Sheltered water.

Mediterranean influence —

Flat, or round bottom
keel, or no keel
Flush plank edge-joined by tenons or draw-tongues
Topside wales, internal stringers
Keelson atop floors
Spiked trunnels and headed bolts
Shell-built.

Baltic —

Round bottom, no keel
Lapped plank, edge-joined by sewing
Green-bent frames lashed to raised plank-cleats
Shell-built
Sheltered water.

39

of the boats was cut must have been over a metre in diameter – these boats were an enormous development on the hollowed-out log boat and demonstrate very sophisticated craftmanship. The strakes are fastened edge-to-edge with lashings of green yew. In the same group is a much later boat, dating from *c.*700–650 B.C., excavated at Brigg on the south shore of the Humber, almost opposite Ferriby. Built in the same general tradition as the Ferriby boats, it probably resembled when complete a scow type river boat similar to the Polish garbet of today. The Ferriby boats were probably used as watermen's boats in the Humber estuary and the considerable area of shallow waters which spread on either side of it in the period during which they were built. They were paddled, or in shallow waters poled, along.

Log-boats dating from as early as the third millenium B.C. have been found on the mainland of Europe, and a log boat dated early in the second millenium has been found in Scotland, but the archaeological, iconographic and literary evidence for the development of the boat in northern Europe between the Ferriby boats and the centuries immediately before the Christian era is almost non-existent, particularly in comparison with the rich evidence for developments in the Mediterranean over the same 1500 years. Only after 500 B.C. does evidence, in the form of remains of boats, begin to become available, and even then it is very sparse. Boat remains, found in Yugoslavia, the Netherlands, Belgium, Germany, Switzerland, France and the south-east of Britain, notably at Blackfriars, give us a certain amount of information about the plank-built boats and ships used in northern Europe over the thousand years between 500 B.C. and A.D. 500.

It appears that there were four principal groups of vessels, two of them flat-bottomed and associated with inland or sheltered water navigation – one group built of planks sewn together at the edges with natural fibres of one kind or another, and the other built of planks not fastened at the edges. The third group comprised boats, built in a tradition perhaps imported from the Mediterranean, in which the vessel, round-hulled or flat-bottomed, was built of planks edge-fastened by wooden pins or tenons. The fourth and last group was quite different, the ancestor of what was to become a great tradition in the northern part of Europe as long as vessels were built of wood. Although only one example has been discovered from this early period (on the Island of Als in southern Denmark), we can assume that these vessels were built of planks fastened at the edges by sewing, but with the edges of the planks overlapping one another.

The migration period and the Viking era

It was this last style of building which was to blossom forth in a multiplicity of variations to comprise the mainstream of European shipbuilding for six or seven centuries. At the same time, however, two other strong local building traditions were to develop which would eventually largely replace it. The boat or ship built of planks overlapped at the edges and fastened together was to develop into the much vaunted Viking ship in all its various forms.

Six archaeological finds give some indications of the process by which this may have happened, though evidence from this early period is far too scanty

The Blackfriars ship — second century A.D. — (Iron Age)

Dug from the Thames at London, 1962. Believed to have been a sailing barge with single mast and square sail. This vessel's hull structure may reflect a pre-Roman, native-British boat-building technique which continued to be practiced during the era of Roman occupation.

Estimated length: 55'
        breadth: 22'
        depth: 7'

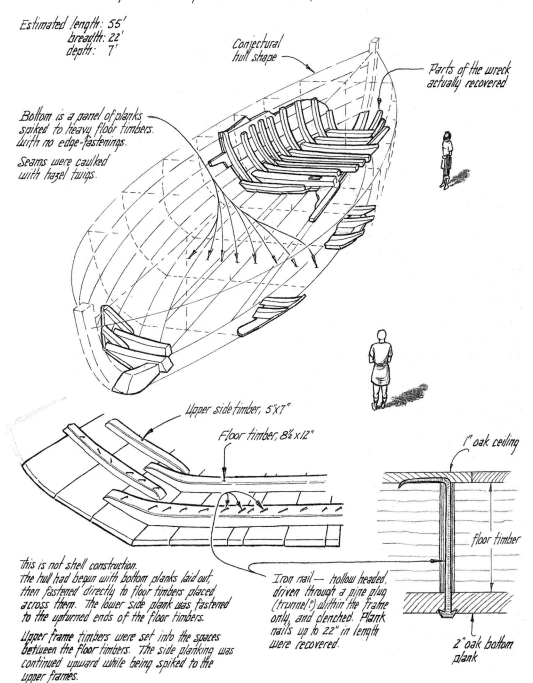

Conjectural hull shape

Parts of the wreck actually recovered

Bottom is a panel of planks spiked to heavy floor timbers with no edge-fastenings.

Seams were caulked with hazel twigs.

Upper side timber, 5"x7"

Floor timber, 8½"x12"

1" oak ceiling

floor timber

2" oak bottom plank

This is not shell construction. The hull had begun with bottom planks laid out, then fastened directly to floor timbers placed across them. The lower side plank was fastened to the upturned ends of the floor timbers.

Upper frame timbers were set into the spaces between the floor timbers. The side planking was continued upward while being spiked to the upper frames.

Iron nail — hollow headed, driven through a pine plug (trunnel?) within the frame only, and clenched. Plank nails up to 22" in length were recovered.

(This drawing is based upon diagrams attributed to Peter Marsden, excavator of the wreck.)

41

Hjortspring Boat —— c.500 B.C. –300 B.C. —

A shell-built Baltic Bronze Age war canoe excavated on the island of Als, Denmark,
in 1921. The oldest known boat-find with overlapping planks. Entirely sewn.
Length: 52½ ft.   Paddled.

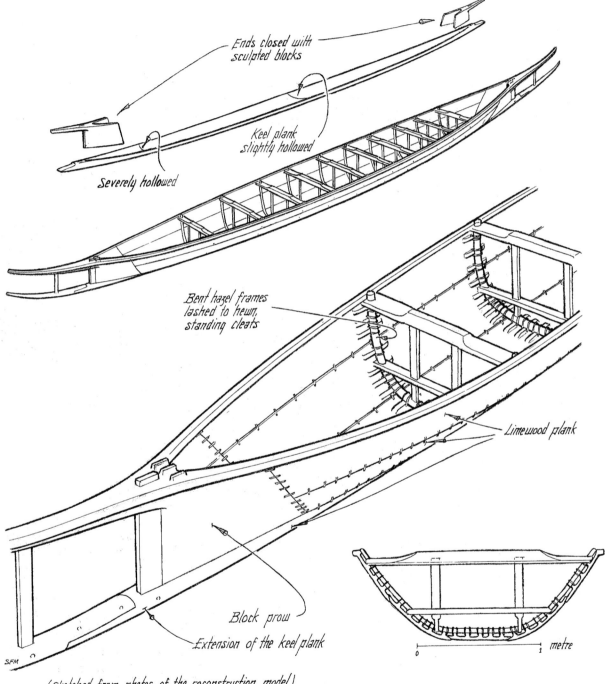

Ends closed with
sculpted blocks

Keel plank
slightly hollowed

Severely hollowed

Bent hazel frames
lashed to hewn,
standing cleats

Limewood plank

Block prow

Extension of the keel plank

metre

(Sketched from photos of the reconstruction model)

42

The Nydam oak boat — A.D. 350-400 — 75 ft. x 11 ft.

Excavated at Nydam, south Jutland, 1864.
Shell-built with nearly full-length plank. Oak throughout.
Earliest recovered oared boat native to northern Europe.
First example of rivet-fastened lap work.

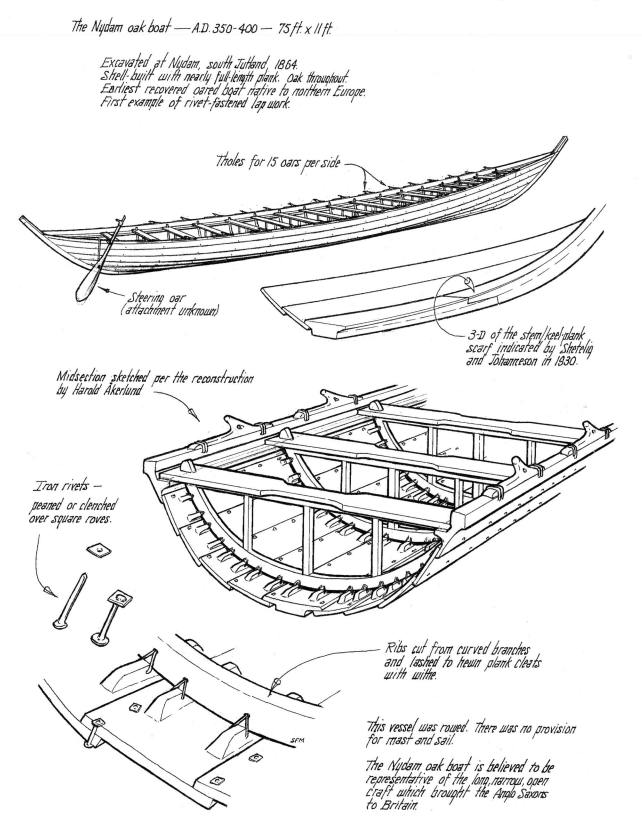

Tholes for 15 oars per side

Steering oar
(attachment unknown)

3-D of the stem/keel-plank
scarf indicated by Shetelig
and Johanneson in 1930.

Midsection sketched per the reconstruction
by Harold Åkerlund

Iron rivets —
peaned or clenched
over square roves.

Ribs cut from curved branches
and lashed to hewn plank cleats
with withe.

This vessel was rowed. There was no provision
for mast and sail.

The Nydam oak boat is believed to be
representative of the long, narrow, open
craft which brought the Anglo Saxons
to Britain.

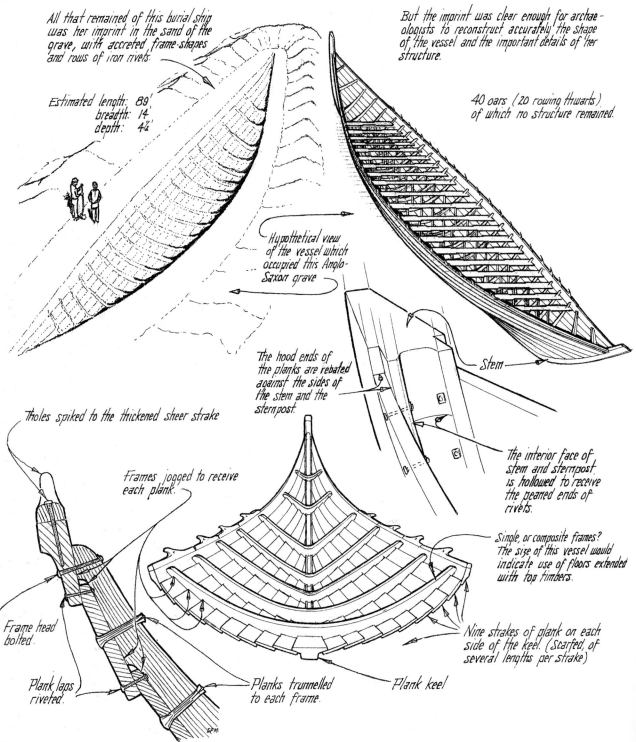

Sutton Hoo ship — A.D. 600 — excavated 1939, 1965-7 — pre-Viking

This vessel is believed to represent the state-of-art boatbuilding technique in the North at the time Britain was occupied by Angles, Saxons, and Jutes.

All that remained of this burial ship was her imprint in the sand of the grave, with accreted frame-shapes and rows of iron rivets.

But the imprint was clear enough for archaeologists to reconstruct accurately the shape of the vessel and the important details of her structure.

Estimated length: 89'
breadth: 14'
depth: 4½'

40 oars (20 rowing thwarts) of which no structure remained.

Hypothetical view of the vessel which occupied this Anglo-Saxon grave

The hood ends of the planks are rebated against the sides of the stem and the sternpost.

Stem

The interior face of stem and sternpost is hollowed to receive the peaned ends of rivets.

Tholes spiked to the thickened sheer strake

Frames jogged to receive each plank.

Single, or composite frames? The size of this vessel would indicate use of floors extended with top timbers.

Frame head bolted.

Nine strakes of plank on each side of the keel. (Scarfed, of several lengths per strake)

Plank laps riveted.

Planks trunnelled to each frame.

Plank keel

44

to make any firm statements. These finds, ranging from the great ship discovered, with its precious contents, as an 'image' in the sand at Sutton Hoo, near Woodbridge in Suffolk, to fragments of a vessel found at Gretstedbro in Denmark, were all built of planks which overlapped at the edges, fastened by iron nails driven through the plank edges and clenched over 'roves' (metal washers). From this practice the name 'clench', 'clencher' or 'clinker' was given to this style of building in the Germanic languages which have contributed so much to modern English, and it is still often used, wrongly, to describe a plastic boat moulded with serrated sides, somewhat resembling a wooden clinker-built boat.

All these finds, which include the famous Nydam boat now preserved at the Schloss Gottorp in Schleswig, demonstrate the use of a central keel-plank rather than a keel. The later boats have more and narrower strakes than the earlier; they also have frames fastened to the planking with wooden pins – 'treenails' – rather than with lashings to lugs or cleats left standing proud when the planks were finished after being split out of the log, as with the earlier boats. All these boats of the pre-Viking and Viking period were built of planks split out of the tree, not cut out with saws.

With the coming of Scandinavian expansion in the late eighth century A.D. this clinker-building tradition began to develop in what are now Sweden, Denmark and Norway. Because of numerous archaeological discoveries, rigorously analysed by Ole Crumlin Pedersen, Arne Emil Christensen and others, we know more about the ships and boats of some parts of northern Europe, particularly the western Baltic area and Norway, at this time – that is, roughly 800 to 1200 A.D. – than we do about the vessels of any preceding period. The traditions recorded in the Icelandic sagas and in the chronicles of the Anglo-Saxons, as well as a certain amount of iconographic material, help to develop the picture we have of Viking vessels still further.

There are at the time of writing some thirty to forty archaeological discoveries dated over a period of 400 years which contribute to our knowledge of shipbuilding. Roughly half of these are vessels of war of one kind or another, perhaps to be compared with the classical longships. The remainder are working vessels – 'round ships' in classical terminology.

Strong identifiable characteristics emerge from an examination of the evidence provided by all these finds. The Viking ships, like those of the classical Mediterranean, were built in shell sequence: that is, the shell of the vessel was built first, of planks fastened edge-to-edge, and the strengthening frames were shaped and added afterwards. But there the resemblance to the classical Mediterranean vessels ends. The clinker-laid strakes, fastened to one another with iron rivets turned over roves, are built around a backbone of keel and stems, the keel being a strong vertical member in contrast with the flat keel-planks of earlier north European vessels. Evenly spaced floor timbers and lower frames were secured to the planking, either lashed to cleats or secured with treenails, but they were not fastened to the keel. Each of these lower frames had a slender crossbar stretching across the boat from framehead to framehead with a structure of 'knees' and upper crossbeams above. The hull thus constructed was symmetrical, or almost symmetrical, fore and aft – 'double-ended' in the terminology used by boatmen in the past to describe such structures – with a keel slightly deeper in the centre than at the ends, blending gracefully into the lower parts of the stem and stern-post. The curve

The Oseberg ship — A.D. 800 — 76 ft. x 17 ft. — an early Viking karve

*Excavated near Tonsberg, Norway, in 1905.   A royal ship, meant for fjord and coastal dispatch work.
The earliest Scandinavian boat-find with provision for mast and sail.*

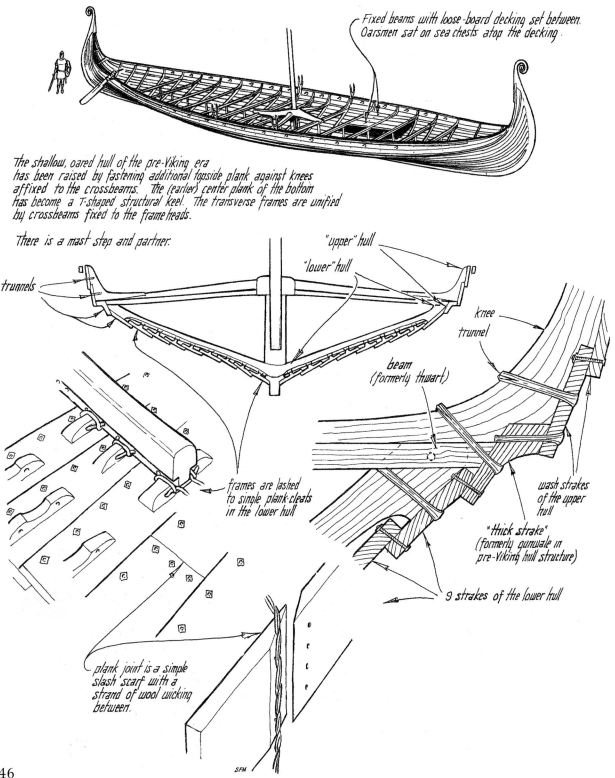

*Fixed beams with loose-board decking set between.
Oarsmen sat on sea chests atop the decking.*

*The shallow, oared hull of the pre-Viking era
has been raised by fastening additional topside plank against knees
affixed to the crossbeams.   The (earlier) center plank of the bottom
has become a T-shaped structural keel.   The transverse frames are unified
by crossbeams fixed to the frame heads.*

There is a mast step and partner.

"upper" hull

"lower" hull

trunnels

knee

trunnel

beam
(formerly thwart)

frames are lashed
to single plank-cleats
in the lower hull

wash strakes
of the upper
hull

"thick strake"
(formerly gunwale in
pre-Viking hull structure)

9 strakes of the lower hull

plank joint is a simple
slash scarf with a
strand of wool wicking
between.

SFM

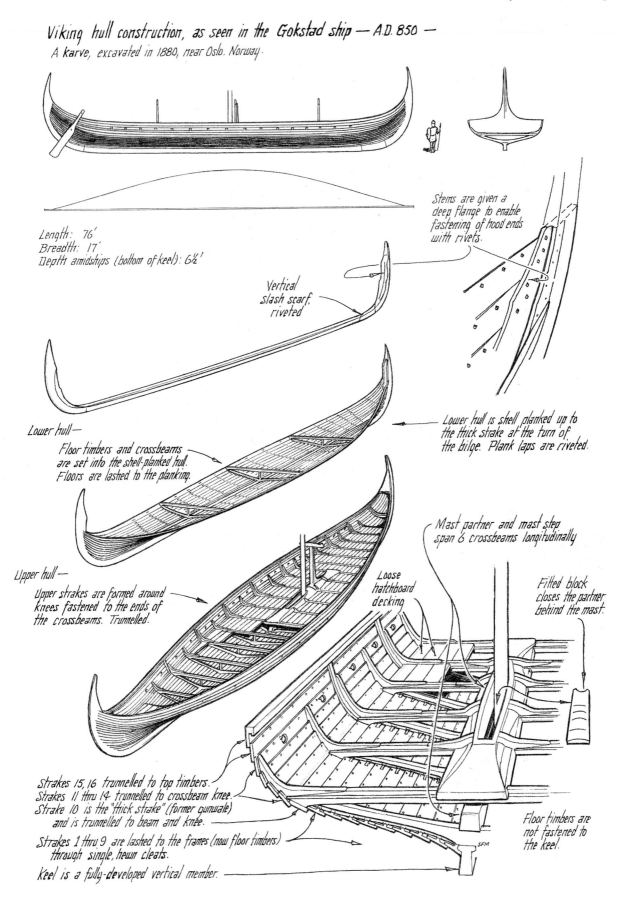

Viking hull construction, as seen in the Gokstad ship — A.D. 850 —
A karve, excavated in 1880, near Oslo, Norway.

Length: 76'
Breadth: 17'
Depth amidships (bottom of keel): 6½'

Vertical slash scarf, riveted

Stems are given a deep flange to enable fastening of hood ends with rivets.

Lower hull—

Floor timbers and crossbeams are set into the shell-planked hull. Floors are lashed to the planking.

Lower hull is shell planked up to the thick strake at the turn of the bilge. Plank laps are riveted.

Mast partner and mast step span 6 crossbeams longitudinally

Upper hull—

Upper strakes are formed around knees fastened to the ends of the crossbeams. Trunnelled.

Loose hatchboard decking

Fitted block closes the partner behind the mast.

Strakes 15, 16 trunnelled to top timbers.
Strakes 11 thru 14 trunnelled to crossbeam knee.
Strake 10 is the "thick strake" (former gunwale) and is trunnelled to beam and knee.

Strakes 1 thru 9 are lashed to the frames (now floor timbers) through single, hewn cleats.

Keel is a fully-developed vertical member.

Floor timbers are not fastened to the keel.

SFM

Skuldelev Wreck #3 — A.D. 1000 —

Recovered from Roskilde fjord, near Copenhagen, in the late 1950's.

Thought to have been a "farm boat" (**storbåt**, in Swedish, today) or general workboat for the private transport of a prosperous farmer, his family, and his men. This vessel probably ranged along the coasts of Zealand.

The modern replica of Skuldelev Wreck #3 has proven the vessel to be too heavy for portaging — as would be required along the Viking river trade routes to the east. The original craft was primarily a sailing vessel with provision for seven auxiliary oars.

Length: 40'
Breadth: 10'-3"

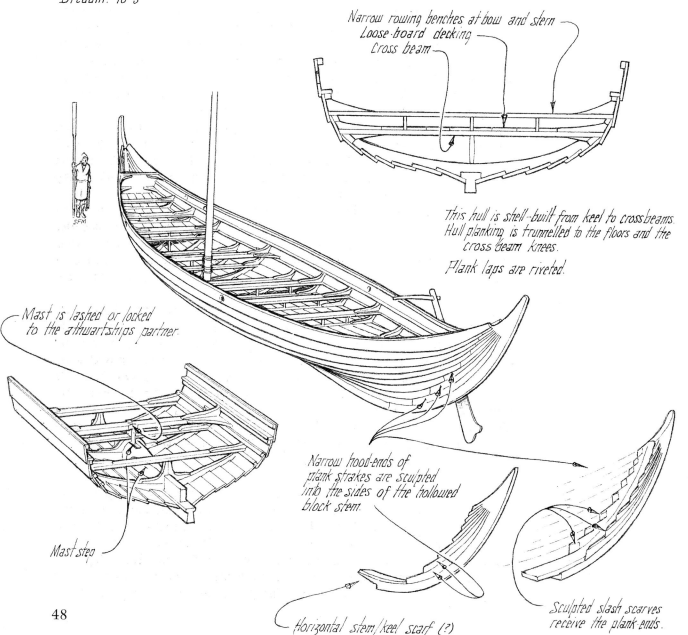

Narrow rowing benches at bow and stern
Loose-board decking
Cross beam

This hull is shell-built from keel to crossbeams. Hull planking is trunnelled to the floors and the cross beam knees.

Plank laps are riveted.

Mast is lashed or locked to the athwartships partner.

Mast step

Narrow hood-ends of plank strakes are sculpted into the sides of the hollowed block stem.

Horizontal stem/keel scarf (?)

Sculpted slash scarves receive the plank ends.

of the sheerline was exceedingly graceful and the vessels were, of course, round-bottomed, with flared sides.

These boats were both sailed and rowed. The oars were either pivoted against single 'thole pins', with grommets to prevent the oars sliding back on the recovery stroke, or put through 'oar ports' in an upper strake. Very little is known of the rigging and sails of these vessels, largely because the natural fibre of which they were made has scarcely survived. A certain amount can be deduced – though such conclusions are controversial – from iconographic evidence, from the examination by naval architects of the sailing characteristics of the hulls, and from experimental work with replicas of Viking vessels. It is apparent from this evidence – and from the seafaring achievements of the Vikings as they are recorded in the Sagas – that they could achieve sufficiently high standards of seaworthiness to fulfil the various purposes for which the ships and boats were built and to support adequately the economic and social needs of the societies which built them. Some of the most hazardous parts of the North Atlantic were crossed regularly. The North Sea was their highway and they sailed through the Bay of Biscay and the length of the Mediterranean. In an easterly direction an extensive trade with what is now Russia, through to the Middle East, was conducted from Sweden, notably from Gotland, via the Åland Islands, the Gulf of Finland and the Russian rivers, in vessels which must on the whole have been smaller and lighter than those used by the western Vikings voyaging in the North Sea and the Atlantic. The vessels in the eastern trade, perhaps not more than 10 metres long and some of them much smaller, sometimes had to be carried by their crews from river to river on their way south from the Baltic to the Black Sea, and on the return journey.

Only recently has study been given to the ways in which the Vikings rowed their ships, either on the long passage to Greenland and on to Labrador and Newfoundland, or on the equally long and perhaps even more arduous routes to the east. Questions of rowing geometry, possible work output, available energy in relation to food consumed, the effects of exposure on crew endurance, and so forth, all need much more research.

Those Scandinavians who went eastwards entered first Finno-Ugrian and then Slavic cultural areas. Those who reached the south coast of the Baltic Sea entered Slav country at once. Dr Smolarek, Director of the Polish National Maritime Museum, who, with his staff, has done much excavation and other research work into the boats of the Vistula and its delta coastal region, is convinced that clinker-building traditions developed in Slavic areas quite independently of their evolution in Scandinavia – and with a number of differences in detail. Dr Smolarek's arguments, although not fully published in English, are impressive, and lend weight to the possibility of very similar types of boats developing quite independently of one another in relatively small areas.

Similarly, the only substantial find of the remains of a Viking Age boat in England, although clinker-built, shows very marked differences from the structures of vessels built in the Viking tradition and found in the Baltic and in Scandinavia. This is the Graveney boat, dating from the early tenth century, found in Kent in a former tributary of the Thames. Taken together with the Slavic finds and using some other evidence this find suggests that the building traditions of the Scandinavian Vikings may have been specialized,

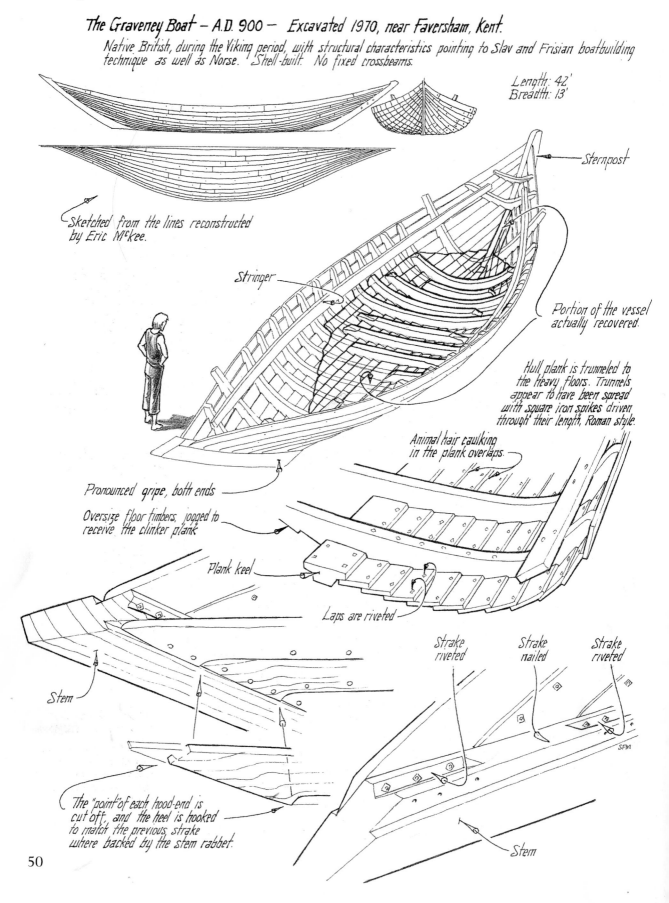

The Graveney Boat — A.D. 900 — Excavated 1970, near Faversham, Kent.

Native British, during the Viking period, with structural characteristics pointing to Slav and Frisian boatbuilding technique as well as Norse. Shell-built. No fixed crossbeams.

Length: 42'
Breadth: 13'

Sternpost

Sketched from the lines reconstructed by Eric McKee.

Stringer

Portion of the vessel actually recovered.

Hull plank is trunneled to the heavy floors. Trunnels appear to have been spread with square iron spikes driven through their length, Roman style.

Animal hair caulking in the plank overlaps.

Pronounced gripe, both ends

Oversize floor timbers, jogged to receive the clinker plank

Plank keel

Laps are riveted

Strake riveted   Strake nailed   Strake riveted

Stem

SFM

The "point" of each hood-end is cut off, and the heel is hooked to match the previous strake where backed by the stem rabbet.

Stem

The Kalmar ship — thirteenth century A.D. — excavated from the old harbor at Kalmar, Sweden, 1934.

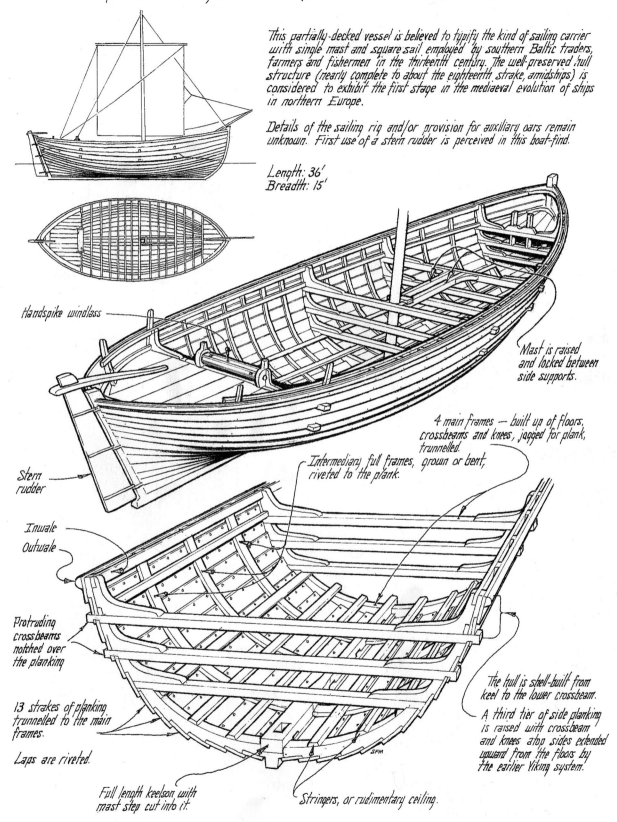

This partially-decked vessel is believed to typify the kind of sailing carrier with single mast and square sail employed by southern Baltic traders, farmers and fishermen in the thirteenth century. The well-preserved hull structure (nearly complete to about the eighteenth strake, amidships) is considered to exhibit the first stage in the mediaeval evolution of ships in northern Europe.

Details of the sailing rig and/or provision for auxiliary oars remain unknown. First use of a stern rudder is perceived in this boat-find.

Length: 36'
Breadth: 15'

Handspike windlass

Mast is raised and locked between side supports.

Stern rudder

4 main frames — built up of floors, crossbeams and knees, jogged for plank, trunnelled.

Intermediary full frames, grown or bent, riveted to the plank.

Inwale
Outwale

Protruding crossbeams notched over the planking

13 strakes of planking trunnelled to the main frames.

Laps are riveted.

The hull is shell-built from keel to the lower crossbeam.

A third tier of side planking is raised with crossbeam and knees atop sides extended upward from the floors by the earlier Viking system.

Full length keelson with mast step cut into it.

Stringers, or rudimentary ceiling.

51

on the edge of a wider north European tradition, rather than representing its principal branch. There may have been a broad tradition of clinker-boatbuilding of which the Scandinavian tradition was only one highly developed part, about which, by virtue of the discovery of remains, we happen to know a great deal more at present that we do about others.

The clinker-building tradition in the post-Viking period

There is iconographic and archaeological evidence available from which something may be deduced of the further development of clinker shipbuilding in the eleventh, twelfth and thirteenth centuries. As the Viking Age drew to a close, clinker-built ships became larger and more complicated. Remains found at Bergen in 1960 revealed a merchant vessel of about 1250 A.D. which was clinker-built, 85 ft long and nearly 30 ft wide. Thirteenth- and fourteenth-century town seals from England, France, Germany, the Netherlands and Poland, carefully executed and often illustrating the ship as the most esteemed indication of a community's prosperity, suggest how the ships developed. These seals show large clinker-built vessels with complex rigging, additional structures built up on the open boat fore and aft (usually referred to as 'castles'), with crossbeams projecting through the sides. This evidence is confirmed by an important archaeological find made at Kalmar Castle in Sweden in the 1930s, revealing several clinker-built merchant vessels from the middle thirteenth to the sixteenth century. They had short fore and after decks and were equipped with windlasses, stern rudders in place of the side rudders of the Viking ships, and upright stems and stern posts.

The fore and after castles were fitted to the vessels to raise the fighting platforms in order that they could be defended against an entirely different type of vessel which was now in the ascendant: the cog. This was a much higher sided vessel than the Viking ships, which gave a great advantage to her fighting men, who could rain arrows and spears down on the decks of the old longships. As a result of this development the use of the old clinker-built ships had come to an end in the early 1400s, though the huge *Grace Dieu*, of which the remains supposedly lie in the Hamble River, in Hampshire, was clinker-built in the early 1400s. Although clinker-building was mostly superseded in the construction of larger vessels, Norwegian coasters, paddle tugs and even three-masted square-rigged sailing vessels were still occasionally clinker-built, even in the nineteenth century, and traditional clinker-building remained normal practice in northern Europe for boats of all sizes right down to the end of wooden boat-building in the second half of the twentieth century.

The rise of the cog

Over the centuries during which round-hulled clinker-building traditions had been developing, mainly in the Baltic basin, at least two other quite different traditions had arisen to the south. Each of these in turn was to result in to

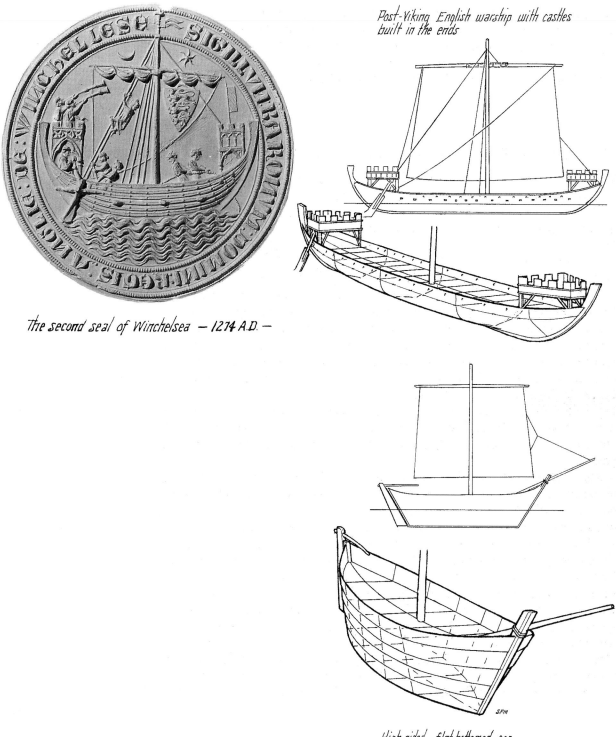

The second seal of Winchelsea — 1274 A.D. —

Post-Viking English warship with castles built in the ends

High-sided, flat-bottomed cog.

SFM

53

The Bremen Cog — A.D. 1380 —

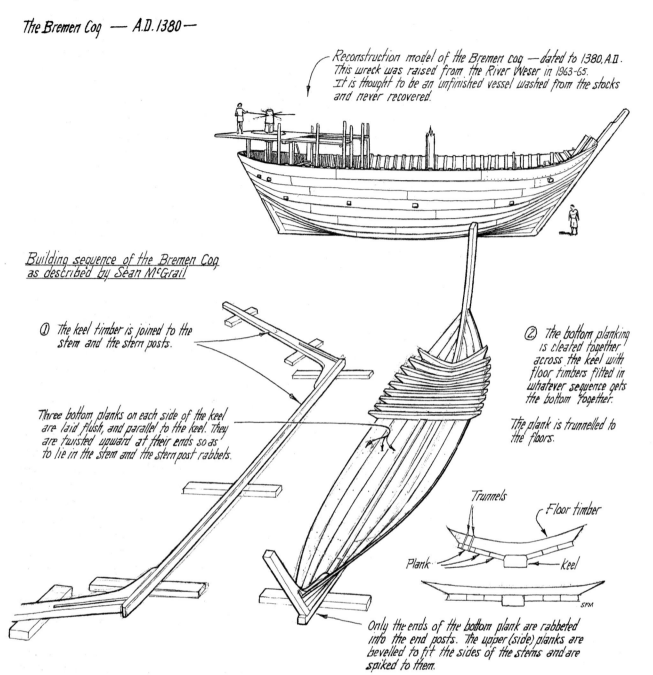

Reconstruction model of the Bremen cog — dated to 1380, A.D.
This wreck was raised from the River Weser in 1963-65.
It is thought to be an unfinished vessel washed from the stocks
and never recovered.

Building sequence of the Bremen Cog
as described by Sean McGrail

① The keel timber is joined to the
stem and the stern posts.

Three bottom planks on each side of the keel
are laid flush, and parallel to the keel. They
are twisted upward at their ends so as
to lie in the stem and the stern post rabbets.

② The bottom planking
is cleated together
across the keel with
floor timbers fitted in
whatever sequence gets
the bottom together.

The plank is trunnelled to
the floors.

Trunnels

Floor timber

Plank

Keel

SFM

Only the ends of the bottom plank are rabbeted
into the end posts. The upper (side) planks are
bevelled to fit the sides of the stems and are
spiked to them.

what for many years would be the most important type of vessel used in western European sea trade. The first of these two was the cog.

The study of the archaeology and history of the wooden ship and boat has not been free from nationalism. Research into the Scandinavian building tradition has produced something of a Slavic reaction in Poland. Britain, for reasons of geography and history, has poor archaeological material in comparison with the Baltic and the Netherlands and the comparable academic emphasis here has been on the study of the development of sewn boats internationally. In Germany, perhaps by way of reaction to the intensive Scandinavian interest in the clinker traditions, the discovery of a very late cog, almost intact, in the mud of the River Weser at Bremen in 1962 has prompted research, largely by Detlev Ellmers, into building traditions in German-speaking areas, revealing that while the Viking ship was slowly developing in the first millenium A.D. a completely different pattern of traditions, equally complex and important, was growing on the North Sea coast and rivers of what are now the Netherlands and Germany, as well as in the Baltic.

As has been explained, the building of flat-bottomed boats of various kinds dates back in northern Europe to the beginning of the Christian era. The double-ended flat-bottomed log-boat, which is believed to have been the cog's remote ancestor, gradually evolved in the area between the Rhine Delta and the Baltic coast into a plank-built vessel with an almost flat bottom, rockered fore, aft and athwartships into a very shallow dish. In some cogs the bottom planks were laid edge-to-edge without overlapping, joined only to the athwartships floor timbers. The sides, joining the bottom at a sharp angle in early cogs, were shell-constructed, with planks overlapping at the edges (but sometimes with the upper edges of the lower planks outside the lower edges of the upper, in reversal of the Scandinavian clinker-building practices). These planks were joined to one another with nails which in many cases were driven through the two strakes and then bent over twice, the point driven back into the wood inside the vessel. These nails have become an indication of the existence of a cog. When they are found, all timber long rotted away, scattered around the seabed or on a shore site, the presence of the last remains of a cog wreck or a cog-building site is probably rightly deduced. From these and other archaeological discoveries, from images on coins and on the picture stones of the middle Baltic Island of Gotland, from literary references and other documentary evidence, the story of the cog has been pieced together, at least in outline.

Cog nails have been found on a shipbuilding site of the seventh century A.D. at Wilhelmshaven at the mouth of the Elbe. Cog nails were found freely distributed in the ninth century strata of the harbour area of Hamburg. One hundred years later, recognizable cogs are shown on the coins of Haithabu, a great trading centre in Schleswig, on the eastern side of the Jutland peninsula, just south of the present Danish/German border. The cog was already then sailing the Baltic Sea.

It seems that Friesian traders from the Rhine delta used the cog, already developed to a degree as a plank-built ship from its log-boat origins, for trading in the sheltered waters of the German coast north to Jutland – waters familiar to readers of Erskine Childers' great maritime spy story, *The Riddle of the Sands*. The shallow, flat-bottomed cogs could work up the little creeks on

The Bremen cog —

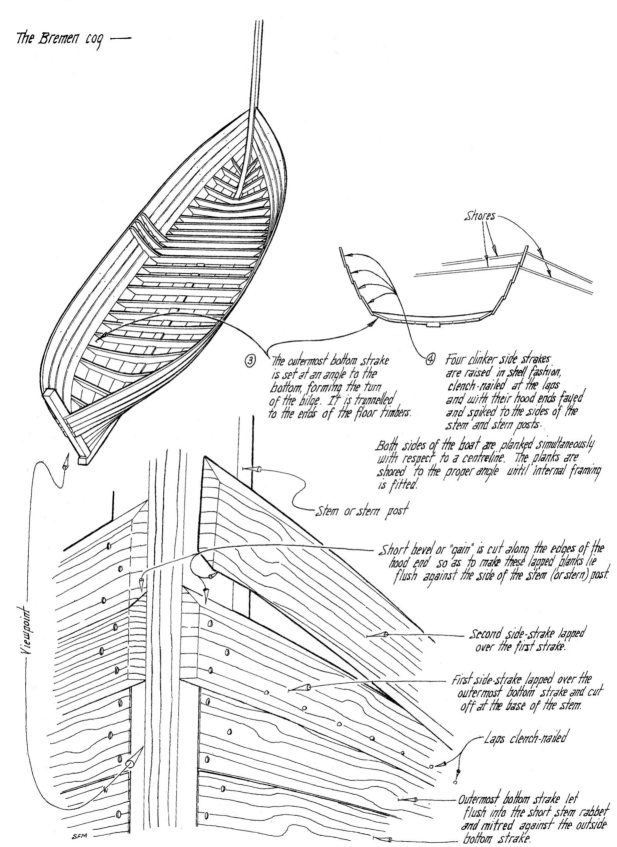

③ The outermost bottom strake is set at an angle to the bottom, forming the turn of the bilge. It is trunnelled to the ends of the floor timbers.

④ Four clinker side strakes are raised in shell fashion, clench-nailed at the laps and with their hood ends fayed and spiked to the sides of the stem and stern posts.

Both sides of the boat are planked simultaneously with respect to a centreline. The planks are shored to the proper angle until internal framing is fitted.

Shores

Stem or stern post

Short bevel or "gain" is cut along the edges of the hood end so as to make these lapped planks lie flush against the side of the stem (or stern) post.

Second side-strake lapped over the first strake.

First side-strake lapped over the outermost bottom strake and cut off at the base of the stem.

Laps clench-nailed

Outermost bottom strake let flush into the short stem rabbet and mitred against the outside bottom strake.

Viewpoint

SFM

56

flood tides, take the ground on the ebb, and load or discharge with pack horses or carts. Then, because of their rockered bottoms, they floated off easily on the flood tide and were not held down by the suction of the mud, as less sophisticated flat-bottomed vessels could be. On the North Sea coast of the Jutland Peninsula, opposite Haithabu on the Baltic side, was the tidal harbour of Hallingstedt. Here the early cogs came and their cargoes were portaged across the 16 km-wide isthmus (thus avoiding the dangerous passage round the exposed Skaw or the long route through the Limfjord) and reloaded into the vessels of Friesian settlers in Haithabu which were, naturally, of the cog type.

These early Baltic cogs appear to have been three or four planks high at the sides with straight stem- and stern-posts, giving them a potential laden freeboard comparable with those of the major Viking vessels found in Norway – the Oseberg and Gokstad ships. Some of them at least appear to have been steered by varying the position of the centre of the hull's lateral resistance and altering the sideways lift provided by the leeboard, by raising or lowering a device secured on one quarter of the cog, rather than using the later orthodox side rudder or the steering paddle of the Scandinavians.

These early cogs sailed far into the Baltic. Cog-nails have been found in Birka, the *entrepôt* port of the Scandinavian trade with Russia, the Middle East and Europe to the south. The site of the port is on Lake Mälaren – at that time, before the subsequent land rise, a great fjärd of the Baltic, west of the island where Stockholm was to be founded. Cogs are pictured on stones and in churches on the island of Gotland, in Finström Church in the Åland Islands and in many other places in Scandinavia and Finland. Across the Baltic, through the Åland Islands and along the south coast of Finland, names like Kuggham, Kuggholm and Kuggsund suggest an extension of cog trading towards the head of the Gulf of Finland. These waters are scattered with other memorials, like the chapel at Lembote in Lemland in the Åland Islands where the crews of cogs perhaps came ashore for refreshment when their vessels were anchored in this obvious sheltering place on the long route east. Later on, Visby, in Gotland, prospered on the cog trade with the east.

The cog trade really developed rapidly with the shifting of dominance from the north to the south coasts of the Baltic following the foundation of the town of Lübeck in the middle of the twelfth century. One current German historical theory suggests the power and prosperity soon to come to Lübeck stemmed from the partnership of well-established Baltic merchants who migrated there with land-based merchants; the latter's resources in Westphalia soon became a component of a trading community stretching eventually from London and Bruges in the west to Bergen in the north, Cologne in the south, and Tallin in the east. Whatever the truth of the matter, this city founded on the Trave marshes was then, as it is now, in frontier country. Today, from the tower of the great church you can look across the levels into East Germany. Then, this same country had recently been captured from the Slavs. The land had no feudal masters. The leading prince in the early Crusade against the Slavs of the southern Baltic was Henry the Lion, and to attract colonists to the new land significant concessions were offered. The result was a north German society somewhat different from that in areas to the south: here the princes' powers were limited and those of the nobles weak. Taxes were paid in lieu of the supply produce and feudal service, so the princes'

The Bremen Cog ———

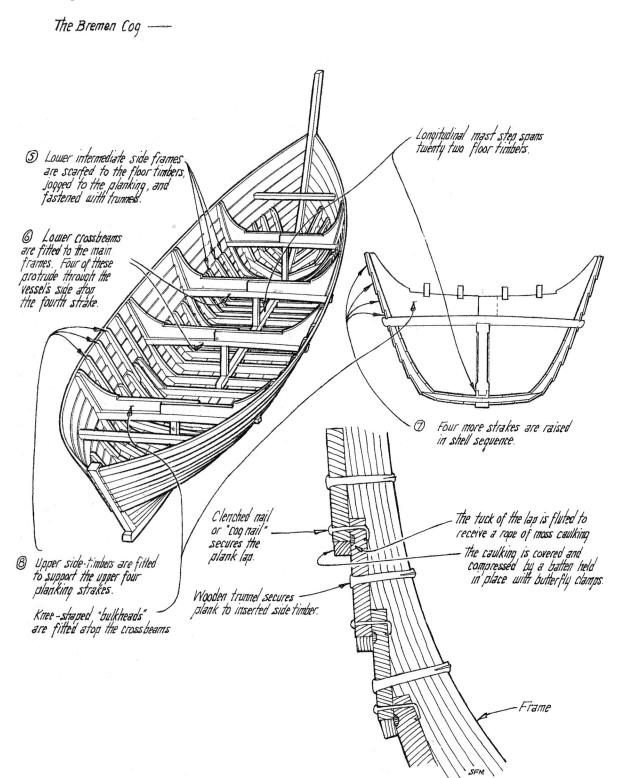

⑤ Lower intermediate side frames are scarfed to the floor timbers, jogged to the planking, and fastened with trunnels.

⑥ Lower crossbeams are fitted to the main frames. Four of these protrude through the vessels side atop the fourth strake.

Longitudinal mast step spans twenty two floor timbers.

⑦ Four more strakes are raised in shell sequence.

⑧ Upper side-timbers are fitted to support the upper four planking strakes.

Knee-shaped "bulkheads" are fitted atop the crossbeams

Clenched nail or "cog nail" secures the plank lap.

Wooden trunnel secures plank to inserted side timber.

The tuck of the lap is fluted to receive a rope of moss caulking

the caulking is covered and compressed by a batten held in place with butterfly clamps.

Frame

SFM

interests became identified with those of the taxpaying classes. Such was the foundation of the commercial society which was to develop at Lübeck and become a great centre of influence.

The vehicle of Lübeck's trade was developed from the indigenous cog, which soon became the predominant type of vessel in north Europe. Within 60 years the cog had grown to be capable of carrying 200 tons of cargo, probably eight or ten times as much as any but the largest vessels in the Scandinavian tradition. Contemporary accounts show that two cogs could carry the provisions of a town for four or five months, together with a garrison force of armed men. No wonder cogs played a crucial part in the 'Baltic Crusades' which opened up the area between the Gulf of Finland and Poland to north German economic exploitation, further increasing the prosperity of the mother city and her satellites. Visby, in Gotland, a necessary staging post until the cogs grew big enough to bypass her, was already under increasing German control. German trading towns were established along the southern shore of the Baltic, many of them adopting the cog as a symbol on their town seals.

The cog grew with prosperity. More and more strakes of planking were added to her sides, and her flat bottom was refined to give curved ends and a more gentle junction with the sides – all changes which made her more seaworthy. In the early 1200s the stern-rudder was adopted and a couple of generations later 'castles' were being built on to cogs to give crossbowmen an overwhelming advantage over opponents at sea. In all her variations the cog was probably cheaper, and certainly easier to build, than her round-bottomed clinker contemporaries. As the remains of cogs dating from the thirteenth century to the late 1400s indicate, some of these vessels were built with sawn planks, cheaper to use than the split planks of the Scandinavian tradition.

By the late thirteenth century the use of the cog had spread to the west coast of France and down to the Mediterranean. The earliest known agreement for the chartering of a vessel in northern Europe, preserved in the National Maritime Museum, covers the carriage of a mixed cargo of grain and wine in 1326 in the cog *Our Lady of Lyme*, by Master Walter Giffard, from Bordeaux to Newcastle-upon-Tyne. The most westerly iconographic evidence for the cog so far noted would apear to be its depiction in graffiti on a slate corner-block found at Crane Godrevy, Gwithian, Cornwall, by Professor Charles Thomas. Two cogs are shown; one is a large vessel with seven strakes, an integral forecastle and an after castle of different structure; the other is a very small cog, or a boat in the cog tradition, with strakes and some sort of cover in the stern. The larger vessel is single-masted; the smaller appears to be two-masted with the foremast stepped in a tabernacle.

The mysterious hulc

Documentary evidence indicates that in the 1300s the cog began to be widely supplanted by a different type of vessel, already well established in northern Europe, called the 'hulc'. Many identified remains of vessels in the Scandinavian round-hulled clinker-building tradition have been examined, and conclu-

The Bremen cog —

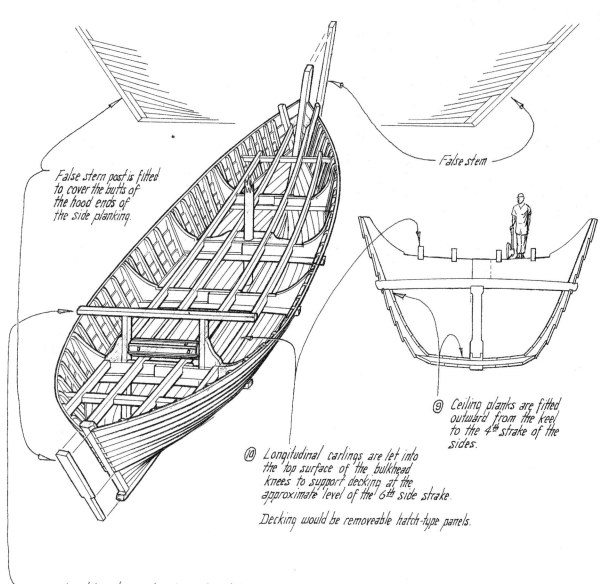

False stern post is fitted to, cover the butts of the hood ends of the side planking.

False stem

⑨ *Ceiling planks are fitted outward from the keel to the 4ᵗʰ strake of the sides.*

⑩ *Longitudinal carlings are let into the top surface of the bulkhead knees to support decking at the approximate level of the 6ᵗʰ side strake.*

Decking would be removeable hatch-type panels.

Athwartships beam atop the windlass bitts is the foundation piece for the after castle.

The mediaeval hulc — Successor to the cog on the north European trade routes. Believed to have been the dominant seagoing carrier of the fourteenth century.

Pictorial representations show a hull banana-shaped in profile, with plank strakes parallel to the sheer and terminating in a horizontal line at both ends of the vessel.

To date there is no archaeological boat find identified as a hulc.

Portion of a carved relief on the twelfth century font in Winchester Cathedral. The vessel is thought to represent a hulc.

*The elusive **hulc** remains an important link in the evolution of vessel structure from shell-built open boats to pre-framed hulls of great size and carrying capacity.*

Let's design a vessel which offers improvement over the mediaeval cog, and which has the general look of the Crusader ship on the Winchester font. We'll call it a "hulc". Bear in mind, however, that no seasoned shipbuilder of any century would accept the unstable look of that ship on the font!

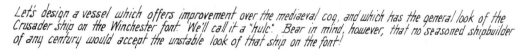

<u>Requirements</u>

① *Fighting platforms be contained within the hull.*

② *Arc bottom and slack bilges for sea keeping ability, and for better continuity of structure between sides and bottom.*

③ *Full ends — to maximize cargo capacity.*

④ *Use of available wide, thick, whipsawn plank in less complicated lapped seamwork than in the cog.*

Modern three-view plan not utilized by shipbuilders for another three centuries.

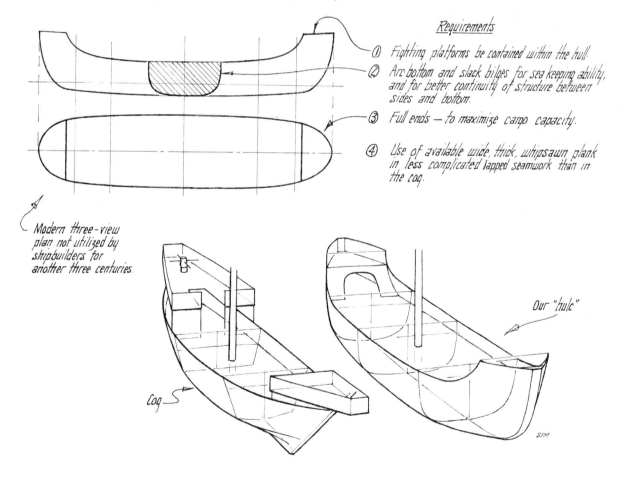

Cog

Our "hulc"

SFM

61

sions published. Cogs have in this way become identified to a degree with a romantic and nationalistic conception of their importance. They have been a focus of German historical interest in the Baltic society which replaced the Viking ascendancy. As yet no identified hulc has been revealed by archaeologists to provide a focus of either study or national pride. When, and if, one is discovered, it may well be in England, for the hulc seems to have been a vessel of the North Sea. Her image appears on town seals and coins in Britain, but not east of the Isselmeer. She is illustrated elsewhere in numerous forms.

The available iconographic material suggests that the hulc was quite different in construction from either the cog or the Scandinavian clinker-built boat. She appears to have been curved both longitudinally and transversely, probably with a long, narrow, flat keel, curved up at the ends, and always without a stem or stern-post. Most of the illustrations suggest clinker-laid planking, running in a uniform curve parallel to the sheer line and bottom, ending on a horizontal line at the ends well above the waterline. This solution to the ever present problem of planking a vessel has also been adopted elsewhere in the world in the course of history, notably in the thousands of big river boats, both rowed and sailed, on which the economy of Bangladesh is totally dependent today, and which appear to be remarkably like the hulc in general form and possibly construction. Such a vessel is completely different from the traditional clinker with stem and stern-posts, and has a characteristic dish-like shape – in profile, something like a banana.

Having described the apparent characteristics of the vessel identified (by Ole Crumlin Pedersen of the Danish National Museum, Detlev Ellmers of the German National Maritime Museum and others) with the type-name 'hulc' as it appears in medieval documents, we must examine very briefly some of the evidence we have for the existence of a distinct shipbuilding tradition, quite different from the traditions which produced the Scandinavian, Slav, or Middle North European clinker-built boats – and quite different from the traditions which produced the cog.

Ellmers believes the hulc to have been predominant in the North Sea as early as the second half of the eighth century, in the form illustrated on contemporary coins of the town of Dorestad, near Utrecht. It has been noted that medieval Shoreham was called 'Hulkesmouth' and that the vessel roughly depicted on its seal of *c.*1295 appears to have some of the characteristics described above. It is largely on this evidence that the name 'hulc' has been given to this type of vessel.

What is quite certain is that medieval craftsmen seeking to illustrate vessels in illuminated manuscripts, in stone-carving, and in fine metalwork, were by the early twelfth century deliberately and carefully depicting a vessel quite different from the clinker-type with stem and stern-post, equally carefully depicted in other contemporary works of art. Let us take a few examples. The Lewes capital of circa 1120 from Lewes Priory, now in the British Museum, depicts scenes from the life of St Peter and in one of them a vessel of the hulc type is very carefully shown. The Worcester Chronicle of *c.*1130–40, in the possession of Corpus Christi College, Oxford, shows an equally carefully depicted vessel of the same type. English enamel plaques dated by art historians to *c.*1170–80, now in the Germanisches National Museum in Nüremburg, show a less carefully depicted vessel which is evidently of the same type. All these vessels have steering oars and one of them a clearly drawn single

Hypothetical hulc. A conjectural reconstruction —

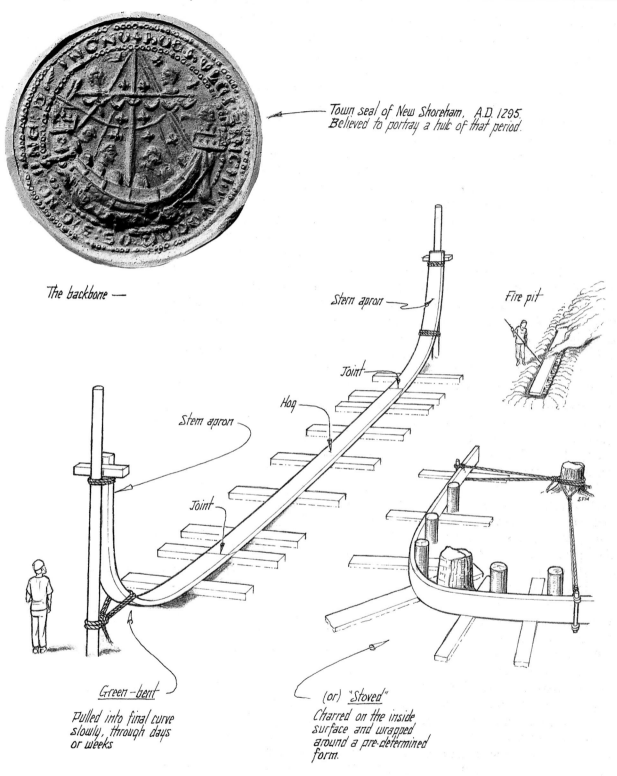

Town seal of New Shoreham, A.D. 1295.
Believed to portray a hulc of that period.

The backbone —

Stern apron

Fire pit

Joint

Hog

Stem apron

Joint

Green-bent

Pulled into final curve
slowly, through days
or weeks

(or) "Stoved"

Charred on the inside
surface and wrapped
around a pre-determined
form.

63

Hypothetical hulc —

Noah and his sons building the Ark.
(Engraving by J. Sadeler from a painting by
M. de Vos. Engraving is dated to 1588.)

The foreground of this fanciful scene is carefully
drawn — as if from shipyard site sketches.
The foreground tools are correct for the artist's period.
That curious bow framework relates astonishingly
well to the needs of the reconstruction below.

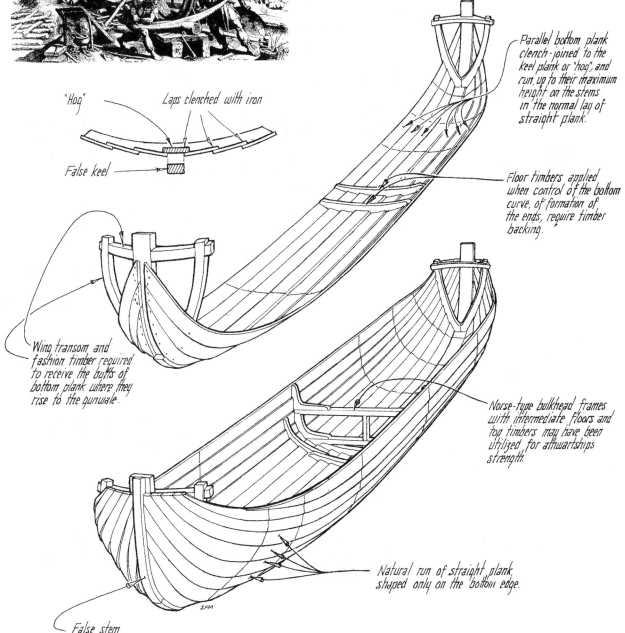

"Hog"

Laps clenched with iron

False keel

Parallel bottom plank
clench-joined to the
keel plank or "hog", and
run up to their maximum
height on the stems
in the normal lay of
straight plank.

Floor timbers applied
when control of the bottom
curve, of formation of
the ends, require timber
backing.

Wing transom and
fashion timber required
to receive the butts of
bottom plank where they
rise to the gunwale.

Norse-type bulkhead frames
with intermediate floors and
top timbers may have been
utilized for athwartships
strength.

Natural run of straight plank,
shaped only on the bottom edge.

False stem

S.F.M.

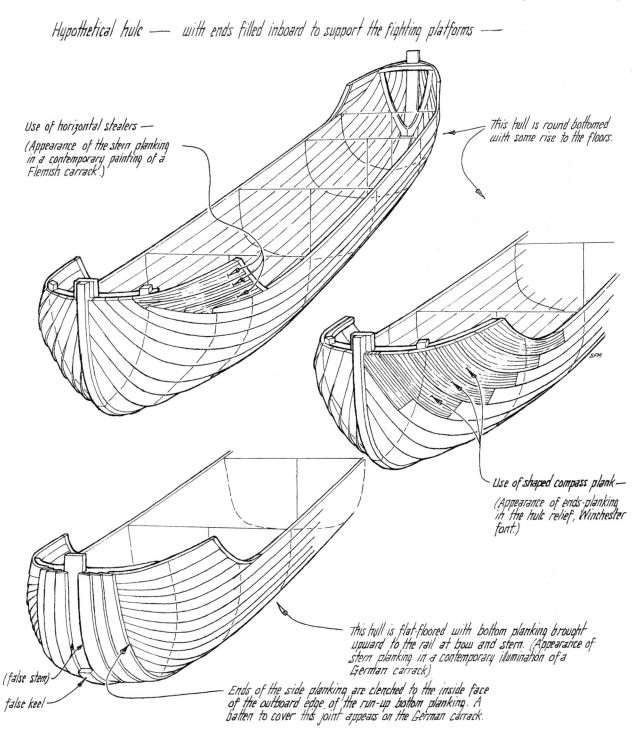

Hypothetical hulc — with ends filled inboard to support the fighting platforms —

Use of horizontal stealers —

(Appearance of the stern planking in a contemporary painting of a Flemish carrack.)

This hull is round bottomed with some rise to the floors.

S.F.M.

Use of shaped compass plank —

(Appearance of ends-planking in the hulc relief, Winchester font.)

(false stem)

false keel —

This hull is flat-floored with bottom planking brought upward to the rail at bow and stern. (Appearance of stern planking in a contemporary illumination of a German carrack)

Ends of the side planking are clenched to the inside face of the outboard edge of the run-up bottom planking. A batten to cover this joint appears on the German carrack.

Our hypothetical hulc is a blunt-ended, round-bilged seagoing carrier. It may be that the hulc "shape" was the first manifestation of a blunt-ended hull for long-haul service. If blunt ends were truly the hallmark of the vanished hulc, then its perpetuation may be seen in the blunt <u>stern</u> of its successor, the carrack, and possibly in the hull forms of the (later) North Sea dogger and the herring buss.

Carrack — Mediterranean —

The Mataró model — c.1450 A.D. —

This is a sailor-made ship model, of a contemporary vessel, which hung in a church near Barcelona for many centuries. It is now on display in a Rotterdam museum.

This votive model is thought to represent a one or two-masted *nao*, or Mediterranean carrack.

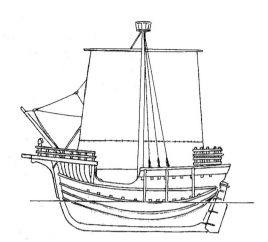

To date there no archaeological boat-finds which are agreed to represent a mediaeval carrack. The *San Juan* find, a Basque whaler of the mid 1500's, is a galleon.

The Mataró model remains the sole-existing three dimensional artefact against which the contorted contemporary pictures of carracks may be judged.

The Mataró model exhibits flush-laid planking on the sides and on the bottom. There is a keel, stem post, and a well-defined stern post. Staving enclosing the forecastle is lapped. The after-castle extends upward from a transom timber atop the stern post.

Conjectural reconstruction ——→

squaresail. The well-known depiction of *c*.1180 of the same type of vessel, on the font of Winchester Cathedral, shows a stern-rudder as does a similar carving at Zedelgem near Bruges; these may well be the first depictions of a stern-rudder so far noticed. All these examples of illustrations of the hulc (except the last) are English.

A distinct type of vessel therefore undoubtedly existed. We can deduce some of her characteristics – and also the reasons for them – but can go no further until archaeological evidence becomes available. Of the hulc's origins we know nothing. Crumlin Pedersen and others, following him, have seen a possible ancestor in the Utrecht boat, an extended log-boat of *c*.900 A.D., but there are few structural characteristics to connect this vessel with the hulc. Equally, there seems little evidence to support the theory that the hulc is represented today by the two-transom boat miscalled a 'pram' by yachtsmen in the English-speaking world. This has none of the hulc's aparent structural characteristics and is at least equally likely to have been developed in comparatively recent years from the willow tree log-boat of the middle Baltic region.

Recent research by Mrs Jones-Baker into the vessels illustrated by graffiti in churches in East Anglia has revealed the images of many vessels which appear to be of the hulc type, associated with river and coastal trade. This may suggest that the hulc developed in Britain from the inland and sheltered-water vessels of the area north of the Thames in the way that the cog developed from similar boats in the Friesian area. Certainly the development of the hulc would seem to be a prime subject for British research and its study should be given priority in anticipation of the inevitable archaeological discovery, which may occur at any time.

The hulc seems to have become predominant in northern sea commerce in the fourteenth century because she was capable of greater cargo capacity in relation to building cost than even the cog (with its definite size limits) at a time when vessels of greater capacity were becoming profitable to operate.

The invention of the sailing ship

The reign of the hulc was extremely short, for by the middle of the next century she had been overtaken by an almost totally new type of ship, capable of development to a degree which was to make her infinitely superior in seaworthiness, sailing ability, size, economy and range of operation to any vessel which had existed before. This new type of ship, which appears to have been developed at roughly the speed with which the aircraft has been developed in the twentieth century, represents one of mankind's most important technical developments, comparable in its long term effects, and the speed with which they came about, with the development of steam power or electricity.

To recapitulate, the overwhelming majority of the vessels which have been discussed in this book so far were entirely shell-built, with planks joined together at their edges and then strengthening frames inserted, shaped to fit the existing hull. The new type of ship was built the other way round. To put it very simply, first a skeleton was erected on a backbone consisting of

Blend of shell and pre-framed structure in a fifteenth century carrack —
(as deduced from the external appearance of the Mataró model)

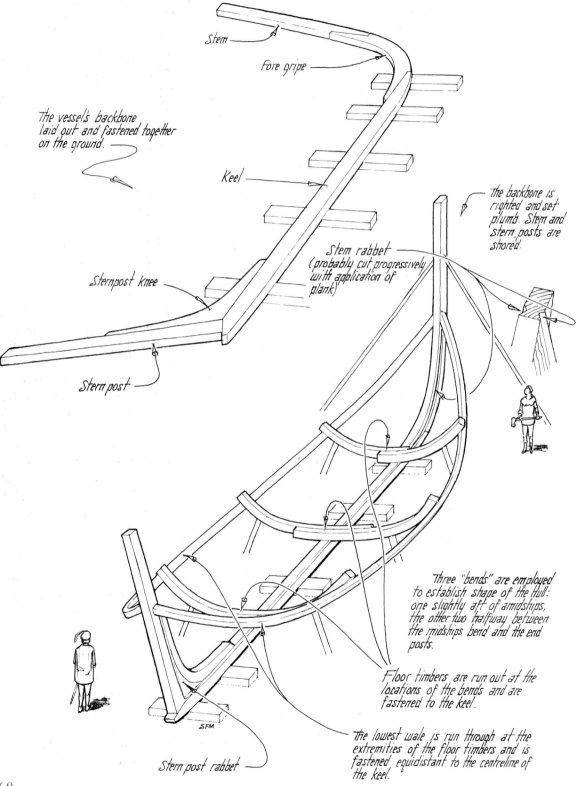

Stem

Fore gripe

The vessel's backbone
laid out and fastened together
on the ground.

Keel

the backbone is
righted and set
plumb. Stem and
stern posts are
shored.

Stem rabbet
(probably cut progressively
with application of
plank)

Sternpost knee

Stern post

Three "bends" are employed
to establish shape of the hull:
one slightly aft of amidships,
the other two halfway between
the midships bend and the end
posts.

Floor timbers are run out at the
locations of the bends and are
fastened to the keel.

The lowest wale is run through at the
extremities of the floor timbers and is
fastened equidistant to the centreline of
the keel.

Stern post rabbet

S.F.M.

keel, stem and stern-post, and then the whole was wrapped round with a skin of planks which were fastened only to the skeleton and *not to each other*. Thus the vessel's shape–her 'design', to use a modern term–was determined by the skeleton, not the planks, as had previously been the case. This was a revolutionary technical change, with profound implications. It enabled bigger and stronger ships to be developed which – and this was soon to become very important – could carry guns and enough supplies and men to make long voyages, even if half the crew died on the way. These ships were easier to maintain than vessels built in any of the shell traditions, but, above all, they were stronger, and the technique was capable of a high degree of development. The shell tradition, because of inherent weaknesses when the boats grew beyond a certain size, could not compete.

We do not know when, where, or even why, the skeleton-building technique developed. There is not much evidence to work with, and what there is is inconclusive. It appears that the technique began on what is now the Biscay coast of Spain and southern France, slowly spreading north-east across Europe. The process probably started in the late fourteenth or early fifteenth centuries.

Until recently it had often been assumed that big vessels of the late sixteenth century were necessarily fully skeleton-built. However, the first examination of the Basque whaler *San Juan* (from the mid 1500s) by the Canadian team under Robert Grenier, at Red Bay, Labrador, appears to show something of a mixture of techniques. Skeleton construction seems here to be groping forward by shell-building methods – as if in the upper part of the vessel the shape was derived from the planking, even though the planks were not joined edge-to-edge but only to the frames; these were made to fit but were not continuous. Here perhaps is evidence that full skeleton construction, and the use of complete pre-erected frames and backbone, may have taken a century or more to develop, perhaps not becoming fully established until the early seventeenth century. The Swedish maritime ethnographer, Olof Hasslöf, suggested this in publications in the early 1970s. Certainly, full skeleton construction was not common in many parts of the world until the present century, and in both Norway and Japan its wide adoption was brought about only with governmental encouragement. One possible source of further information, the Swedish warship *Wasa* of 1628, is unfortunately too magnificently complete to have provided detailed evidence yet about her construction.

This book is principally concerned, as its title suggests, with the *structure* of wooden ships, rather than their rigging and fittings. It must be noted, however, that at roughly the same time as the development of full skeleton construction another revolution in shipbuilding took place. Hitherto all ships had been rigged with either a single squaresail on one mast, more or less amidships – like the Viking ship, the cog and the hulc – or with one or two triangular lateen sails, like many south European vessels.

There are illustrations which seem to indicate the use of three masts dating from the fourteenth century, such as the ships in the picture for the month of June in the manuscript of *De Sphaera estense* from about 1350, now in Modena (Anna-Lisa Stigell, *Kyr Kans Teckan och Arets Gång*, Helsinki, 1974). But from the middle 1400s onwards, illustrations of ships with three masts began to appear widely on manuscripts, church walls and bench-ends, on

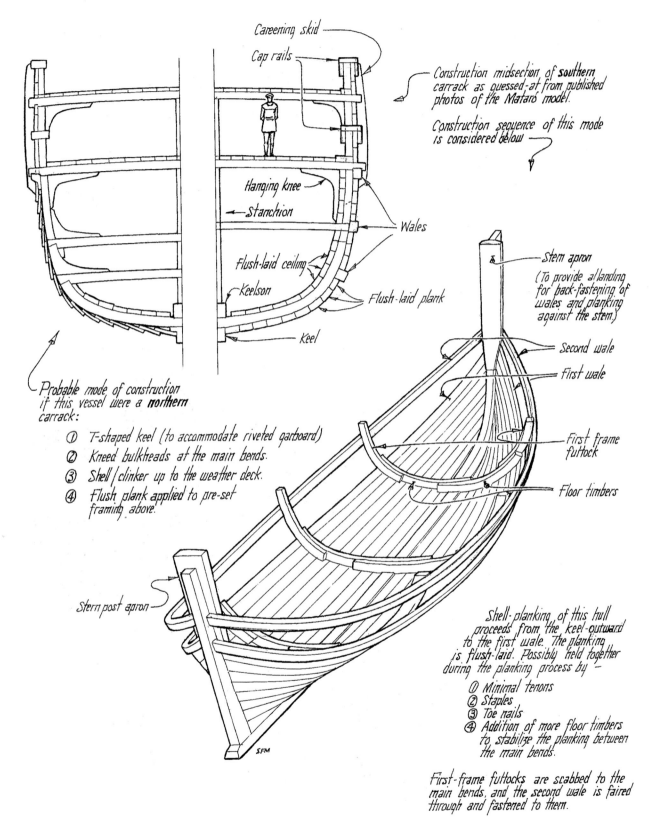

Conjectural reconstruction of a fifteenth century carrack —

Careening skid

Cap rails

Construction midsection of **southern** carrack as guessed-at from published photos of the Mataró model.

Construction sequence of this mode is considered below —

Hanging knee

← Stanchion

Wales

Flush-laid ceiling

Keelson

Flush-laid plank

Keel

A

Probable mode of construction if this vessel were a **northern** carrack:

① T-shaped keel (to accommodate riveted garboard)
② Kneed bulkheads at the main bends.
③ Shell / clinker up to the weather deck.
④ Flush plank applied to pre-set framing above.

Stem apron
(To provide a landing for back-fastening of wales and planking against the stem)

Second wale

First wale

First frame futtock

Floor timbers

Stern post apron

SFM

Shell-planking of this hull proceeds from the keel-outward to the first wale. The planking is flush-laid. Possibly held together during the planking process by —

① Minimal tenons
② Staples
③ Toe nails
④ Addition of more floor timbers to stabilize the planking between the main bends.

First-frame futtocks are scabbed to the main bends, and the second wale is faired through and fastened to them.

Conjectural reconstruction of a fifteenth century carrack —

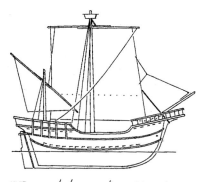

Two-masted carrack —A.D. 1400 —

Mid-frame beams are placed across the hull to stabilize the bends at the second wale.

Intermediate floor timbers are set across the keel for passive backing of the bottom planking.

The keelson is run-in atop the floors. It is bolted through the floor timbers to the keel.

Intermediate first futtocks are set between the floors to raise active framework to the second wale.

Top timbers and deck beams are applied to the bends in order to provide form-work for fairing-through the sheer wale.

The bend-frames are unified with stanchions and hanging knees.

Intermediate top timbers extend the active framing to the sheer wale and beyond.

The hull is planked and ceiled to the sheer wale.

Intermediate beams of the main deck are set in place.

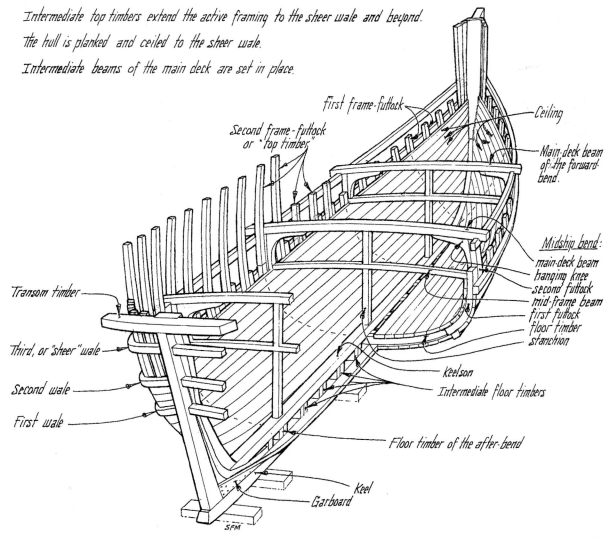

First frame-futtock

Second frame-futtock or "top timber"

Ceiling

Main-deck beam of the forward bend.

Midship bend:
main-deck beam
hanging knee
second futtock
mid-frame beam
first futtock
floor timber
stanchion

Keelson

Intermediate floor timbers

Transom timber

Third, or "sheer" wale

Second wale

First wale

Floor timber of the after-bend

Keel

Garboard

SFM

71

Conjectural reconstruction of a fifteenth century carrack —

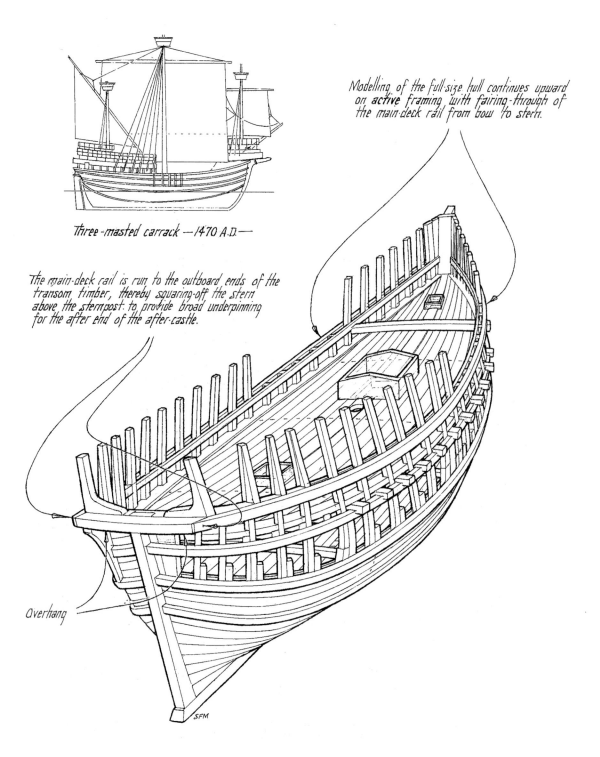

*Modelling of the full-size hull continues upward on **active** framing with fairing-through of the main-deck rail from bow to stern.*

Three-masted carrack — 1470 A.D. —

The main-deck rail is run to the outboard ends of the transom timber, thereby squaring-off the stern above the sternpost to provide broad underpinning for the after end of the after-castle.

Overhang

SFM

Conjectural reconstruction of a fifteenth century carrack —

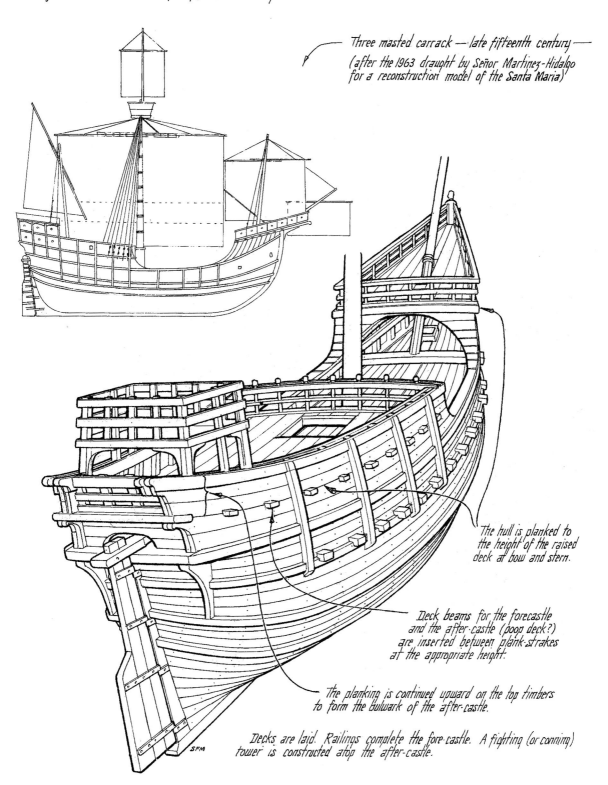

Three masted carrack — late fifteenth century —
(after the 1963 draught by Señor Martinez-Hidalgo
for a reconstruction model of the Santa Maria)

The hull is planked to
the height of the raised
deck at bow and stern.

Deck beams for the forecastle
and the after-castle (poop deck?)
are inserted between plank-strakes
at the appropriate height.

The planking is continued upward on the top timbers
to form the bulwark of the after-castle.

Decks are laid. Railings complete the fore-castle. A fighting (or conning)
tower is constructed atop the after-castle.

SFM

The caravel —— c. 1490 A.D. ——

Of Mediterranean origin. Believed to have developed from an open, flush-planked, single-lateen fishing craft. By the mid 1400s, the caravel had evolved into a decked, square-sterned, three-masted vessel well suited to the needs of world explorers: small (60 to 76 feet in length), of shoal draft, weatherly, easy to handle, and swift. The hull of the caravel is believed to have been fully pre-framed.

Present knowledge of the caravel is mostly from research conducted by José Maria Martinez-Hidalgo, former Director of the Museo Maritime, Barcelona.

One, two, or three-masted lateen.

Square-rigged, fore and main, for Atlantic exploration.

The foregoing illustrations attempt to show the steps by which European and Mediterranean experience with hull structure and sailing rigs became amalgamated in a workable sailing ship for global exploration and ocean-crossing transport in the fifteenth century A.D.

With this beginning established, we can now turn our attention to wooden merchant ship-building at its zenith —— in the closing decades of the nineteenth century.

coins, on pottery and on seals, and eventually in paintings. The first two aft from the bows were equipped with square sails, the third mast with a lateen sail. Documentary evidence shows that three-masted vessels were in use in Britain as early as 1420. There is a Norwegian woodcarving on a 'calendar stick' in the Norwegian Museum of Art showing a three-masted cog dated from its inscription to as early as 1457. In Pyttis Church in south-eastern Finland there is a clearly depicted three-master from the early 1500s.

The spread of the three-masters into northern Europe was rapid. Because pictures show the masts of ships clearly, but tell us little or nothing of their construction, we know far more about the progress of this second revolution than the first, the development of skeleton construction. By the end of the fifteenth century the three-masted wooden sailing ship was fully established. Her frames may not have been continuous and she may have been built partly using shell techniques to develop her shape. The birth of this entirely new type of vessel has rightly been called 'the invention of the sailing ship'.

This invention was one of the most important events in European history. The wooden sailing ship was from now on to play an increasing part in human affairs. Not until the eighteenth century was there to be a similarly revolutionary development in shipping – the adoption of the schooner rig, simpler, handier and more manouverable than the square-rigged sailing ship. This was a development in rigging and sails only, and not in fundamentals of hull construction.

What developed in the 1400s was a vessel strong enough and seaworthy enough to sail almost anywhere, given sufficient time, with an acceptable rate of casualties from starvation, disease and accident among her crew. More than that, because she was simply constructed, from natural materials, and had nothing about her which could not be made by carpenters and blacksmiths on board, using materials either carried on ship or readily available almost anywhere in the world, this 'space capsule of the Renaissance', unlike twentieth-century space capsules, was practically self-supporting. Requiring only a safe, sheltered harbour to which she could return from time to time and where she could be put ashore for the skilled craftsmen in her crew to repair and refit her, she could sail almost indefinitely. Within limits, the simpler and smaller she was, the less dependent she was on a base on shore and the greater her range and the potential duration of her operations. Given a good master, good crews and some good fortune, she could achieve almost anything that could be required of her. The three-masted skeleton-built sailing ship was the vehicle which gave European man his predominance. Within a century or so of her first appearance she had encircled the globe and completely changed man's view of the world. Of course there were many other factors, the absence of which would have weakened or prevented European hegemony, but without this sailing ship it most certainly could not have happened.

The ultimate demonstration of the capability of the small, wooden, three-masted square-rigged sailing ship occurred in the late eighteenth century, when Captain James Cook, using ordinary merchant vessels taken out of the North Sea and Baltic trades, well fitted-out and equipped and provisioned from Naval dockyards, explored more of the earth's surface than any other human being had ever done before. He solved almost all the remaining geographical mysteries without losing a single vessel or any significant number of men – except on one occasion, from chronic infectious diseases picked up on land. On his second voyage, Cook's ship operated for three years without support, often in the extreme conditions of the southern oceans and in latitudes varying from the tropics to the deep Antarctic.

From the early sixteenth century onwards until the commercial development of the compound engine for steamships and the availability of cheap iron plate for shipbuilding in the mid 1860s, the wooden sailing ship played a very large part in the economic developments and the movements of people which laid the foundations of Western society. It is certain that without the wooden sailing ship, industry and international trade could never have developed as they did in the nineteenth century.

part two

the Building of
a wooden ship

3 the slipway

The construction of skeleton-built wooden sailing ships went on for many centuries in most countries of the western world. It is impossible to talk in general terms about wood shipbuilding – except very superficially – because methods of construction varied greatly from age to age, from country to country and from place to place in each country. The crafts of wood shipbuilding must be discussed as they were practised at specific places at specific times. Wood shipbuilding was a very complex craft and the more the subject is examined the more complicated it is seen to have been. A full description in detail of the building of a three-decker of the late eighteenth century would require several volumes.

We have tried to overcome such difficulties in this section of this book by describing the building of a relatively small, relatively simple ship–a schooner 75 or so feet in length of about 60 tons net register and able to carry about 120 tons of cargo – in a typical shipbuilding community situated in the south-western part of Britain. The description of the community and its locality is built up from a number of places in a limited geographical area. The methods used in the building of the schooner, as described by us, were all actually used in south-western England in the late nineteenth century. The yard which is described was in south Devon and 'Master' was a north Devon man who migrated across the county after serving his apprenticeship there. This description gives a basis for understanding what was involved in wood shipbuilding. Bigger ships were more complicated, but the processes involved in constructing them were basically the same. Later on in this book we shall give a few specific examples of different techniques used in building larger vessels in several different communities in Europe and North America, as well as in Britain.

In the second half of the nineteenth century, the country in the West of England around our yard was partly industrialized, with mines, quarries, mills, forges, ropewalks, sawmills and wagon builders, as well as numerous farms and prosperous commercial gardens. There was no railway into the area and the bulk products of the mines and quarries, and the imported goods needed to support the various industries – coal, fertilizer, machinery, grain for the water mills and timber for the mines and the builders – could not be carried in horse-drawn wagons along the rough roads for long distances. The river, with its considerable tidal rise and fall, was the natural highway, both for ships bringing and taking cargoes to and from distant ports and for the movement of goods from the port at the river mouth to the villages upstream and downstream. Some cargoes were moved by sailing barge from the local

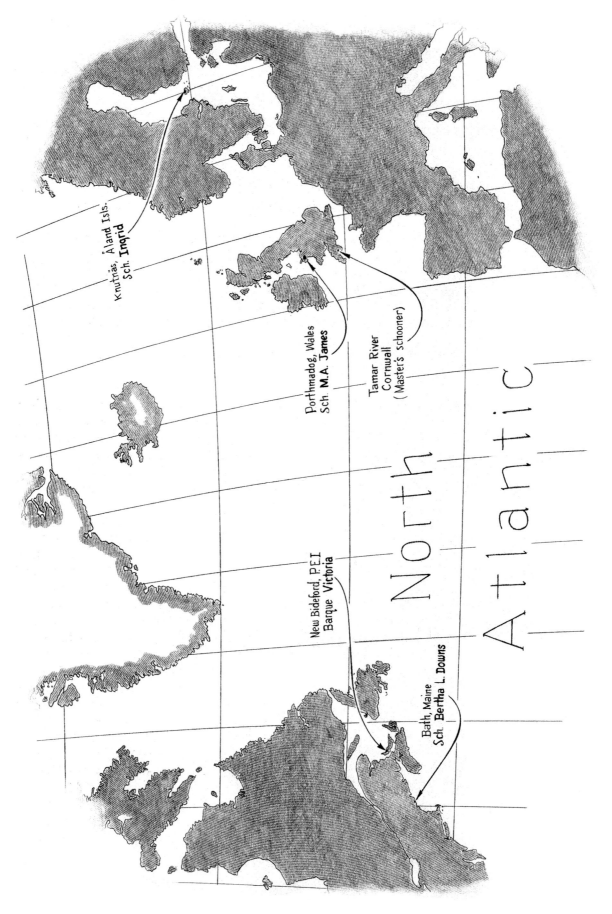

Knutnäs, Åland Isls.
Sch. **Ingrid**

Porthmadog, Wales
Sch. **M.A. James**

Tamar River
Cornwall
(Master's schooner)

New Bideford, P.E.I
Barque **Victoria**

Bath, Maine
Sch. **Bertha L. Downs**

North

Atlantic

roadside wharf to another, or even from farm to farm, on the river and the estuary.

The shipyard, like many in Britain, was dependent on local labour. Travel was possible only by horse, on foot or by boat, and many shipyard workers walked up to 12 miles daily to and from their work, which lasted from 6.00 in the morning until 6.00 at night, and until 4.00 on Saturdays. Sunday was the only day of rest. The crafts of the shipyard workers were learned through apprenticeship; since this was usually seven years long, and boys who were not going to take to the work for one reason or another were weeded out at an early stage, there were few poor craftsmen.

The craft was indeed everything, and a boy as he grew up would hear talk of very little else, at home, in the family, in the public house or at work. Nine-tenths of the conversation when men gathered together probably concerned their trades. There were few distractions from this. It is doubtful whether the widespread dissemination of high manual skills which character- ized the wooden shipbuilding industry could ever be achieved in modern society. There are too many distractions which have destroyed the habit of talking, not least about the skills of a trade. Time off on Sundays was often taken as an opportunity for craftsmen to build their own boats, for sale, work or pleasure. In such an environment a man with a gift for the craft could develop a degree of skill which may seem incredible today, as we are conditioned to different attitudes to work and to totally different working conditions.

These men were often deeply religious, usually non-conformist, and saw in the Bible the answers to life's problems. They were suspicious of innovation and they were insular in outlook. Despite their lifelong involvement with water more often than not they could not swim: tombstones in local churchyards give convincing evidence of the all too frequent result of this. Families followed the same trade, generation after generation. Nothing that could possibly be of use was ever thrown away.

Work was continued out of doors all the year round, though protective clothing in the modern sense was unknown. There was no material available that could successfully keep out the rain. Drying was done after work at home around the fire when everyone went to bed, which was often around 7.30 or 8.00 in the evening in winter, in order to save fuel and candles. To be wet, cold and exhausted from a 12-hour day in bad weather out of doors was a very common experience for both men and women. The usual clothes for men were a flannel or twill shirt without a collar, and a belt with braces keeping up a pair of heavy woollen cloth trousers. The leather boots the shipyard workers wore were constantly wet as the tide lapped at the part of the yard in which work took place. A flat cap or a seaman's cap was worn with a top coat, the latter often very old. Woollen scarves were worn for further protection against both the wet and the cold. These, with home- knitted jumpers as a thermal layer between the top coat and the body, were the uniform of the shipbuilder and it is not surprising that many of them suffered in middle age from rheumatism, acquired from years of literally steaming in wet clothing.

Housing was primitive, washing was difficult, and grimy hands with callouses were chapped and marked with prominent black lines. Endless heavy manual work brought short tempers to the home at night. Children

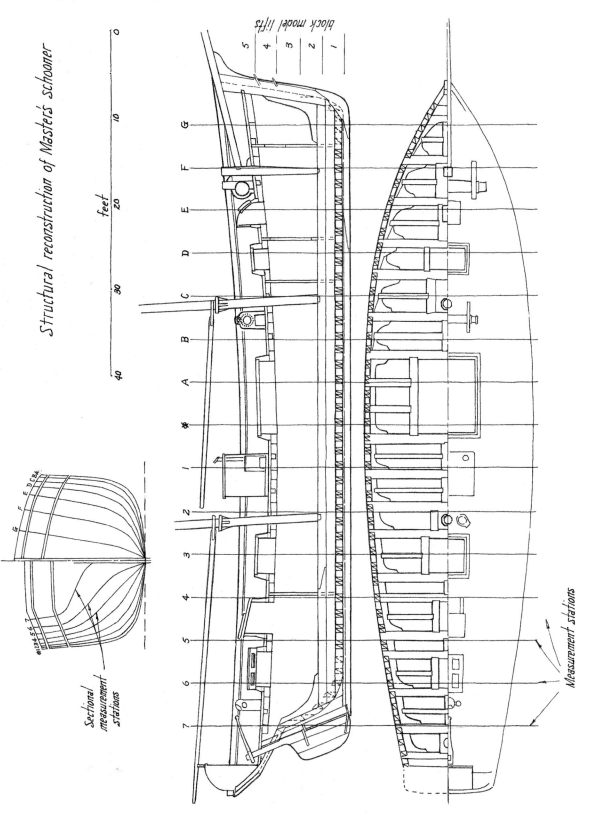

Structural reconstruction of Master's Schooner

block model lifts

feet

Sectional measurement stations

Measurement stations

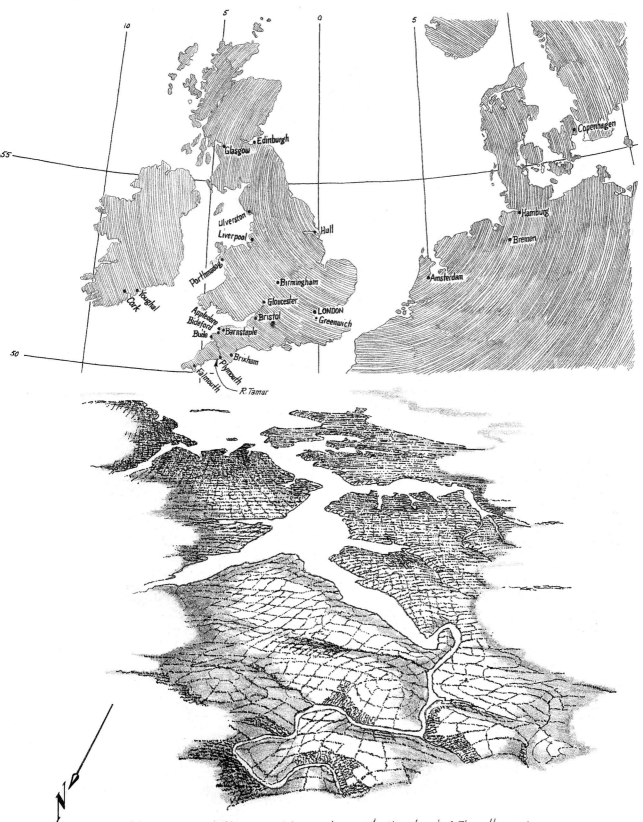

River Tamar — looking seaward from upstream. The Channel port of Plymouth occupies the estuary, top left. Master's shipyard was on a foreground reach of the river.

were put to bed early so that the father would not be disturbed. Often children saw their fathers only when they were allowed to visit the yard, or on Sundays. Saturday was the night to drink, but even then most of the conversation in the public house probably touched on work in one way or another.

Families lived not far above the poverty line, often in crowded conditions. Tuberculosis was very common. Women worked in the house, caring for their large families and continually stoking the stove that smoked and deposited smut everywhere, posing an endless cleaning problem. They were adept at most heavy domestic chores, like chopping wood and breaking up coal and carting it to the stove, and many of them worked in the fields or did heavy surface labour at the mines for some of the year at least. By every door was a foot-scraper, but, nevertheless, mud from the dirt roads was brought into the house over clean slate floors. It got into every corner and the continual fight against it got on many housewives' nerves, sometimes to the point of obsession. Baths were taken in a trough or a tin bath on the kitchen floor in front of the stove. In many families nobody ever bathed properly – they only washed themselves down outside in the scullery.

The shipyard workers and their families usually had very few possessions. Many men when they died left only the tools of their trade and a pocket watch which had been handed down from generation to generation. Worn with a gold chain on very special occasions for most of the time it was kept in a box, stored as a lifelong possession and a possible capital asset. One pair of best boots and a black suit completed the personal possessions of many of the shipwrights and journeymen. Few of them owned their own cottages and they went on working into their seventies because there was no provision made for retirement, either by their employers or by the state, and they did not expect any. Sickness or disablement was a disaster that could lead to poverty. Failure to keep in employment could be equally disastrous. The employer, who could both hire and fire at will, was all-powerful.

Conditions in the country around our yard were alleviated, in comparison with less favourably placed maritime communities, by close connections between shipping and farming, and by the general possession of gardens by even the poorest people, which, through the growing of vegetables, effectively increased the head of the family's average earnings to 12/6d (62½p) per week. There were a number of men in the neighbourhood who cultivated land for part of the year and went to sea in vessels in which they had shares at times when the work on the land could be done by the women alone. In this way the community around the yards resembled some communities in northern Europe where farming and seafaring were combined as occupations, a situation described in Swedish as 'allmogeseglation'-literally 'peasant seafaring', but perhaps best translated as 'rural shipowning'. This kind of occupational pattern was unusual in Britain, though it also developed in north Devon and in Atlantic Canada.

Sons joined fathers or worked elsewhere as soon as they were able, which meant from the age of 6 or 7 in school holidays and from 12, or at the best 14, full-time for the rest of their lives. Daughters went out to service at the same age, or to local shops or small factories, or even to the mines. They were paid a pittance for working very long hours. The Dowager Lady of the local landowning family lived in a nearby big house. When her carriage

Midship half-section of Master's schooner ———

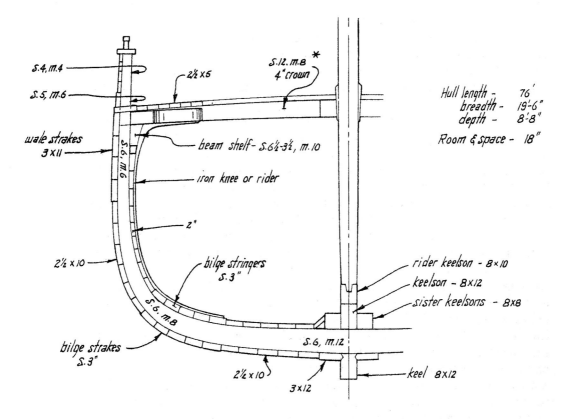

S.4, m.4

S.5, m.6

2½ × 5

S.12, m.8 *
4" crown

wale strakes
3 × 11

S.9, m.6

beam shelf - S.6½-3½, m.10

iron knee or rider

2"

2½ × 10

bilge stringers
S. 3"

S.6, m.8

bilge strakes
S. 3"

S.6, m.12

2½ × 10

3 × 12

S.6, m.12

rider keelson - 8 × 10

keelson - 8 × 12

sister keelsons - 8 × 8

keel 8 × 12

Hull length - 76'
breadth - 19'-6"
depth - 8'-8"

Room & space - 18"

* "s.12, m.8,, 4"crown" ———

"s.12 means <u>sided</u> twelve inches.
"m.8 means <u>moulded</u> eight inches.

<u>Siding</u> is the term for the straight-cut <u>thickness</u> of
squared timber stock.

<u>Moulding</u> (as marked from moulds or patterns) refers to
the front and back faces of the same timber in defining
the curve or shape to be cut by the shipwright.

These particular numbers describe a deck beam cambered 4" across
the hull amidships, placed with its greatest dimension flatways.
The cambered faces would be marked from the deckbeam mould. The
other two sides are straight.

85

passed by, girls on the road had to curtsey. Many a girl felt the coachman's whip across her shoulders because she was slow to show proper respect. The interests of men and women were very different because the roles imposed on both sexes to ensure survival were different, and these roles were all absorbing. It was a consequence of this that at such social gatherings as there were, mainly associated with chapel, men and women formed separate groups.

These economic and social conditions left some young men with the determination to break out of their inherited position at almost any cost. Some succeeded, in varying degrees, through owning shares in the vessels in which they sailed or through successful enterprise in their crafts on land. A few became millionaires, at home or abroad. Others became comfortably placed small capitalists, owning vessels or shares in vessels, as well as houses and land ashore. Some emigrated to North America. Others set up as master craftsmen on their own account and some succeeded in business. These were men with both determination and luck. Inevitably they were always starved of capital. They knew the risks they ran, but they were exceedingly knowledgeable within the narrow limits of their trade, hard-working and also secretive. They developed into very hard taskmasters, demanding as an employer every ounce of respect and effort because their only chance of success lay in exploiting the labours of others as well as themselves to the utmost. Such a man was the Master Shipwright and proprietor of the local shipyard.

In the yard, 'Master', as he was known to all his employees, was held in awe. He was always on hand and, in the local vernacular, he 'eyed' all activities. When a rebuke was in his view necessary his tongue was as sharp as an adze. His defence was attack, and the men who worked so hard for him were goaded all day long. But he led by example and he was as skilful or more skilful than anybody else in the yard, grasping an adze or a maul to show someone the proper way to complete a job. If Master said 't'was right', it was right. The fortunes of the yard were in his hands, everything in the daily running of it, the speculation, the finance, the professional knowledge and the administration, as well as the hiring and firing which was the basis of his great power and position in the community.

The hiring was not difficult. Education was discounted. If a job came up, a lad who was a potential apprentice and over the age of 12 left school immediately. Getting a job in the trade was the most sought after object of any young man. Not only did training in a trade mean reasonably certain employment, it meant also that a lad of ability had some sort of challenge to save him from the boredom of unskilled work. A young worker prepared to serve a long apprenticeship and learn new skills, taking in his stride many rebuffs and by sheer practical ability striving to earn an honest living, was the ideal employee in Master's view. Such a boy in his turn might after many years rise to be an employer himself. While he was an apprentice he was bound to obey his master, undertaking, in the words of one document surviving in the locality of Master's yard, that:

'he shall not contract matrimony within the said term (of seven years), he shall neither buy nor sell, he shall not haunt Taverns or Playhouses, or absent himself from his said Master's service day or night unlawfully. But in all things as a

Hull design: worked out by the master builder in a half-hull block model —

If the block model is made to scale at .,
3/8"=1'-0", then the assembled block is 28½" long.
The width is 3¼". Depth, (to accommodate
the rise of the ends) is 4½".

The five lifts would be carefully sided
to a thickness of 7/8".

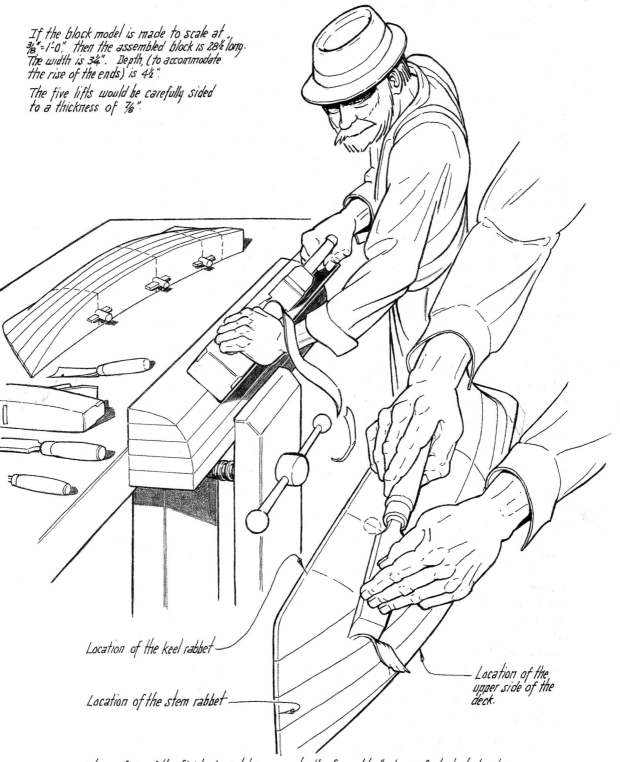

Location of the keel rabbet

Location of the stem rabbet

Location of the
upper side of the
deck.

The surface of the finished model represents the framed hull shorn of plank, bulwarks,
and external protrusions of the keel, stem, and sternpost.

faithful apprentice he shall behave himself towards his said Master at all times during, the said term.'

The shipyard comprised a sloping stretch of river-bank with hard shingle where the slope went down into the water. At the top of the slope, under a row of trees, were two long narrow sheds, roughly built of corrugated iron and open at the ends nearest the water, and one stone shed with a slate roof. The yard was more or less four-square north, south, east and west, with the river, which flowed from east to west here, washing its north side at high water. In the north-west corner of the yard, but still well above the normal tide line, was a steam chest, the purpose and working of which will be described later. This was the total fixed equipment of the yard. Its working capital was wrapped up in the store of metal for fastenings and in the large stocks of timber. Long straight planks and baulks lay pointing north and south between the open ends of the sheds and the water. Curved timber and smaller stuff for ship's frames lay in the south-west corner of the yard, and there was also a raft of seasoning timber baulks and logs kept in the water off the north-west corner.

Vessels under repair could lie on the 'hard' where it sloped well below the high-tide line. By tipping them either inwards or outwards the whole of their bottoms on one side or the other could be worked on, except for the time around high water. The tidal area was sufficient for two or three vessels to be worked on at the same time. The actual site where the new vessels were built was on the eastern side of the yard, between the stone shed and the water.

The yard, like almost all others of its type – and like much larger yards building bigger vessels in nineteenth-century Britain – had no power of any kind. It had no steam-saw or crane; everything was moved and hoisted into position using blocks and tackles, sheerlegs and any other device which fitted the occasion and the muscles of the yard gang. The yard gave to the casual visitor an impression of chaos. So did almost every other contemporary wood shipbuilding yard in Europe or North America. Whatever it looked like, however, although not consciously planned in terms of maximum convenience and minimum labour, the yard still approached this state. Each man used his own tools. Little or no rent, and no rates, were paid for the site, which, before it was filled up and levelled on the slope to make the yard, was a very marshy stretch of grass, subject to periodic tidal floodings.

The yard was organized principally for repairing ships, because most of the business involved repairs, rather than the building of new ships. In this also the place was typical of wooden merchant shipbuilding yards in Britain in the late nineteenth century. Repair work was in constant demand, not only because of accidents and the normal wear and tear on vessels (which led very hard lives indeed), but also as a result of the maintenance standards imposed through the administration of the Merchant Shipping Act by the local Board of Trade representatives, the surveyors, and by the classification organizations, such as Lloyd's Register. The requirements of these two bodies gave plenty of work to good yards and this was usually more profitable than the building of new ships.

Of course, building, particularly of boats, usually continued though progress might be erratic, with frequent interruptions when the labour force was

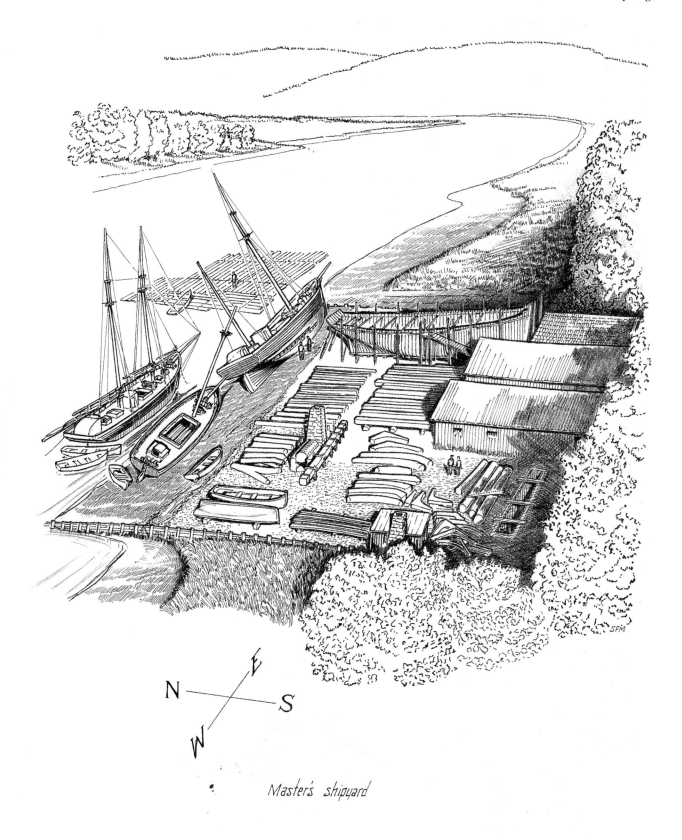

Master's shipyard

switched to repair work. This was most likely to happen when a new vessel was built on speculation, on the yard's own account, to be sold when completed. With this kind of building, work was often done when repair work was slack. It represented a long-term investment which also kept the craftsmen, who were probably the yard's most valuable single asset after its stores of timber, together and in work.

The Master Shipwright who ran the yard did both speculative building and building to order. Let us take a case of the second kind and imagine him approached by a potential customer from down the river. This man is a shipmaster and shareholder and he and some associates, his wife, a brother, a local grocer and a brickworks company, are putting up money for a new schooner, to be employed initially in a contract trade for the brickworks. The potential owner knows very well what he wants, and specifies his requirements orally, as 'a vessel like the *Annie Giffard* you built a couple of years ago, but I want her a little fuller in the body to carry fifteen tons more in the same length'. Master might then say something like, 'The berth at the brickworks is silting up and they don't do nothing about it. We'd better give her more beam and try to get a foot off the draught of the *Annie Giffard*.'

Master would thereupon get down the half model from which the *Annie Giffard* and a number of other schooners had been built and decide what changes were needed to meet the requirements of the new vessel. Master was a product of a stage of technology in which information was not conveyed by means of drawings. Nowadays, of course, everybody thinks on paper or, increasingly, through the computer. All planning begins on the drawing board and any big building project, be it a ship, a house, a factory or even a small boat, requires literally dozens, perhaps hundreds, of drawings. But Master and his customers and the men who worked with him thought of their vessels in three dimensions from the very beginning, and the half model was the first concrete manifestation of a new schooner.

The half model was on the scale of one-quarter inch to the foot and it represented one half of a vessel, sliced down amidships fore and aft from deck to keel, so it was in fact a scale model of half the hull. The block from which it was carved was made up from sanded layers of fine yellow pine planking, each seven-eighths of an inch thick. The layers were fastened together with wooden pins driven into holes drilled right through all the layers, so that the finished block was as strong and could be carved as easily as a piece of solid natural wood. The model was carved out from the laminated block with chisels and, for reasons which will become apparent later, it represented in shape and scale dimensions the inner rather than outer surface of the vessel's planking. It indicated the dimensions of the ship's skeleton, rather than those of the planked-up vessel.

Since the half model largely determined the shape of the finished vessel, its production called for craftsmanship of a high order. It could be judged, by those accustomed to doing so, both visually and by drawing the tips of the fingers over the surface. Indeed, this was the best way of detecting small irregularities and kinks in the curves of the after part of the vessel which were not readily apparent by eye, but which would loom irredeemably large in the finished vessel. In the half model the builder determined the all-important carrying capacity and sailing characteristics of the new vessel. Indeed, the half model determined her very viability as a working ship by

Lift block-model —

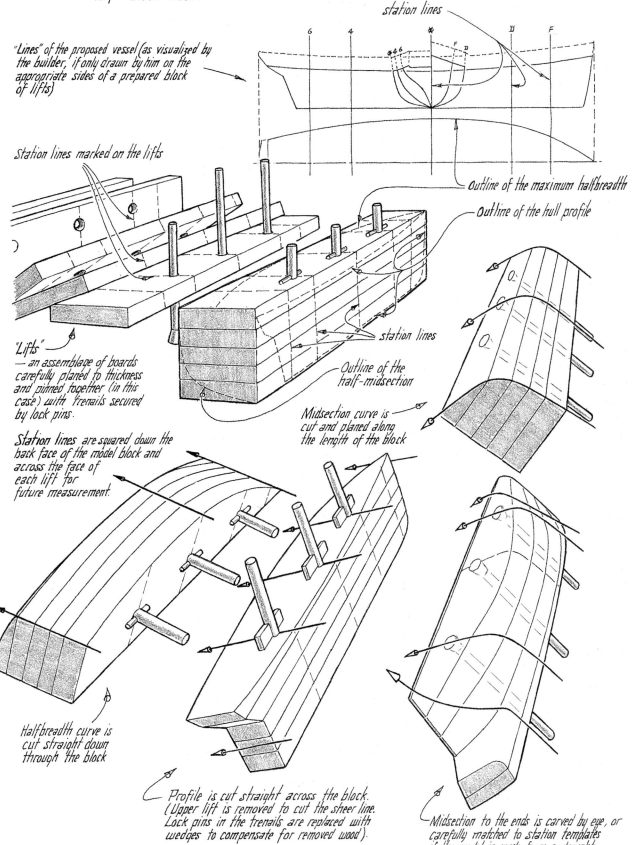

station lines

"Lines" of the proposed vessel (as visualized by the builder, if only drawn by him on the appropriate sides of a prepared block of lifts)

Station lines marked on the lifts

Outline of the maximum halfbreadth

Outline of the hull profile

station lines

"Lifts"
— an assemblage of boards carefully planed to thickness and pinned together (in this case) with trenails secured by lock pins.

Outline of the half-midsection

Midsection curve is cut and planed along the length of the block

Station lines are squared down the back face of the model block and across the face of each lift for future measurement.

Halfbreadth curve is cut straight down through the block

Profile is cut straight across the block. (Upper lift is removed to cut the sheer line. Lock pins in the trenails are replaced with wedges to compensate for removed wood).

Midsection to the ends is carved by eye, or carefully matched to station templates if the model is made from a draught.

such points of design as whether she would float laden with the keel parallel to the water line, a most desirable characteristic in a vessel which had regularly to lie aground on the ebb tide, often laden with heavy cargo.

The half model was sometimes the subject of a good deal of discussion. The shipbuilder, the managing owner and the shipmaster would argue with one another, while the model itself was chiselled and sandpapered here and there, in the forepart and afterpart, until a shape was achieved which satisfied everybody. Then the half model was·ready for use as the basis for the design of the vessel. For reasons which will become apparent later the dimensions of the finished vessel did not necessarily accord exactly with those scaled-up from the half model and in many small details she might be different. But, nevertheless, the half model was fundamental to a ship's design and could often be recognized instantly by men familiar with the ships that had been built from it.

There were, in fact, several different types of half model and several different ways of deriving the shape of a vessel's frame from them. Some models were carved from solid wood and some made up of cut out half-frame shapes glued by their straight edges to a board representing the centre-line of the vessel and shaped to her profile. Developing the shape of the kind of half model Master used into the shape of the full-sized vessel was difficult, and we will describe the process at its simplest. The wooden pins that held the model together were knocked out so that it fell apart into its four or five layers. Each of these, on its top surface, represented in shape a 'waterline' of the vessel – her shape at a given depth if she was sliced horizontally. With our particular schooner, built for trading into a tidal berth, floating with the keel parallel to the waterline both when laden and when light, the layers of the half model did in fact represent almost true waterlines.

By measuring the width of each of the layers of the half model in turn, first amidships and then at the same distance for each layer forward and aft of amidships, and plotting the measurements scaled-up to full size on the wooden floor of one of the sheds (made up from square-edged board laid level) the rough shape of some of the frames of the vessel could be drawn in chalk, or scribed out in scratches made in the wood with a sharp tool. The yard men would then lay off each of the breadths of the layers of the half model in turn, scaled-up to full size from a centre-line which represented the vertical centre of the vessel from mid-keel to mid-deck. In this way they derived the shape of perhaps ten or a dozen of the thirty or forty frames, which, like the bones of an animal, would act as the schooner's skeleton. They would determine her shape and be the main source of her strength when she was built. This is why the half model, which was the source for the frame shapes, represented the dimensions of the skeleton, and not those of the fully planked-up vessel.

While the model was under discussion and the hull was being lined up on the floor, Master would be busy at several other things. He would view the ground, sloping downwards to the water, on which the vessel was to be built, ensuring that the overall length was sufficient. The ground would have to be tramped or rammed to compact the top surface so that the blocks which would take the weight of the keel, and eventually of the whole vessel, could be laid with their tops level and would not sink into the ground. He also had

92

Design information given by the half-hull block model —

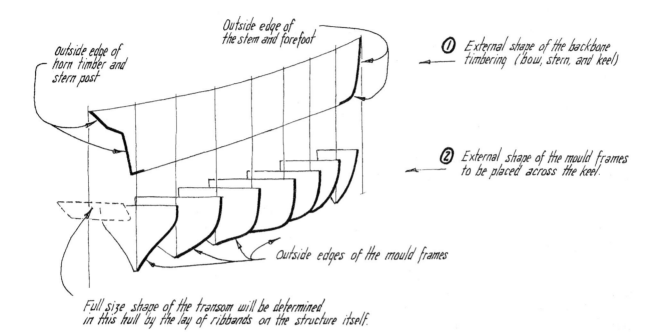

Outside edge of
the stem and forefoot

Outside edge of
horn timber and
stern post

① *External shape of the backbone
timbering (bow, stern, and keel)*

② *External shape of the mould frames
to be placed across the keel.*

Outside edges of the mould frames

*Full size shape of the transom will be determined
in this hull by the lay of ribbands on the structure itself.*

to satisfy himself that the angle at which the slipway was to be led into the
water was right for the eventual launching of the vessel.

Master would also have to acquire the additional stocks of timber needed
for the building of the ship. He already had stocks in the yard, some of which
had been lying there for some years, bought when they were available cheaply
or left over from previous building work. But for the new vessel he would
need much more timber. For this he turned first to local dealers in the town
at the mouth of the river from whom he bought red pine which had come
from Scandinavia in baulks. He also bought pitch pine which had been
brought across the Atlantic from Pensacola on the Florida Gulf in wooden
barques – three-masted square-rigged vessels – owned by sea-farers in the
then Russian Åland Islands in the Gulf of Bothnia. This timber was made
into rafts and brought up the river on the flood tide, in the charge of a local
tug, hired for a very small charge. For the rest of the timber Master would
have to turn to other local sources. In a 16-foot clinker-built boat he had
built himself he rowed about three miles downstream from the yard, to a
quay with a timber yard and a saw-mill. There, Master personally chose local
wood for the frames of our new schooner – mostly English oak. This timber
was then moved to the edge of the quay and eased over into the river. Master
himself lashed it together into rafts and the tide took it, tended by his men
in boats, up to the yard, where it was hauled ashore.

Full size layout of the ends of the vessel as scaled along the lifts on the flat back side of the half model —

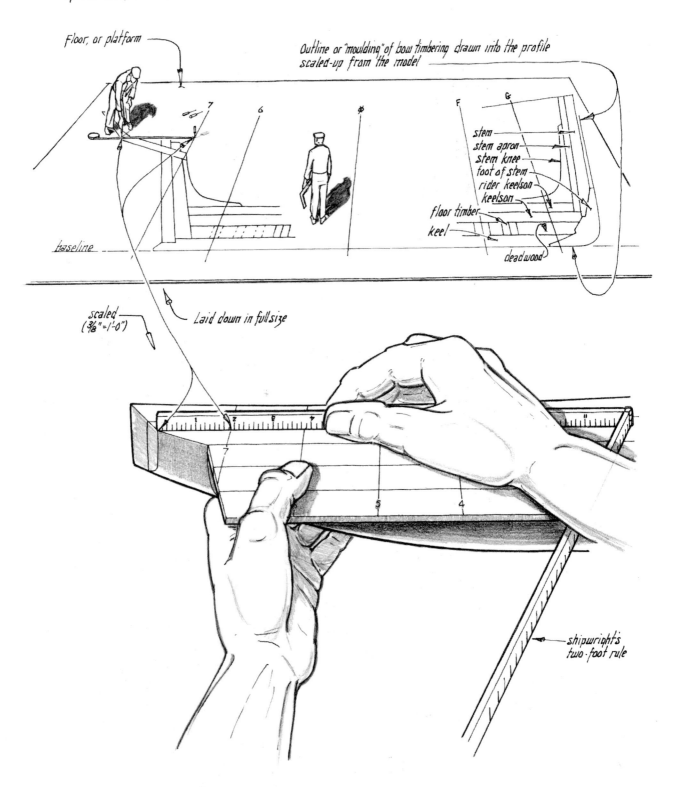

Floor, or platform

Outline or "moulding" of bow timbering drawn into the profile scaled-up from the model

baseline

stem
stem apron
stem knee
foot of stem
rider keelson
keelson
floor timber
keel
deadwood

scaled
(3/8" = 1'-0")

Laid down in full size

shipwright's two-foot rule

Crossectional curves of the hull obtained directly from the lifts of the block model —

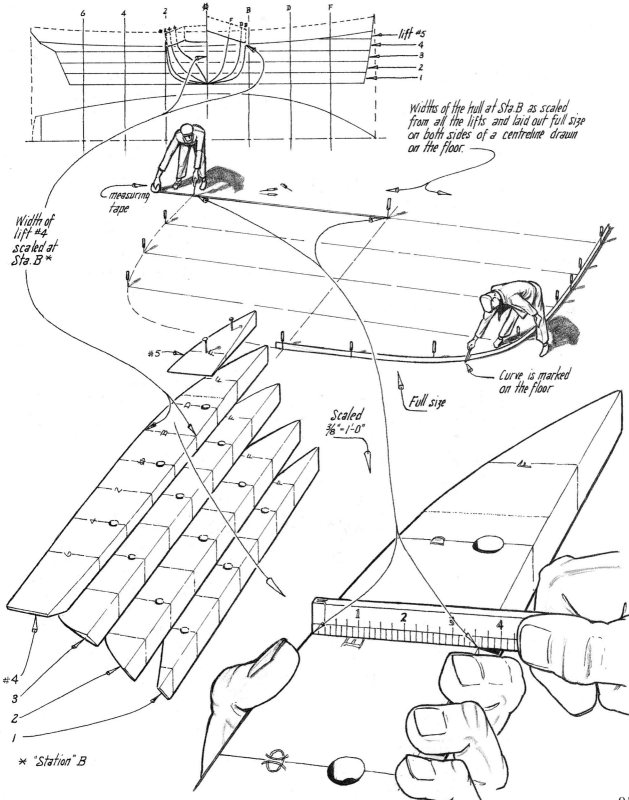

lift #5
4
3
2
1

Widths of the hull at Sta.B as scaled
from all the lifts and laid out full size
on both sides of a centreline drawn
on the floor.

Width of
lift #4
scaled at
Sta.B *

measuring
tape

#5

Curve is marked
on the floor

Full size

Scaled
⅜" = 1'-0"

#4
3
2
1

* "Station" B

1   2   3   4

95

The scrieve board ——————

These three regions of the block model must be plotted accurately in plane views,
full size, in order to pattern timber and control the shape of the structure:

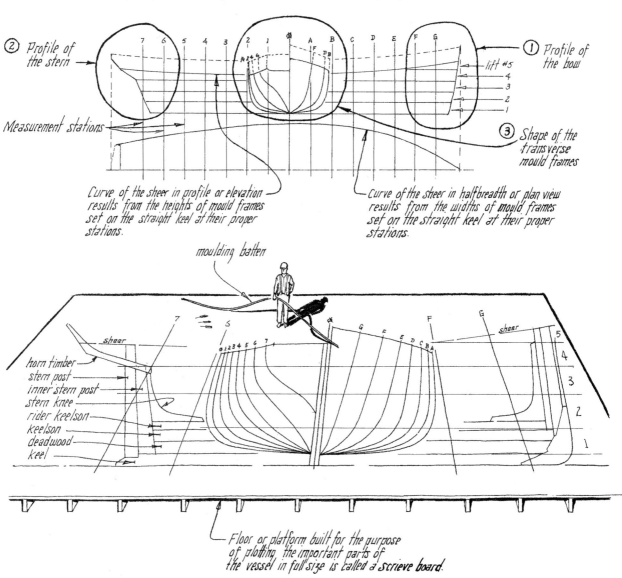

② Profile of the stern →

① Profile of the bow

Measurement stations

③ Shape of the transverse mould frames

Curve of the sheer in profile or elevation results from the heights of mould frames set on the straight keel at their proper stations.

Curve of the sheer in halfbreadth or plan view results from the widths of mould frames set on the straight keel at their proper stations.

moulding batten

horn timber
stern post
inner stern post
stern knee
rider keelson
keelson
deadwood
keel

sheer

sheer

Floor or platform built for the purpose of plotting the important parts of the vessel in full size is called a **scrieve board**.

Patterns ——

—Thin boards shaped to the pencilled outlines of the backbone timbering and to the sectional curves in the fullsize layout.

It is from these patterns that the backbone and mould frame members of the vessel are marked out and cut to assure that the parts of the frame lock together as accurately as they are drawn on the lofting floor.

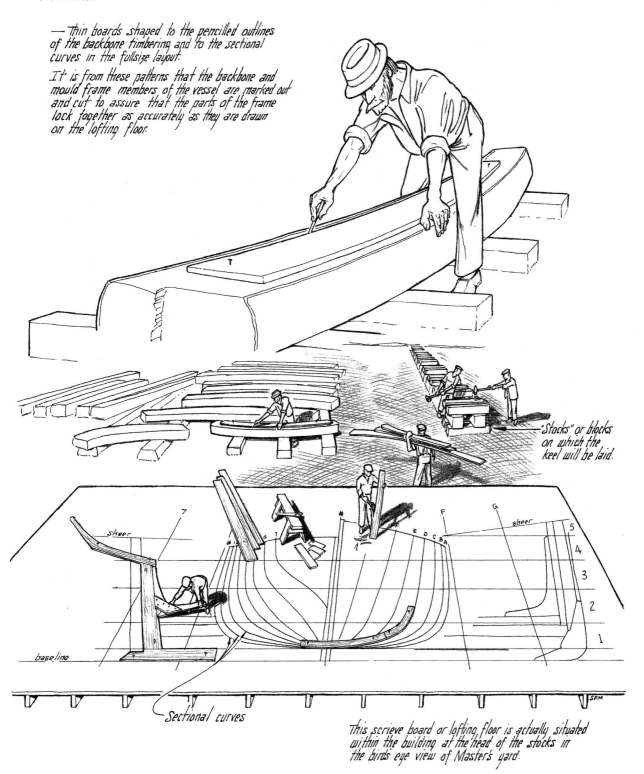

"Stocks" or blocks on which the keel will be laid.

sheer

sheer

5

4

3

2

1

baseline

Sectional curves

This scrieve board or lofting floor is actually situated within the building at the head of the stocks in the birds eye view of Master's yard.

The new vessel was to have a keel of local elm, framing of the local English oak, and a keelson cut from a massive teak baulk sold off from the breaking-up of an old wooden warship. The deck beams, stem, stern post and the massive timbers of the transom, the knightheads and the aprons were all to be of English oak with one or two pieces from the woods adjoining the yard. The outside planking was to be of English oak and pitch pine, though American elm was sometimes used, as was also English elm for the lower planking. The 'ceiling', the planking lining the inside of the vessel, was all to be of pitch pine from Pensacola. The decks were to be of the Scandinavian red pine.

Master's next job was to lay his keel. This he did on a series of massive wooden blocks placed with their centres about a metre apart and each a metre deep (so that there would be plenty of room to work under the schooner as she grew on the slipway), running down in a gentle slope towards the line of the highest spring tides. On these blocks the English elm keel was made up from two pieces, scarfed together. The logs were selected from the stock floating in the river and hauled up to the slipway. The massive timbers, eight-inch sided, were cut from the logs with pitsaws, each eight feet long and a foot broad in the centre, and the whole faired with adze and planes.

All the big sawing jobs were done at the sawpit situated at the back of the yard, high up under the trees on the west side where the water-table was lowest. There, the pit was least likely to fill up with water in rainy weather or in times of very high tides. The pit was lined with planks; it was long and narrow and about two metres deep. The timber to be converted was heaved and shoved into place over the pit with levers, with tackles, and with sheerlegs where necessary. On the pit it rested on beams sometimes on rollers, wedged to the correct angle if it was going to be cut on a bevel. The pit was manned by two men, the top sawyer and the 'pit boy'. The work was done by both; the top sawyer's principal function was to guide the blade, the pit boy's to bring it down with force to make a three-inch bite on each stroke. It was extremely hard work for both, especially for the boy, who lived all the years of his apprenticeship under a rain of sawdust. One elderly shipwright in Gloucestershire remembered even girls and women working in the local sawpits in the 1860s. Another recalled:

> I and another sawyer had to saw a huge log down to half inch boards. We used to go home at night with armpits raw from the sawing. Father would tell us 'Rub some Fuller's Earth into it, that will help it'. And that is what we used to do.

Richard Huxtable served several years apprenticeship in the shipyard of Robert Cock and Sons of Appledore in north Devon when wooden schooners very like the one being described were built there in the early years of this century. In 1975 he recorded

> And we boys as apprentices we had to take the worst job then, in the pit itself. The sawyer would come along and take the tree out, square it off all ready and line it up, and then he would put his chalk line along the top and he would come down underneath and he would put a series of chalk spots along, and you were supposed to stick to these.
>
> You hadn't been down there very long before you couldn't see what you were doing, sawdust down your neck, sawdust everywhere, it was a hard job, that was,

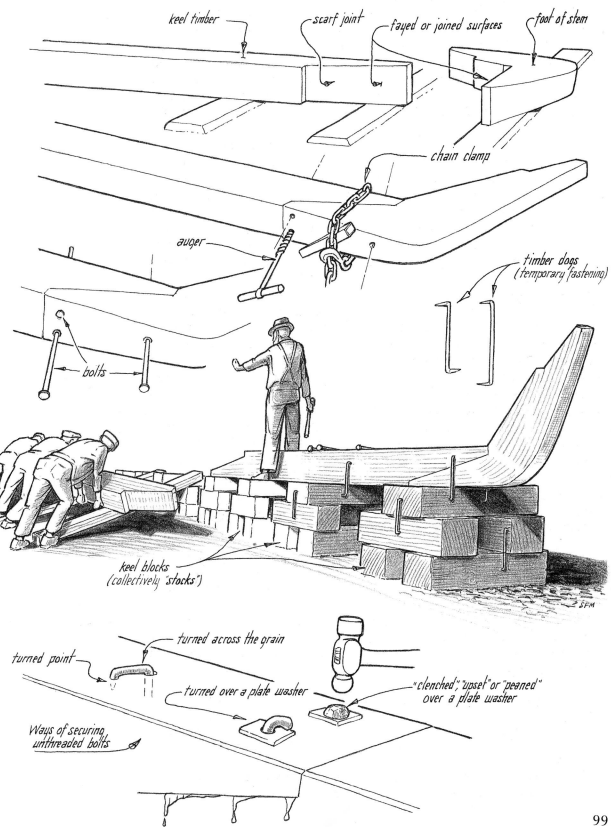

The keel —

keel timber

scarf joint

fayed or joined surfaces

foot of stem

chain clamp

auger

timber dogs
(temporary fastening)

bolts

keel blocks
(collectively "stocks")

turned across the grain

turned point

turned over a plate washer

"clenched", "upset" or "peaned"
over a plate washer

Ways of securing
unthreaded bolts

99

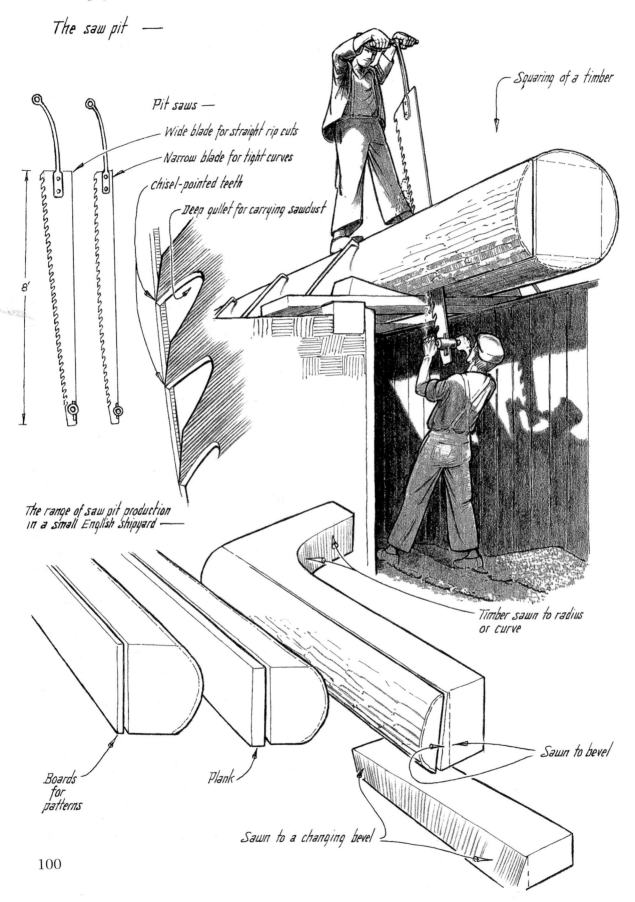

The saw pit —

Pit saws —

Wide blade for straight rip cuts

Narrow blade for tight curves

chisel-pointed teeth

Deep gullet for carrying sawdust

8'

Squaring of a timber

Timber sawn to radius or curve

The range of saw pit production in a small English shipyard —

Boards for patterns

Plank

Sawn to bevel

Sawn to a changing bevel

100

always down there, you know, you would be standing up to your knees in sawdust, your throat would be full of sawdust, and everything else.

The sawyer would square it off and cut off the first slab till he got the size of the planking he wanted and then we would start cutting the planks out from that, which was hard graft.

If it was too dark to work in the winter about your job in the dock or on the deck of the ship, it would be your job to go out and carry the timber in under the sheds. They'd stack it in the dry and you can understand boys of my age, 14, 15, as you were walking along with a 30-foot plank on your back and a chap the other end, your knees would go up and down like a yo-yo.

It was certainly hard graft for 3 shillings and 6 pence a week, that was what I was paid at first. It was a seven-year apprenticeship, 9 shillings and 6 pence I think, or somewhere round 9 shillings in the last year, and then you graduated up to the wonderful sum of 19 shillings for a journeyman. Then, if you were a good chap they would keep you on, but otherwise 'goodbye'.

All the grown men in the yard were extremely skilled with tools, and spent a significant part of their working time simply keeping them sharp. As sawyers they could cut heavy timber for many feet on a chalk line, or even the scratch of a thumbnail. In fact Master himself is said very rarely to have used a pencil. They had a special facility for predicting the changing shape that would be assumed by timber between two measured points. The pit saw, although a coarse tool in appearance, was capable in the right hands of relatively fine work.

The saw pit was only one of several ways of mounting timber for the pitsaw. Almost equally common in England, and more common the world over, was a raised staging on to the top of which the material to be sawn was hoisted with levers and tackles. The top sawyer stood on the staging, the pit boy in the open underneath. This method was used when the site for sawing was a temporary one, and it was not worth digging and lining a pit, or when the water table was too high for a pit, or the ground too hard or frozen to dig one.

The construction of the keel of the new schooner would take up all Master's personal attention, since everything else in the building of the vessel depended on it. To ensure that it was laid 'straight and true' the keel blocks would be lined through and levelled, thus ensuring a true basis for future measurements. If necessary the two elm baulks which comprised the keel had to be clamped to the blocks and even into the ground to secure them against twist and misalignment as they dried out. In the summer heat, elm keels were known to lift off the blocks and 'fly'. Once this happened, wetting, clamping with irons wedged over the twisting elm and weights were used to counteract the twist of the offending grain pattern. The favourite means of wetting was to use sacking, soaked in salt water, and the process continued until sufficient frames had been erected on the keel for their weight to overcome the twisting.

Once the keel was in position on the blocks the next stage was the erection of the stem and stern-posts. Master would mark out the stem and the stern-posts on big pieces of timber, selected in the case of the stem for the natural curve of growth, which in turn were manhandled over to the sawpits. They were sawn into shape and finished off with adzes, then hauled back across the yard and lifted into position at either end of the keel with sheerlegs. They were then secured in position with props and pinned to the keel, so that for

Stem and stern posts —

the first time something approximating to the eventual profile of the finished vessel became visible.

This is a simple description. In fact, of course, the process was more complex. The oak stem was traditionally shaped with a fullness to the top. It was also given a little curve, a reduced version of the graceful curve of the stems of some bigger sailing ships. After it had been shaped with pitsaw, adzes and planes, rebates (long slots, locally called 'rabbets' or 'rabbits') were cut down each side with chisels. These were to receive the fore ends of the planks of the vessel's skin and ensure a fair, watertight structure in which the end grain was covered and protected. The ends of the planks, where water could easily penetrate the structure, were especially vulnerable to rotting.

The whole great shaped piece of timber forming the stem was then carted to the slipway and hoisted up, shored and secured and then checked for plumb. As with the alignment of the keel, this was very important indeed, since if it was not done properly the whole finished vessel could be distorted.

At the stern the oak post, later to carry the rudder, was similarly shored into position and held to the keel with temporary tie battens. Master would make a detailed sketch in chalk of the make-up of the 'dead wood', the timber built up in the angle between the keel and the stem and stern-post to weld the whole together into a continuous backbone. The oak deadwood was cut from grown oak bends and adzed and planed to be fair with the stem and keel. As all this was going on a long rabbet was cut on each side of the keel to take the inner edges of the garboard strakes, the lowest planks of the skin of the vessel, the planks next to the keel on either side. These rabbets were continuous with the rabbets on each side of the stem.

To fasten the stem and stern-posts to the keel and to their respective deadwoods, 'bolts' were used. These bolts were iron bars an inch or more in diameter, hot-dip galvanized, or heat-steeped in bitumen, tar or linseed oil, preferably the former, which were driven with sledge hammers and very great skill into holes previously drilled out with hand augers right through the mass of timber.

These holes were slightly smaller in diameter than the bolts driven into them in order to ensure that the latter had a tight hold on the timbers and fastened the assembly together permanently. Indeed, in the middle of the present century, when old wooden schooners could be found abandoned and falling to pieces in remote harbours all around the coast of northern Europe and north eastern America, the stem and stern-post assemblies were usually the last part of the vessel to fall apart.

Now the time had come to begin 'framing up' the new schooner – building up her ribs, which determined her final shape, into a skeleton to be clothed over later with planks. The frame shape had to be derived from the full-sized drawing which Master himself had made on the floor of the wooden shed from the half model in the way already described. There were several different ways of converting the full-sized drawing into the shape of the actual frame. For a vessel the size of the schooner, and up to perhaps 200 tons or so net register, the frames were made up from five or seven pieces of timber. First there were the 'floors', the bottom part of the frame, which went right across the keel and provided the flat underbody of the vessel amidships, shaped as the vessel fined away at bow and stern. These were notched underneath

The rabbet —

This is a groove cut along the side of the keel and upward along the stem and the stern post to receive the squared edge of the plank adjoining the keel as well as the hood ends of all plank which terminate on the end posts.

The rabbet is normally roughed-out while the backbone timbers are not yet joined and are easy to get at. It can be cut quite accurately into unassembled timbers when the ends of the hull have been well developed in the fullsize layout on the scrieve board.

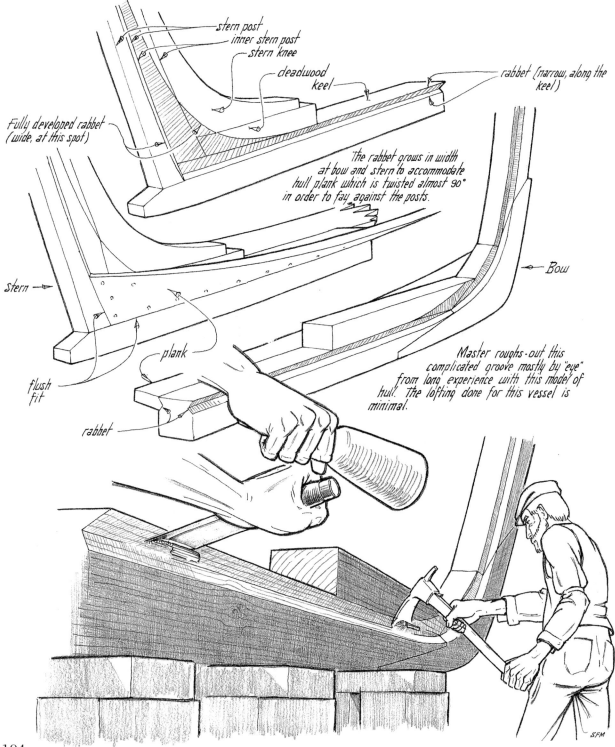

stern post
inner stern post
stern knee
deadwood
keel
rabbet (narrow, along the keel)

Fully developed rabbet (wide, at this spot)

The rabbet grows in width at bow and stern to accommodate hull plank which is twisted almost 90° in order to fay against the posts.

Stern

Bow

plank

flush fit

rabbet

Master roughs-out this complicated groove mostly by "eye" from long experience with this model of hull. The lofting done for this vessel is minimal.

SFM

104

Boring for bolts in the backbone timbering —

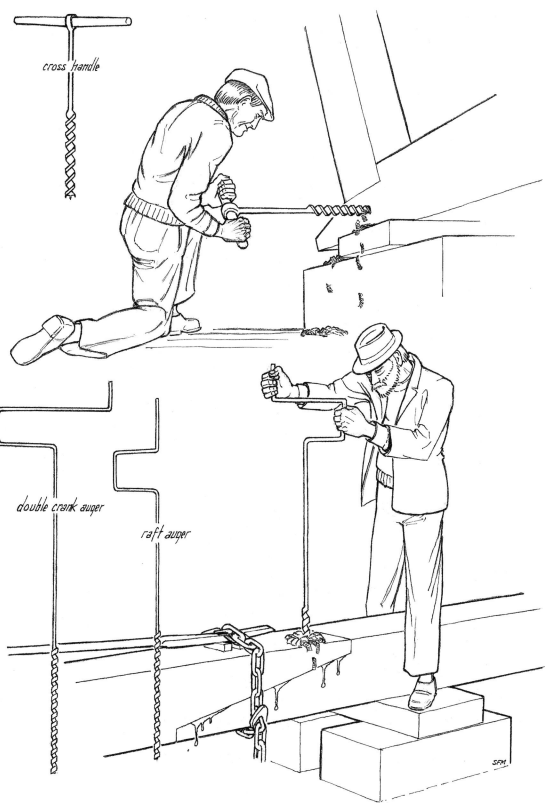

cross handle

double crank auger

raft auger

Non-threaded bolts — driving and heading —

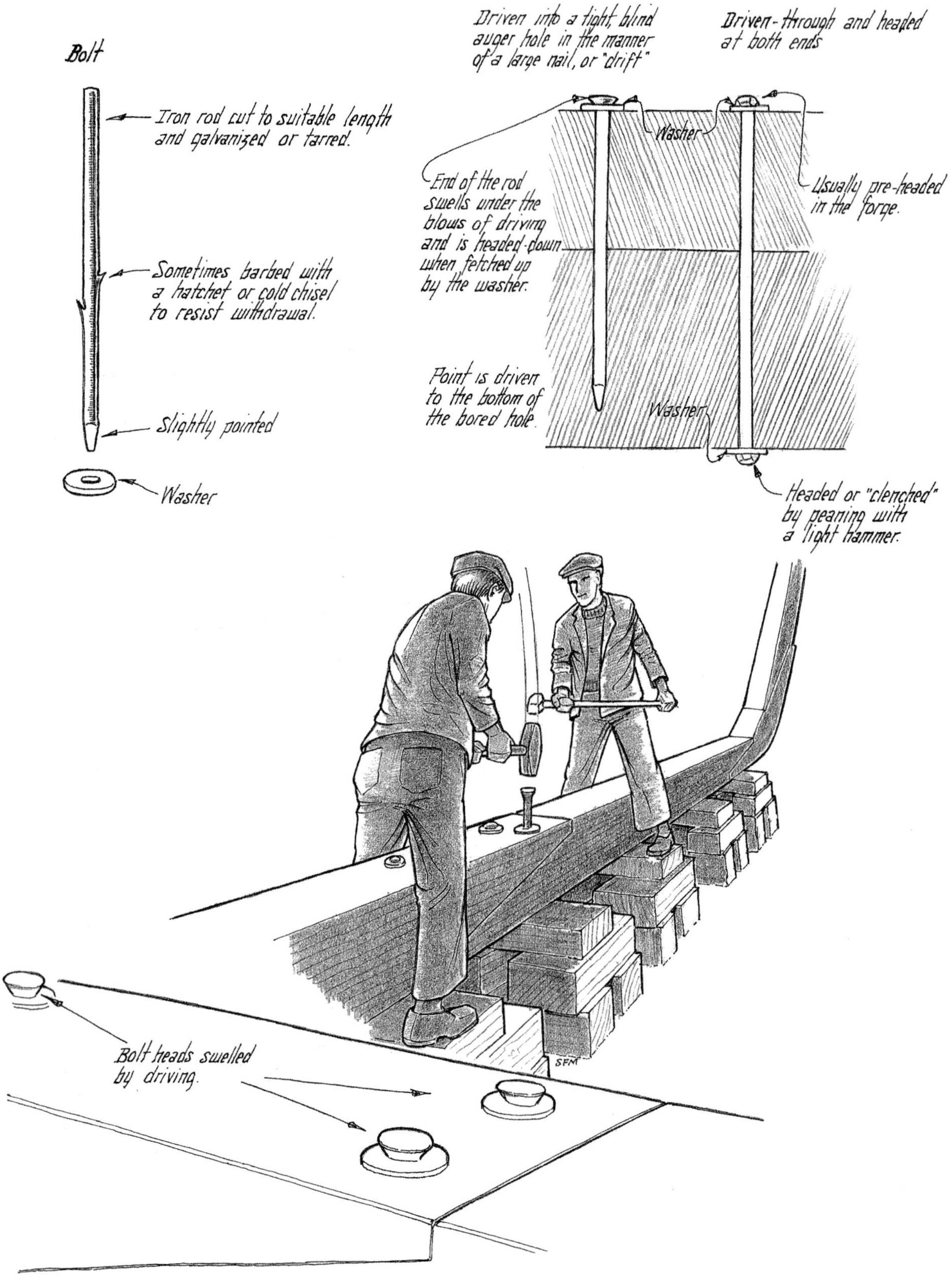

Bolt

Iron rod cut to suitable length and galvanized or tarred.

Sometimes barbed with a hatchet or cold chisel to resist withdrawal.

Slightly pointed

Washer

Driven into a tight blind auger hole in the manner of a large nail, or "drift"

Driven-through and headed at both ends

Washer

End of the rod swells under the blows of driving and is headed-down when fetched up by the washer.

Usually pre-headed in the forge.

Point is driven to the bottom of the bored hole.

Washer

Headed or "clenched" by peaning with a light hammer.

SFM

Bolt heads swelled by driving.

Sawn, paired, transverse frames —

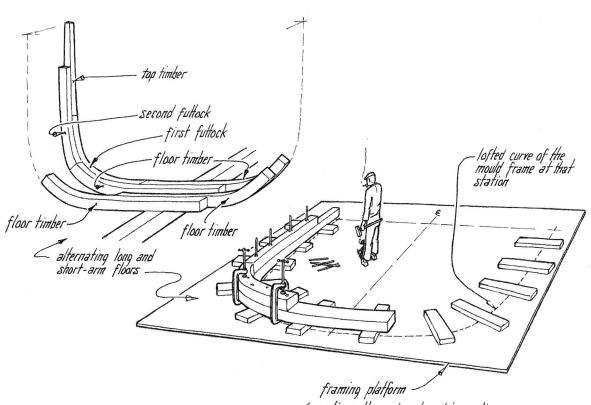

top timber

second futtock

first futtock

floor timber

floor timber

floor timber

alternating long and short-arm floors

lofted curve of the mould frame at that station

framing platform
(sometimes the scrieve board is used)

top timber

third futtock

second futtock

first futtock

(single) floor timber

107

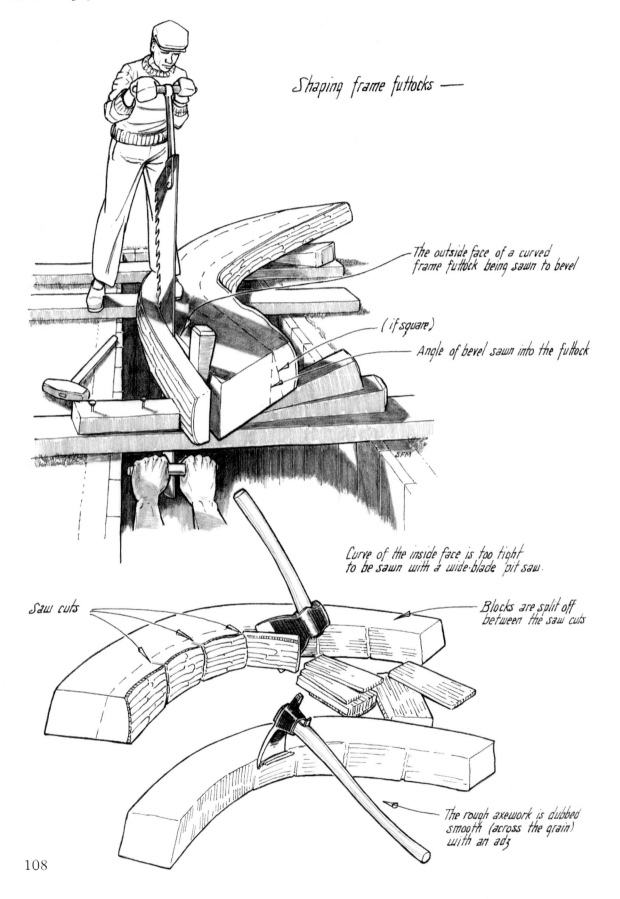

Shaping frame futtocks —

The outside face of a curved frame futtock being sawn to bevel

(if square)

Angle of bevel sawn into the futtock

Curve of the inside face is too tight to be sawn with a wide-blade pit saw.

Saw cuts

Blocks are split off between the saw cuts

The rough axework is dubbed smooth (across the grain) with an adz where they rested on the keel and on top where the keelson, the massive inner keel, would rest upon them. Next there were the 'futtocks', two or three for each frame on each side, making up their side pieces. The topmost futtock of each side was usually called the 'top-timber'.

Master would make up moulds of light, thin board using the drawing on the floor of the wooden shed (which, it will be remembered, was adjacent to the sawpit) and then select from his timber stock which piece to use for which part of each individual frame, before marking the shape off in chalk using the mould. The timber was then manhandled across to the sawpit and roughly cut out by the sawyers. They could get the shape of the outside of the curves of the frames without much difficulty, even though the pit saw itself at its centre part was about a foot (a third of a metre) wide. The inside curve was much more difficult and the sawyers put in a series of sawcuts designed to make it easy to finish this off with adzes.

In almost all vessels the frames tapered: the floor timber or timbers reduced in size on either side of the keel and each futtock in turn tapered further. In a schooner 90 feet long the floors were about a foot square where they rested on the keel, tapering to 8 inches where they joined the futtocks. The futtocks themselves tapered from 8 inches to 5 or 6 inches at deck level. The complex frames of a barque, a square-rigged vessel of say 700 tons, 170 feet long, were much more massive, tapering from perhaps 18 inches at the keel to 8 at deck level.

4 the skeleton

Some explanation of the types of timber used in the building of wooden sailing vessels is now necessary, particularly with reference to the transverse frames which gave form to the hull, the making and fitting of which was really the heart of the whole building process.

The merchant shipyard was entirely dependent for its survival on Master's judgement and experience in the selection and purchase of suitable timber. The business could not carry the losses incurred as a result of acquiring poor timber which was condemned by customers and official surveyors. Master bought the trees either as they stood in the woods or as they lay where they had been felled. Alternatively he bought them from local timber merchants. For compactness and resistance to cleavage, resisting a strain, supporting a weight and resistance to splintering when damaged, English oak was considered by wooden shipbuilders in Britain as superior to all other timber. There were, however, different qualities, even of this fine timber, and the shipbuilder had to be constantly alert when selecting trees for felling. Autumn- and winter-cut oak when well seasoned lasted indefinitely, but it was more usual to fell oak in the spring, when the sap was running, because it was easy to strip off the bark (in the nineteenth century this had marketable value for tanning leather and was also used as the base for the waterproofing of sails, rope and nets).

After the tree was felled, the branches and twigs were lopped off and the trunk was measured for girth and cubic content. It was then hauled along the ground to the waiting timber carriage, in some areas known as a 'tug', parbuckled on to it and then hauled to the shipyard by a team of heavy working horses. Timber was measured in loads, a load being the quantity which could be drawn by a one-horse cart, roughly the equivalent of 1 ton weight (40 or 50 cubic feet). A book could be written solely on the labour and skills required to transport timber of this size across rough country to the shipyard.

On arrival at the yard the rough logs had to season before being cut over the sawpit, so there was always a great deal of capital locked up in the stock. The timber was stacked in such a manner as to allow free circulation of air over the exposed surfaces, but it also had to be protected from the direct rays of the sun and the rain. One year for every inch of thickness was said to be the minimum for full seasoning, but ideally the timber would not be worked until a decade had passed after the tree was felled – an ideal seldom achieved in small yards, of which there were very many in Britain, Europe and North America.

110

The "square frames" or "square body" of the vessel —

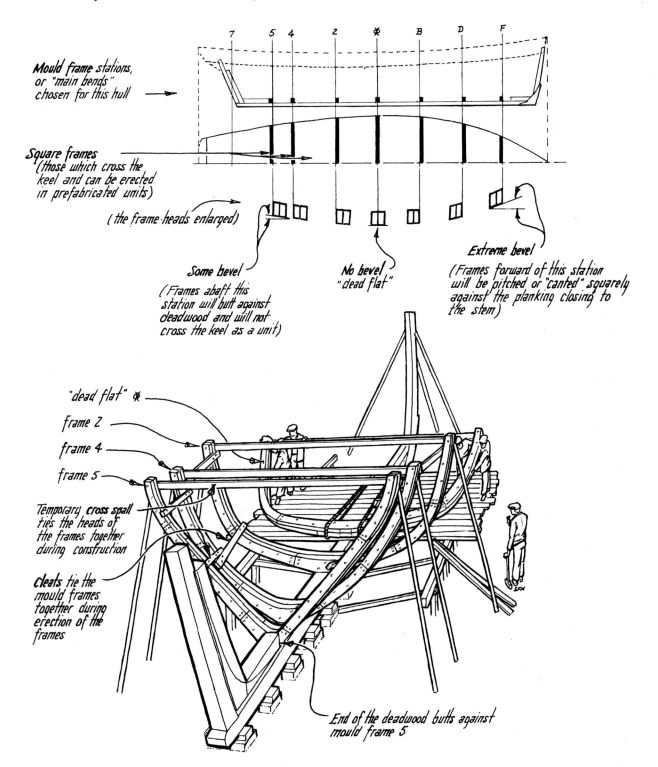

Mould frame stations, or "main bends" chosen for this hull

Square frames (those which cross the keel and can be erected in prefabricated units)

(the frame-heads enlarged)

Some bevel (Frames abaft this station will butt against deadwood and will not cross the keel as a unit)

No bevel "dead flat"

Extreme bevel (Frames forward of this station will be pitched or "canted" squarely against the planking closing to the stem)

"dead flat" ⌀

frame 2

frame 4

frame 5

Temporary cross spall ties the heads of the frames together during construction

Cleats tie the mould frames together during erection of the frames

End of the deadwood butts against mould frame 5

The test of Master's judgment came when the timber was put to the saw, adze or plane. Then the effect of the soil in which the tree grew, the exposure to the prevailing wind, periods of drought, and many other circumstances which influenced the quality of the timber, became apparent for the first time as the timber was worked. About one-third of the timber in its rough state was lost in siding and squaring – shaping the timber in preparation for cutting into planks or frame-pieces, beams or knees. Some 75 per cent of the dressed timber used for building a wooden sailing vessel was required for the main framework or skeleton. The rest went on knees, fillings and the planking of the hull.

Before the introduction of iron knees in wooden ships in the 1820s, it was reckoned that a load-and-a-half of timber was required for every ton of merchant shipping. After the use of iron knees became almost universal, a 200-ton vessel could be built of some two-thirds of a load of timber per ton; a vessel between 100 and 200 tons, the sort of ship described in this narrative, of three-eighths of a load per ton, and smaller vessels of up to half-a-load per ton.

It is a myth that only well-seasoned high-grade timber was used in wooden shipbuilding. In most cases the type and quality of timber put into a vessel depended upon the depth of the owner's purse, how quickly he wanted the vessel built, and the stock of timber that was immediately available in the shipyard to complete the job to an acceptable standard. However, *if* an owner could afford to specify that only the finest seasoned timber should be used in his vessel, and English oak which had been seasoning for years in the yard was used for the main framing, and *if*, at this stage, the vessel could stand a few months longer on the building slip with her frames raised (technically, 'in frame'), but unplanked, for the air to circulate around, then a strong and durable vessel would result. This sometimes happened by accident, if a vessel was built on speculation and stood in frame for some time (sometimes even for years) while repair work went forward.

The skeleton of a wooden vessel was composed of a backbone consisting of a longitudinal keel with a vertically raised stem-post secured to its fore end; a similarly placed stern-post at its after end; and a series of vertically disposed transverse ribs or frames bolted to the keel at equidistant intervals between them. This backbone was strengthened by the fore and aft deadwood connection between the keel, stem and stern-posts, and, after the frames were positioned, by an inner keel or keelson bolted on top of them through to the outer keel. As the building went on the skeleton so formed was tied together by deck beams, 'lodging knees', 'hanging knees', 'breasthooks', the beam shelf and clamps; then a skin of longitudinal strakes of planking was fastened to the outside faces of the frames to form a watertight hull. A similar skin of planking called, somewhat oddly, the ceiling, was also laid on the inner frame faces. The deck was laid on the deck beams. The whole together formed a unit without undue stress in any one part.

The main problem confronting the wood shipbuilder was the construction of the transverse frames which governed the shape of the vessel. If it had been possible to find, cut, transport and work suitable timber of a size and curvature sufficient to make a frame from one, two or even three pieces of timber, wood shipbuilding would have been greatly simplified. The impossibility of obtaining such timber, even for the smallest wooden vessels, forced

Bow and stern formed with "ribbands" —

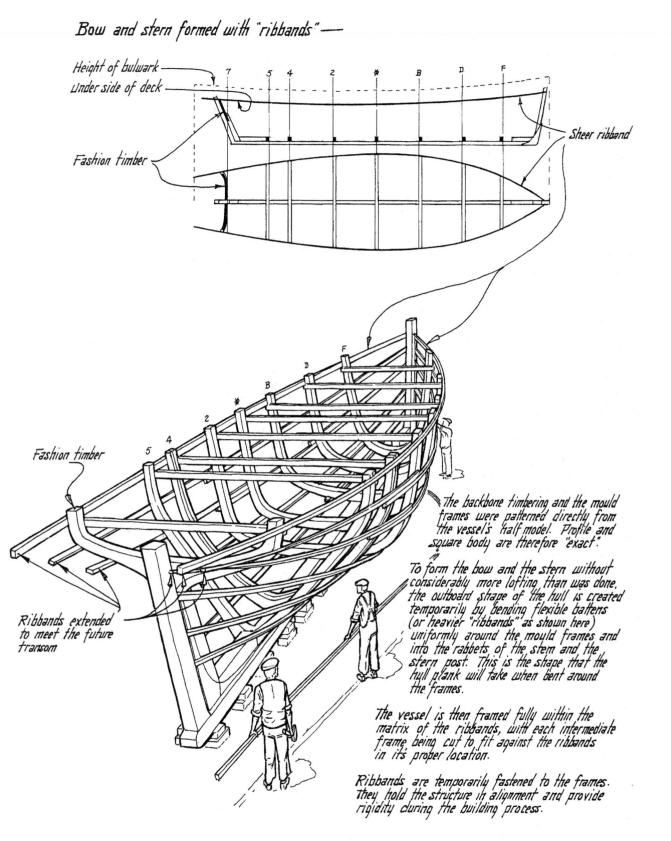

Height of bulwark
Under side of deck

7 5 4 2 ✳ B D F

Fashion timber

Sheer ribband

Fashion timber

F

D

B

✳

2

5 4

Ribbands extended
to meet the future
transom

The backbone timbering and the mould
frames were patterned directly from
the vessel's half model. Profile and
square body are therefore "exact".

To form the bow and the stern without
considerably more lofting than was done,
the outboard shape of the hull is created
temporarily by bending flexible battens
(or heavier "ribbands" as shown here)
uniformly around the mould frames and
into the rabbets of the stem and the
stern post. This is the shape that the
hull plank will take when bent around
the frames.

The vessel is then framed fully within the
matrix of the ribbands, with each intermediate
frame being cut to fit against the ribbands
in its proper location.

Ribbands are temporarily fastened to the frames.
They hold the structure in alignment and provide
rigidity during the building process.

113

Sawn, single, transverse frames ——

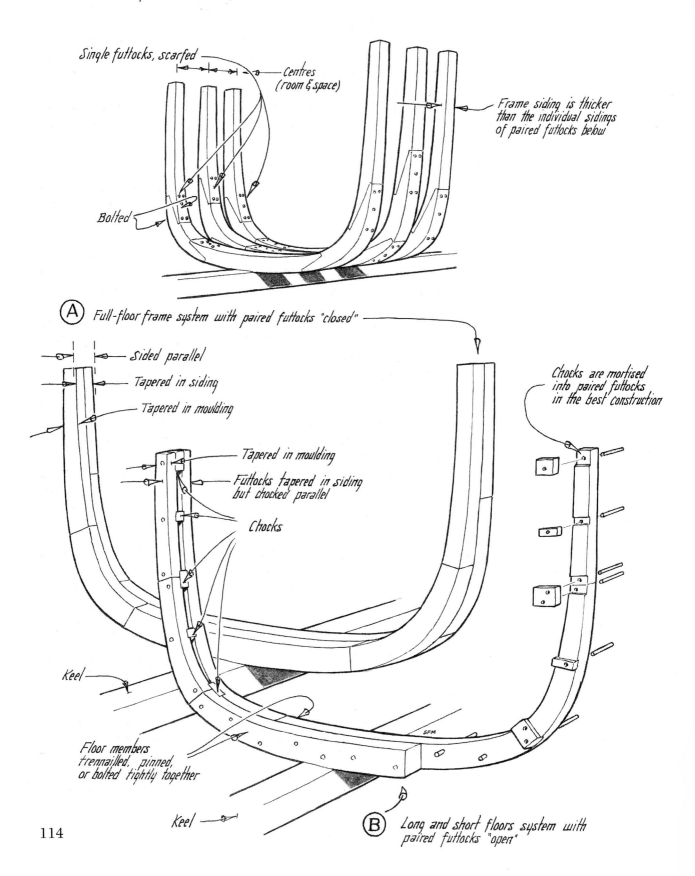

Single futtocks, scarfed

Centres (room & space)

Frame siding is thicker than the individual sidings of paired futtocks below

Bolted

(A) Full-floor frame system with paired futtocks "closed"

Sided parallel

Tapered in siding

Tapered in moulding

Chocks are mortised into paired futtocks in the best construction

Tapered in moulding

Futtocks tapered in siding but chocked parallel

Chocks

Keel

Floor members trennailled, pinned, or bolted tightly together

Keel

(B) Long and short floors system with paired futtocks "open"

114

the shipbuilder to make his frames of several pieces of timber, joined together in such a manner as to allow the run of their grain to follow the curvature of the frame as closely as possible.

Over the centuries, shipbuilders developed many methods of overcoming the consequent difficulties in producing a strong frame structure. By the late nineteenth century many yards in Britain and Europe and most yards in North America were using a system which perhaps first evolved in the Royal Dockyards during the Napoleonic Wars. There were many variations of detail, but basically the system involved the building of frames in *pairs*. Each single frame was made up of several parts–the floors, futtocks and top pieces–the ends of which were cut off square and butted against one another, perhaps fastened with wooden pins to hold them in position during construction. The paired frames were then fixed together with horizontal bolts, often with chocks placed in between them (but never between the floors and first futtocks, which were bolted hard against one another), to keep them a little apart so that the air could circulate freely. In this way the two frames together comprised the basic units of the ship. Separately they fell into their constituent parts; together they formed an immensely strong structure. It is not an easy structure to describe in words, but the drawings make it very clear.

Not all shipbuilders used this framing method, even in the late nineteenth century. In cases where large timber was still readily available, single frames of greater siding than the lighter, doubled frames with the constituent parts fastened together, were still used.

Because the shipbuilder was forced to construct his frame from several separate pieces of timber, every butt joint between them was a potential source of weakness; so, he arranged the butts in each unit of the paired frames so that they were as far apart from each other as possible in the vertical plane, and also from the butts of the adjacent frames, obtaining what is technically described as a 'good shift of butts'.

A glance at the drawing opposite will show that with a series of square butt frames composed of full floors (which reached from bilge to bilge) and the required number of futtocks and top timbers, the resultant line of consecutive butts from fore to aft have but one timber between each of them.

In order to increase the distance between each butt a system of framing was introduced in the construction of naval vessels during the second half of the nineteenth century, and subsequently used in building merchant vessels. In this system, a 'filling frame' composed of long and short arm floors (long on one side of the vessel, short on the other), and the required number of futtocks and top-timbers, was placed between two full-floored frames, as shown here. This system of framing ensured that in any line of consecutive butts there were at least three timbers between each butt; it also meant that the difficulty of obtaining the curved timber required for full floors was lessened.

Owing to the curvature of the bow and the rounding-off of its immersed section into the lower part of the stem-post, the space available for framing lessened considerably from deck level to keel in the fore part of the vessel. As a result, the frames placed square across the keel, as described above, could not be continued for the whole length of the vessel, due to lack of room. There would also have been a great wastage of timber resulting from obtaining

Cant frames —

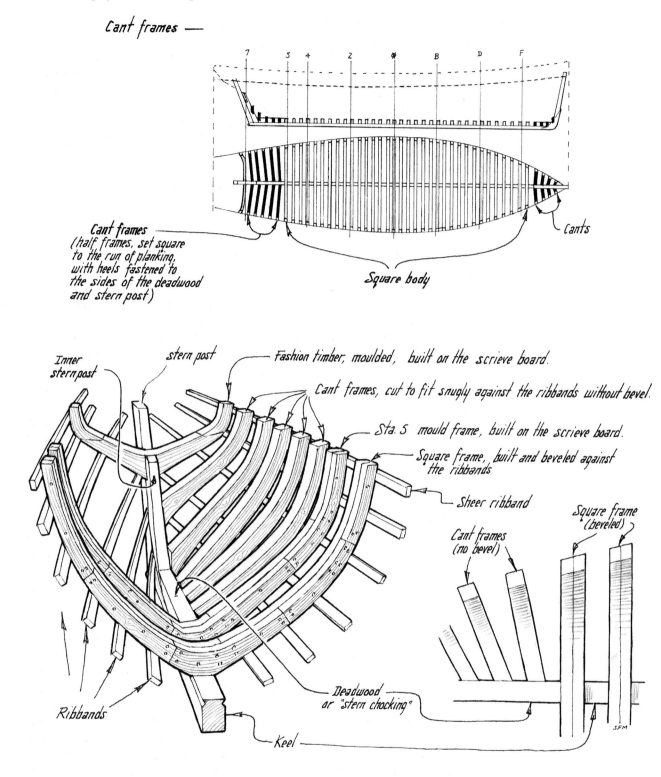

Cant frames
(half frames, set square
to the run of planking,
with heels fastened to
the sides of the deadwood
and stern post)

Cants

Square body

Inner
stern post

stern post

Fashion timber, moulded, built on the scrieve board.

Cant frames, cut to fit snugly against the ribbands without bevel.

Sta. 5 mould frame, built on the scrieve board.

Square frame, built and beveled against
the ribbands

Sheer ribband

Cant frames
(no bevel)

Square frame
(beveled)

Deadwood
or "stern chocking"

Ribbands

Keel

SFM

the acute bevelling of the frame faces necessary to allow the outer and inner planking of the hull to lay square to it.

In order to overcome this problem Master would have arranged what are known as 'cant timbers' or 'cant frames', to fill up the required spaces between the most forward square frame and the stem-post, in a manner similar to the use of staves in a cask. Unlike the square frames, with their timbers placed athwart the keel and disposed vertically, the cant timbers, while still keeping their sides vertically disposed, had to be gradually inclined one by one as they were positioned in the form of a quarter circle to meet the stem-post, the side of which lay in a fore and aft direction.

The cant timbers were fastened to the keel and the deadwood with bolts which secured their heels on opposite sides of the ship. These bolts were placed alternately high and low to avoid the structural weakness resulting from a line of bolt holes.

Cant frames did not have floors, of course, but their futtocks were made up in the same fashion as that used in the building of square frames. Consequently, there would be only one timber between two consecutive butts in the same line, but this was compensated for by the greater length of the futtocks, the timber for which could be more easily obtained owing to the reduction in curvature of the transverse section of the vessel at her extremities. Indeed, in some small vessels the whole of one side of a cant frame could be made of a single timber, cut to a gentle curve on its outer side.

The cant frames of the after body, abaft the furthest after square frame, were disposed in a similar manner to those at the bow. Unless the vessel had a straightforward flat transom stern (like many of the smaller Danish wooden sailing vessels) the assemblage of timbers abaft the stern-post were of a complex character which varied according to the particular shape of stern required–whether transom counter, eliptical counter, pointed or 'pink'. Again the drawings help to explain these differences.

'Room and space' was a technical expression used by wood shipbuilders to describe the distance by which the frames of a vessel were separated along the keel, forming the skeleton of the hull. This was the distance between the 'centres' of any two adjacent frames, the centre being defined as the joint between the floor and the first futtocks. In the case of closed joint frames (without chocks between them) the timbers continued to be in contact with each other right up to the sheer line. In the case of open joint frames (with chocks) the only timbers in contact with each other were the floor and first futtocks. Beyond them, in larger vessels, the diminishing sidings of the second, third or fourth futtocks and top timbers created an ever increasing gap, so that in a well constructed frame the spaces between the timbers at the sheer line were equal to their sidings. The space between the timbers allowed a free current of air to circulate on both sides of them, thereby helping to prevent the premature decay which could occur in vessels with a closed joint frame.

Before deciding on the room and space for our schooner, Master had to consider carefully the purpose for which she was being built. The spacing of the frames had a great influence on the weight and strength of the hull, and Master would have to cut the total weight down to the minimum compatible with the strength required. The less the weight, the more paying cargo would be carried on the proposed draught – and cargo-carrying was the primary function of the working wooden sailing vessel.

The equal spacing of the ship's frames was ensured by reference to the full-sized drawing on the mould-loft floor. The measurements were transferred to the keel by the use of a rod, called, in the shipbuilders' jargon, the 'station' or 'room and space staff'. In naval vessels and merchant ships of superior quality each paired square frame (i.e. all but the cant frames) was connected to its neighbour laterally with frame-bolts. The advantage of this system was the rigidity which it gave to the separate frames and the greater strength which this lent to the whole vessel. A disadvantage of this method of construction was the time and extra labour required to drive in the frame-bolts, as well as the extra cost of materials and the increased weight of the ship. These factors largely precluded the use of this system in most merchant shipyards. Master certainly could not have afforded to use it for our schooner, which was being built on a contract at a price of £850. The whole assembly of timbers, composed of floors, long and short arm floors, first, second, third and even fourth and fifth futtocks, and top timbers, was sometimes described by shipbuilders as a 'frame of doubled timbers', and not as a 'double frame' or a 'paired frame'.

Master would always endeavour to construct a vessel of sufficient strength and quality to satisfy the prospective owner. He also had to satisfy the official surveyor's requirements for the statutory registration of the ship with Board of Trade, meeting the terms of the Merchant Shipping Acts. The shipbuilder also had to meet the demands of the surveyors who would classify the schooner for insurance. Naturally, he did all this at the minimum cost to himself, in order to maximize his profit.

To achieve this end, the shipbuilder would use his judgement and skill in selecting and converting the curved timber required for the frames from the lumber which he had in stock. The ideal form of the new vessel's hull had to be carefully weighed against the ability to build it with the resources available. The shipbuilder's experience would allow a small deviation from the original design, or alteration in the scheme of construction within the limits imposed by good shipwrighting, which might allow the use of otherwise redundant timber, avoiding the need to purchase more. For this reason, all wooden sailing vessels, even those built from the measurements obtained from the same half-model, differed slightly in dimensions and structural details. As a result, and because other deviations were made from the half model (such as the placing of extra frames amidships to lengthen the vessel and increase her carrying capacity), surviving half models today can very rarely be checked exactly with the registered dimensions of actual vessels.

In the case of the new schooner built in Master's yard, relatively few frames had their shapes derived from the half model, via the drawings on the shed floor. Of the thirty-six or so in the finished schooner perhaps eight or nine, or at the most a dozen, were built up, paired and then hoisted into position complete. The rest were built up and shaped on the floor timber as it rested on the keel. There were very special reasons for this.

As has already been explained in Chapter Two, building a vessel by erecting a skeleton of frames and covering it with a watertight skin of planks is an extremely difficult process. The description here is of the process at its simplest, as it was conducted by unsophisticated but highly skilled craftsmen, working in a small, simple shipyard, building small, simply constructed vessels. The bigger the ship, the more were the problems; the finer the shape, then again on the whole, the more problems.

Our Master was a boatbuilder as well as a shipbuilder and indeed the greater part of his income over the years was derived from boatbuilding and repairs to vessels. When he constructed his clinker-built boats he used a much older (to him more *natural*) technique, which was the very reverse of that which he used in building schooners. He began, of course, by building the shell of the boat – the outside skin – from planks, each carefully shaped and fitted, and joined to its neighbour edge-to-edge, as all vessels were built before the technical revolution of the fifteenth century. By this process Master would build the empty shell of the boat first, into which he would insert strengthening frames, shaped to fit the shell and deriving their shapes from its shape. The creation of the shell was the work of supreme craftsmanship – almost an act of sculpture. Master could see the boat grow under his hands, through his skill in shaping the planks from which it was constructed. His boats were the ultimate form of personal expression for him.

Shell building, with many, many variations, was the way in which most of the world's vessels were built until very recent years. Ships of relatively large size continued to be built in this way – like huge overgrown boats, if you like – until well into the second half of the twentieth century in some parts of the world, such as Scandinavia, Bangladesh and even Japan.

It is most difficult to build a vessel by shaping her skeleton and covering it with a skin of planks which are not joined together at the edges. Vessels built in this way can be much bigger and more durable than edge-joined vessels, able to carry heavy cargoes, in rough seas and under arduous conditions of loading and discharging, for years on end with a minimum of maintenance. When they are being built, such vessels are not 'sculpted' by the builder; on the contrary, the design commitment is chiefly made, not as the vessel grows on the slipway, but in the half model from which the leading frame shapes are derived, by whatever process. Vessels built in this way were not susceptible to much alteration. The determination of the frame shapes, right through from the half model to their erection on the keel, was an extremely difficult process and mistakes could be very costly. The result could be spoiled timber, or at best an unsatisfactory vessel, incapable of earning a reasonable living for its owner; perhaps even, at worst, it could be potentially dangerous. In the words of a real Master Shipwright, Tom Perkins:

> The complete skeleton gives the full shape of the half block model, and is checked constantly for line and size as work proceeds. It is in the framing operation that most care is needed since there are many pitfalls along the way, which can give rise to all sorts of misalignment if the operation is not co-ordinated.

It was entirely natural that Master – whose boats were so well built for their various purposes that he was well known for them around the coasts of Britain–should have done all he could to make the above process as flexible as possible, allowing the vessel to grow to shape under his hands as he went along. Of course, the scope for deviations from the half model was restricted. The vessel's basic shape was determined by the model, but by going some way back towards 'natural' boatbuilding (the shell method) Master was able to introduce a degree of liberty in the shaping of the finished hull. He could simplify the process of converting the half model's shape into frame shapes

The framing of some typical sterns —

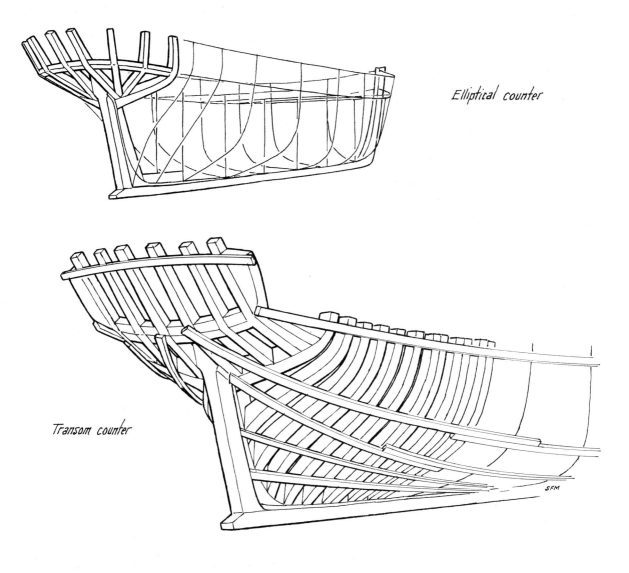

Elliptical counter

Transom counter

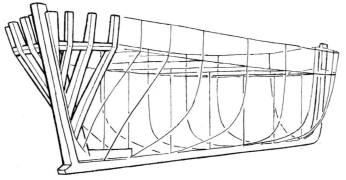

"Barrow flat"

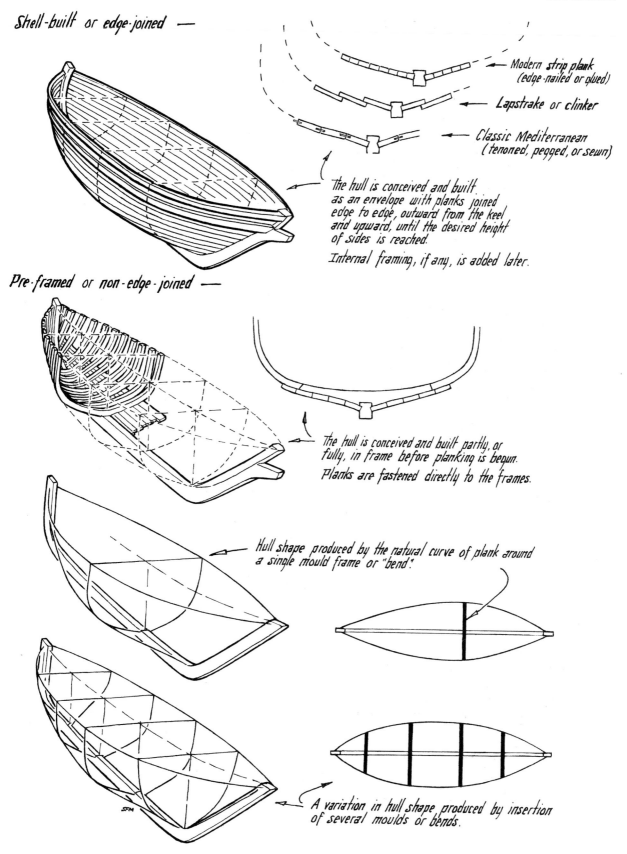

Shell-built or edge-joined —

→ Modern strip plank
   (edge-nailed or glued)

→ Lapstrake or clinker

→ Classic Mediterranean
   (tenoned, pegged, or sewn)

The hull is conceived and built
as an envelope with planks joined
edge to edge, outward from the keel
and upward, until the desired height
of sides is reached.

Internal framing, if any, is added later.

Pre-framed or non-edge-joined —

The hull is conceived and built partly, or
fully, in frame before planking is begun.
Planks are fastened directly to the frames.

Hull shape produced by the natural curve of plank around
a single mould frame or "bend".

A variation in hull shape produced by insertion
of several moulds or bends.

SFM

(and reduce the risk of expensive errors) by shaping many of his frames to fit the full-size vessel, rather than the other way round.

A shipbuilder could make a single frame, shaped within a limited range of variations based on his own and his predecessor's experience, depending on the basic characteristics required of the finished vessel, and then erect this frame on the keel somewhere amidships. He could then work slowly forward and aft, shaping every third of fourth frame by eye alone, erecting it and stringing thin flexible battens around the outside of the frames where the outside planks would eventually be fitted. From the curves assumed by these battens the builder would determine the shapes of the intermediate frames by making up moulds, cutting out the frames with pit saw and adze, fitting and finishing them on the keel as the skeleton grew. Such methods, with some variation, were practised all over the world by relatively unsophisticated shipbuilders for as long as wooden vessels were built.

Our Master's own particular method was to derive up to a dozen frame shapes from the half model, fairly evenly distributed along the run of the keel, and then 'mould up' the remaining twenty to thirty frames. Thus he built the schooner to some extent as he would have built a boat, doing some of his shaping, not through the forming of the outer skin, but through observing shapes assumed by the battens under tension.

Tom Perkins explains the process of making and erecting frames derived from the 'scrieve board',

> Moulds were sometimes made in thin battens of wood and shaped on the scrieve board to give an overall frame pattern. These followed the completed overall shape, and on them would be marked the lengths required to cut all the hooks, and the floor-butts were lined in to the correct angle of turn in the frame required, and so the job was simplified by producing something which could be laid on the converted timber, and the timber just scribed to the pattern required by each frame component. Pattern-making was indeed a trade of its own, since middle lines, curves and datums all had to be understood.
>
> Constructionwise it is interesting to note that the floor, or solid oak piece of the frame across the keel, is placed on the foreside of the framing from the middle line to the stem, and on the after end of the frame to the transom, a counteracting strength factor for longitudinal strengthening as well as transverse.
>
> Framing is an exercise in 'eyeing' and lining, for the correct faying [fitting] of the outside planking to the finished frame, the accuracy of the lay of the plank to the framing, gives the fastening a better hold on the frame. Erecting the frames from a midship position and working from there, forward and aft positioning, the skeleton takes shape. Across the top of the frame is fastened a board or 'cross-paul', to box the frame shape for rigidity. Outside, substantial softwood battens, called 'ribbands' and 'hairpins', are nailed at about three foot intervals around the frame's external face to the keel; these battens give an indication of the frame fairing as the skeleton grows forward and aft. The centre of the frames is marked on to the cross-paul already boxing the frame unit, and plumbed down to the centre line of the keel to ensure the line of building is being held, and prevent the vessel from being built with a kink in the bow or stern. On the floor of the frame the keel position is marked, and the plumbing should meet on the centre line for both markings.

There was one other major difficulty involved in building by the method of erecting a skeleton and wrapping a watertight skin of separate planks around it: the frames were made up out of square sections of timber, around

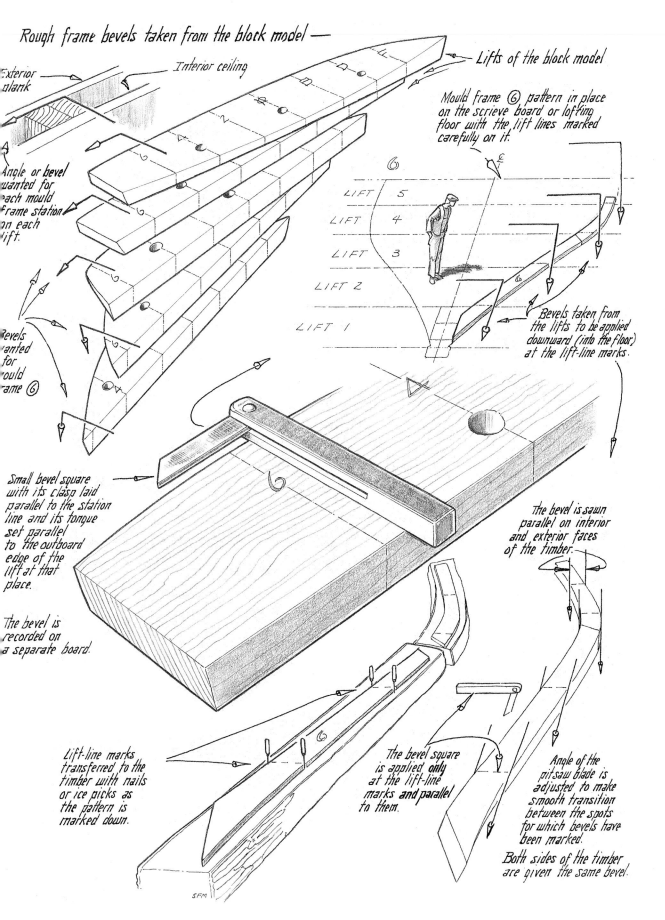

Rough frame bevels taken from the block model —

Exterior plank

Interior ceiling

Lifts of the block model

Angle or bevel wanted for each mould frame station on each lift.

Bevels wanted for mould frame ⑥

Mould frame ⑥ pattern in place on the scrieve board or lofting floor with the lift lines marked carefully on it.

6

LIFT 5
LIFT 4
LIFT 3
LIFT 2
LIFT 1

Bevels taken from the lifts to be applied downward (into the floor) at the lift-line marks.

Small bevel square with its clasp laid parallel to the station line and its tongue set parallel to the outboard edge of the lift at that place.

The bevel is recorded on a separate board.

The bevel is sawn parallel on interior and exterior faces of the timber.

Lift-line marks transferred to the timber with nails or ice picks as the pattern is marked down.

The bevel square is applied only at the lift-line marks and parallel to them.

Angle of the pitsaw blade is adjusted to make smooth transition between the spots for which bevels have been marked.

Both sides of the timber are given the same bevel.

SFM

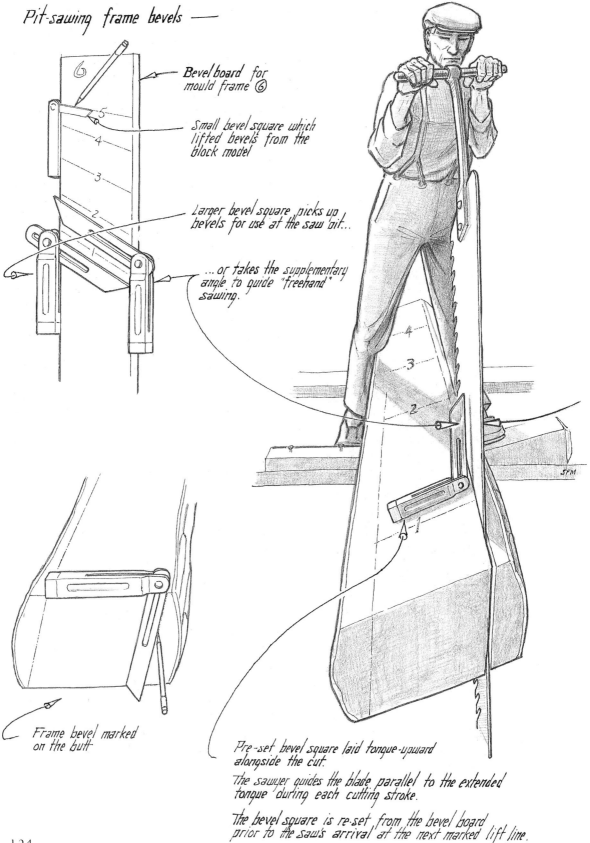

Pit-sawing frame bevels —

Bevel board for mould frame ⑥

Small bevel square which lifted bevels from the block model

Larger bevel square picks up bevels for use at the saw pit...

...or takes the supplementary angle to guide "freehand" sawing.

Frame bevel marked on the butt

Pre-set bevel square laid tongue-upward alongside the cut.

The sawyer guides the blade parallel to the extended tongue during each cutting stroke.

The bevel square is re-set from the bevel board prior to the saw's arrival at the next marked lift line.

which you could not wrap planks. The frames' faces had to be sloped, or 'bevelled', that is, cut away on their fore sides in the fore part, and on their aftersides in the after part of the vessel, so that the planking skin would fit snugly to them. To our Master, building his schooner with frames of double timbers, each of roughly eight-inch siding, the process presented no great problem. The frames could be roughly bevelled with the adze before they were erected, then further worked with the adze to angles derived from the smooth run of the battens when they were in place, and finally finished off with the adze as the planking proceeded. The process was rarely so simple, however, as Tom Perkins explains:

> Bevels on the framings' faying surface were noted on the scrieve board's full-size plan, and these bevels increase going forward and aft from the amidship frame. Forward framing loses $1\frac{1}{2}$ inches of its inside faying surface to get home in the turn to the stem. Frame construction with square heads and heels that butted on the joining faces as from the floor to the second futtocks often gave rise to devious grain patterns, that made fairing an art rather than an everyday task. Many tradesmen were adapted to a particular skill with tools, and it usually fell to Charlie or Ted, who knew the bevel by eye and a winding batten, gradually monopolizing this particular task. As 'Master' once remarked he had a good eye before, but it must have been closed when he joined this 'un. It was repetitive skill, or doing a job you had more 'feel for', that led to a competitive struggle to become as good or better, when work was allotted perhaps to the same men over and over again. There is no doubt 'the rule of thumb' came into its own, often on fairing the frame line.
>
> During the skeleton's construction, fairing of the frames externally would proceed with adze and plane, by the 'ship party' and their apprentices. To fair under the schooner meant lying on your back, and working overhead, a trial of patience and strength, worsened by rain splashing in your face or the uncomfortable lay in the tide-line aft which could add to the slipway problems. 'Laying sacks' were gathered and dried in the shops or over the steam box when operative.

All the work of building a small wooden sailing ship in our yard would have been done by six or seven men besides Master himself. Once they were old enough, and had completed their informal apprenticeship, the heart of the labour force would always have been Master's three sons, Tom, Harry and Lewis. The rest would have come and gone over the years, but there would nearly always have been relatives of one kind or another in the yard gang.

Youths not in the family would serve a more formal seven-year apprenticeship at the yard. This was hard work, but it was almost always shipwrighting or work closely associated with shipwrighting, such as shifting timber, clearing up the sheds, and preparing or sharpening tools. In the course of the years the young man, if he had a flair for the trade, would gradually begin to acquire a remarkable degree of skill with his tools. This skill was the product of the concentrated interest of men with few distractions and few other outlets for their nervous energy than the exercise of their trade—a professional concentration often enhanced by the additional limitation of outside interests imposed by illiteracy.

5 the hull is completed

While the framing process continued on the slipway, timber would have been prepared for the keelson, deadwood and stem-knee. Ideally, a keelson was made from a single tree trunk with a siding (after squaring) of, say, 14 inches by 14 inches. Usually, for lack of long enough timber, it had to be made up from two pieces scarfed together. In the West of England, surplus timber from the Naval Dockyard at Devonport could be used if transport could be found to move it. Pitch pine was the best ordinary timber for the job, since it had good longitudinal strength and could withstand the occasional soaking in bilge water which was inevitable from its position in the vessel.

After rough sawing at the sawpit the keelson would be dragged and levered on rollers across to the slipway. In the case of our schooner, the keelson was a single piece of timber, over fifty feet long, so moving it about the yard was a job which called for the strength of everyone there. Alongside the slipway it would be 'blocked up' then adzed and planed to shape, lying on the insides of the floors to meet with the rise of the bow section, and aft to lay to the stern-post, rising again to the shape of the stern as required. On top of the keelson would be fastened the 'rider keelson'.

In the words of Tom Perkins:

Since the skeleton of the vessel as now constructed was cross-braced and batten-tied longitudinally the keelson could be lifted and lowered into the floor line, that is, lined through, faired with the keel. The keelson was bored by hand augers which made a very tight fit for the securing bolts which were driven through the keelson into the floors and down into the keel, sometimes as a blind fastening– that is, like a nail, not right through the keel, sometimes a through one.

The top keelson was parallel to the keel throughout its very long length. Afterwards the deadwood [which had already been shaped] could be manhandled to the fore foot stem position and bored and fastened off with through fastenings clenched over reinforced washers under the clenched ends, to secure them permanently in place. A good eye was needed to drill the holes, since the stem face was only three to four inches in width and it was no good to let 'Master' see the hole come through the side of the stem, or similarly through the side of the keel – and the hole, drilled by hand, might be three feet long.

Again, probably the same gang bored all the holes for the underwater fastenings for the stern-knee as well, having taken in their stride the complete frame line with the keelson. 'Plum jobs' in wood shipbuilding did not mean a relaxation of the workload, but an added responsibility and pride to do the job 'proper', since below the waterline all faults were magnified, as eventual 'taking up' with the swelling of the soaked wood was not enough to combat 'poor shipwrighting'. To be an apprentice to the 'bottom men' meant learning your trade the hard way,

keelson and horn timbers —

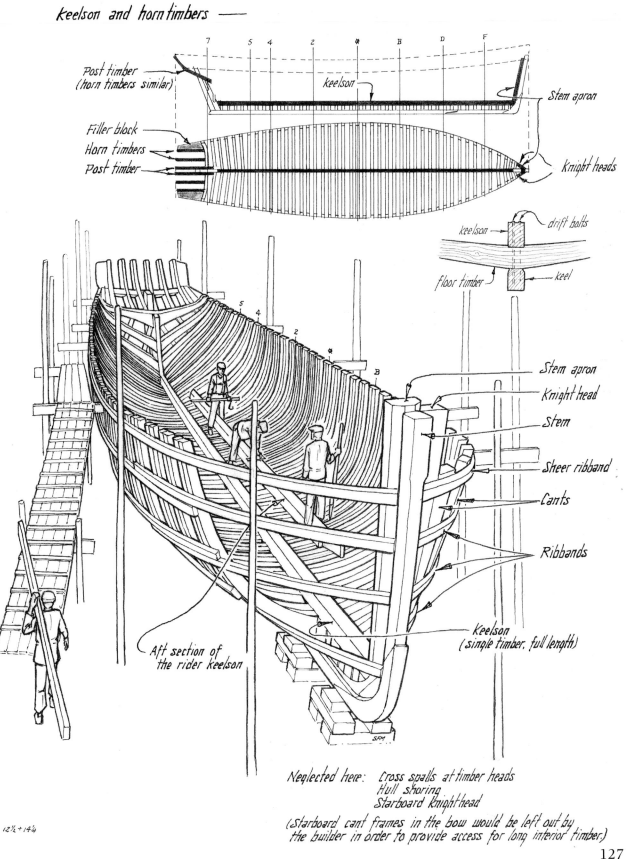

Post timber
(horn timbers similar)

Filler block

Horn timbers

Post timber

keelson

Stem apron

Knight heads

keelson

drift bolts

floor timber

keel

Stem apron

Knight head

Stem

Sheer ribband

Cants

Ribbands

Keelson
(single timber, full length)

Aft section of
the rider keelson

Neglected here: Cross spalls at timber heads
Hull shoring
Starboard knighthead

(Starboard cant frames in the bow would be left out by
the builder in order to provide access for long interior timber.)

12½ + 14¼

127

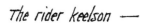

The rider keelson —

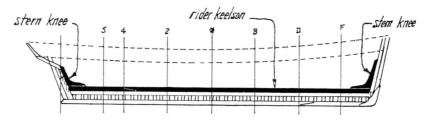

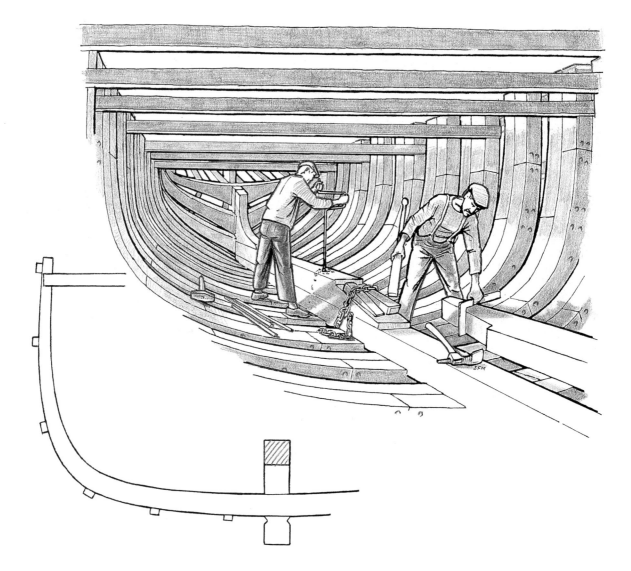

cuffed and kicked, with sharp words to remind the boy of his indentured apprenticeship in no uncertain manner.

Further building required the storeman to lift out the cut, rose-headed, heavy galvanized nails with which the planks were fastened to the frames, some of them still made by the blacksmith of the yard, made with a chiselly point and then dipped in hot tar. Planking could then commence. The labourers assembled the scaffolding that had laid ready for the job. They nailed and tied with ropes all the sections that gave the lift to enable the shipwrights to put around the 'sheer strake' – the topmost plank – and the strake below that would carry the bolts right through from the inside of the beam shelf at this level to the outside of the planking. The steam box would be fired, sawdust and scrap wood feeding the hungry boiler, and the shipwrights setting off the line on the frames, while others made the planking from converted timber in the shed.

Fitting garboards —

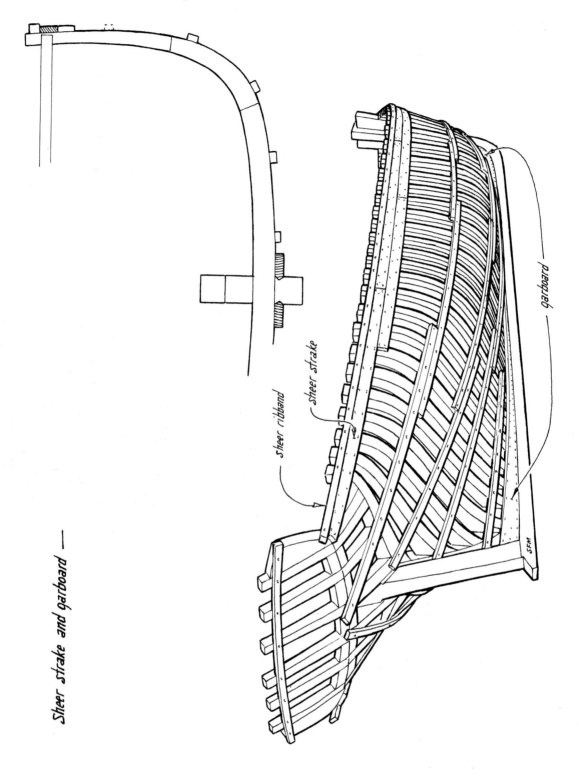

Sheer strake and garboard —

The steam box —

'Setting off the line of the frames' comprised the 'dubbing', that is the fairing of the frames by adze to ensure that the planking fayed well to them. In a big yard, those working on the dubbing had to keep one jump ahead of the plankers.

The steam chest or box was at the north-west corner of our yard, well above the water. It was a heavy wooden trunk, two feet square in section, with doors at either end, and about 30 feet long. Steam was let into the chest from a boiler alongside, fired with timber scrap. The steam chest itself was made up from oak planks, with a brick-built furnace and chimney. Planks were inserted, several at a time, with timber stops between them to keep them apart; the end of the steam chest was then closed and the doors jammed with old rags to make it reasonably steam-tight. The steam then flowed in from the boiler; when thoroughly soaked in this fashion, the planks became relatively soft and pliable. They would also be very hot when they were drawn from the steam chest by three or four men and carried rapidly over to the adjacent slipway, so the carriers had to have thick pads on their shoulders. (As a former sawyer remembered in 1946, 'At Appledore you had to be careful you didn't leave your coat lying around or they would snatch up that as well!') The planks were then shoved, shouldered, wedged, shored and clamped into place. This final fitting had to be done at speed, before the planks cooled, dried and became rigid again. At many yards it was a point of professional pride and good practice to avoid sending the same plank back twice to the steam chest.

The next task was to bind together the skeleton of keel, stem and stern-post, and frames and keelson at the top at the sheer line of the vessel, producing a stable structure which would not distort while the rest of the outside planking, as well as the decks and the internal planking (called the ceiling) were fixed. In the words of Tom Perkins again:

A rigid sheer would strengthen the hull considerably and prevent any racking from the ship's inclination on the slipway, or any tendency of the whole structure to twist while it lay on the blocks. Inside the frame heads, the line of the beam shelf was scribed in, following the sheerline of the deck, and clamps were positioned for immediate usage. 'Master' would be busy superintending the new work, eyeing, and advising where scarfs could best be made in the line of the beam shelf and how they should be alternated port and starboard so as to give maximum strength. Scarfs in the beam shelves at the same distance aft port and starboard would form a natural hinge around which the completed vessel could work in a seaway.

With the top planking on, from stem to transom, eased to the bow and stern by steaming, the nailing would commence to ensure a rigid line. Inside the hull the shipwrights would manhandle the beam shelf into position, still hot from the steam box, and busily bore and bolt each frame, one fastening up and one down to avoid splitting.

The massive beam shelf, the topmost member in the inside lining of the vessel on which the transverse deck beams rested, was of about ten inches by three inches in cross-section. It was traditional to bevel the lower edge to reduce by sight its ungainly thickness. The ideal beam shelf went down one side of the vessel in one complete length, but pitch pine of such length was growing hard to find so scarfs became inevitable. The scarf ratio was at least three to one, sometimes a little more, and through bolting would be continued, as well as additional fastenings through the scarfs, down through the beam shelf's width.

Beam shelf —

Beam shelf

Hooked vertical scarph joint

S.FM

The whole framework was now steaded up, since the line from stem to transom was complete inside and out.

The ship would now be ready to receive the deck beams which would hold her in shape athwartships and complete the skeleton. Tom Perkins continues the story:

Since the hull was now 'framed up', the transverse strength could be built in, in the form of beams to carry the decking fore and aft. The first two beams to go in were the main cargo hatch beams at each end of the main hatchway, (the hole through which cargo was loaded and discharged). The positions of these were critical since they defined the size of the hatchway in overall length from the beam forward to the beam aft and therefore the size of the largest object that could be put in the vessel's hold. The cross-section of these beams, to give a reasonable camber to the decking forward and aft, was about 12 inches by 8 inches, and beams of English oak served for this purpose. The shapes of the beams with a $3\frac{1}{2}$ to 4-inch camber over 19 feet was marked off on the baulk of oak which was trimmed with axe and adze and faired by planing so that the camber coincided with the top of the sheer strake. This datum of the sheer strake's top edge allowed later for the laying of the waterways of English elm. The beams were finished with a bevel to the lower edges, a finish prided in craftsmanship to lighten the look of the heavy completed work. Six men could easily manhandle the beams into the housing prepared on the beam shelf, port and starboard.

Deck beams were curved to give the deck its necessary camber, so that the vessel spilt water, whether from sea or rain (which, if it lay in pools on the decks, would have rotted them in no time). Horizontal oak lodging-knees bound the beams to the frame heads; vertical iron hanging knees, made up at the blacksmith's shop by yard workers, tied the beams through their lower surfaces to the beam shelf and the planking inside the vessel.

The whole structure of the skeleton was now complete and the new vessel was ready to be planked up, inside and out.

Planks would be cut out at the sawpit from squared baulk pitch pine and from English oak or elm. The pitch pine would have been rafted up the river from the seaport town at its mouth, already squared with 16-inch sides; the local elm and oak logs would already have been cut into planks at the sawmill, but with no trimming and the bark still on them.

It is obvious that the shaping of the planks of a wooden ship was a highly skilled job, since the linear distance around the frame from the keel to the deck level amidships was always very much greater than the same distance measured up the outer face of a frame three-quarters of the way forward or aft; and it was greater again than the total height of the stem and the stern-post, where each successive run of planking was necessarily terminated. Since for reasons of strength each strake (that is, each run of planking from bow to stern) had to be continuous (though each could be made up of a number of separate planks), the strakes therefore had to be wide amidships, tapering away progressively fore and aft.

In Tom Perkins's words:

"Under the schooner now the shipwrights were setting out for the outside planking, and roughly marking the outside frame face with 'Master' giving the final orders to keep her 'wide under' and 'fine in' the fore foot to give a straight line with wide English elm boards of 10 inches width and standard 2 inches thickness. Sometimes the number of planks were scribed on to the half block in a 'mock up' to determine

134

Deck beams, lodging knees —

centerline blocking

carlings

beams

lodging knees

Use of the block model in establishing the layout of hull planking —

The block model provides a useful mandrel upon which to line off the run of plank and to determine the number of plank strakes required to cover the full size hull. An aesthetically pleasing layout of hull plank is easier to establish at the small size of the model than on the staging-cluttered structure.

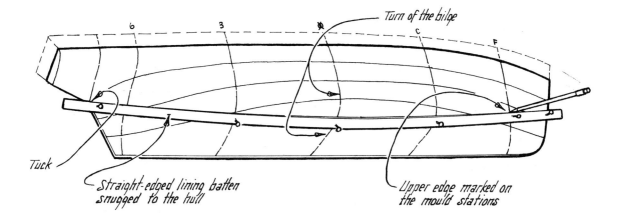

Turn of the bilge

Tuck

Straight-edged lining batten snugged to the hull

Upper edge marked on the mould stations

Run of plank is determined by stretching a wide, limber "lining" or "fairing" batten along the length of the hull, starting at the tuck where the sternpost joins the horn timber, and ending at an appropriate height on the stem. What is sought is a location where the whole batten lies snugly against the hull without hanging off at one edge or the other. On this kind of hull the batten will normally course along the turn of the bilge, or slightly below it, amidships, in a fair run from the tuck to a similar height on the stem.

The fair curve given by the upper edge of the batten is marked on the station lines of the model and (later) on the mould frames of the vessel. Plank widths are laid off above this line to the sheer, and below it to the keel rabbet.

Number of plank is then determined by dividing the hull's maximum girth (at ⌀ here) by the width of available plank stock. If 10" plank is used, 21 strakes of plank result, on each side of the keel, for Master's schooner. Nine strakes lie below the faired line through the tuck at ⌀. Twelve above.

Width of plank at any location is determined by stepping off the 21 plank spaces at that particular girth and by measuring the widths of the units found.

Lining off plank on the block model ——

1. The frame mould at widest midship girth is marked from rabbet to sheer in equal spaces representing the average width of available plank stock. Spaces for 21 planks of 10" width are stepped off with dividers.

Bottom of the transom

Aft edge of the fashion timber

Sheer line

Stem rabbet

Horn timber rabbet

Lining batten

Stern post rabbet

Plank #9 (upper edge)

keel rabbet

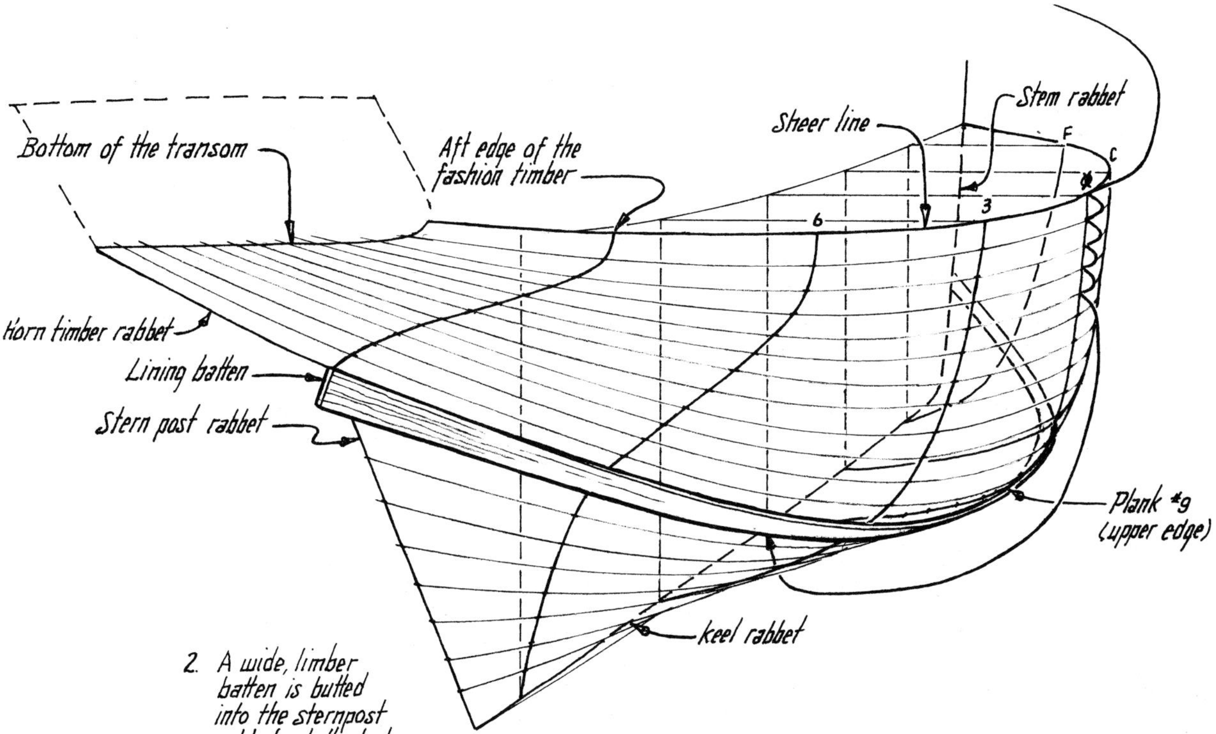

2. A wide, limber batten is butted into the sternpost rabbet at the tuck and is run forward along the hull, lying tightly to it, without hanging off at one edge. A "fair" run of the batten from the tuck will usually lie just along, or under, the turn of the bilge in this type of hull. Forward of midship (ϕ) the lining batten is encouraged to rise to a location on the stem of corresponding height to that at the tuck.

3. The builder notes (in this case) that the upper edge of the snugged-down lining batten passes close to the 9th mark out from the keel on the midship mould frame ϕ. This mark represents the upper edge of plank #9 spaced outward from the keel.

4. The upper edge of the lining batten is now scribed down on the mould frames, the stem, and the sternpost. Equal spaces — 12 above, 9 below — are stepped off with dividers away from the lining batten surmarks. These are the plank-widths sought at each marking station. They will be widely spaced in the midship section and closely spaced in the ends.

The same lining-off with batten and dividers will be done on the full size hull. Use of the block model for this purpose saves a good deal of climbing and shifting of battens at the building site.

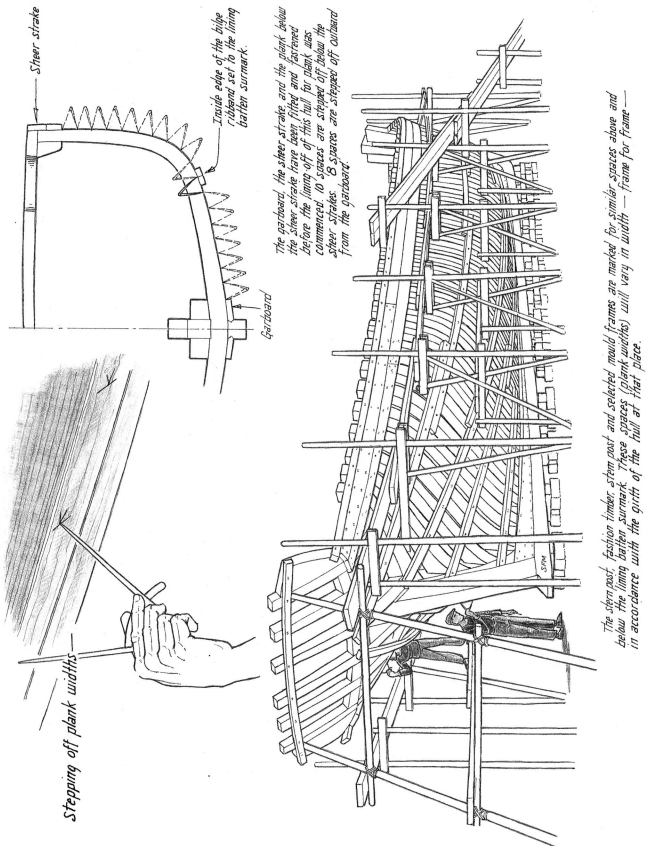

Sheer strake

Inside edge of the bilge ribband set to the lining batten surmark.

Garboard

Stepping off plank widths

The garboard, the sheer strake and the plank below the sheer strake have been fitted and fastened before the lining off of this hull for plank was commenced. 10 spaces are stepped off below the sheer strakes. 8 spaces are stepped off outboard from the garboard.

The stern post, fashion timber, stem post and selected mould frames are marked for similar spaces above and below the lining batten surmark. These spaces (plank widths) will vary in width — frame for frame — in accordance with the girth of the hull at that place.

SFM

138

Lining off the hull for plank —

With the plank widths established, the corresponding plank-edge marks are faired-through along the length of the hull with a limber fairing batten. Small adjustments are made so that no jogs, hollows, or otherwise "un-fair" places occur along the planed edge of any plank. As each line of marks is faired, the plank edge is scribed onto the frames so that exact plank widths may be picked off at any place during the planking process.

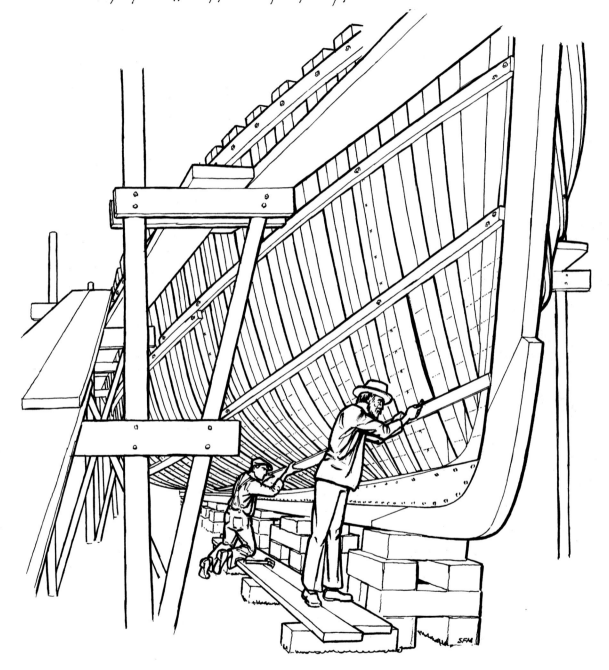

Rose-headed planking spike —

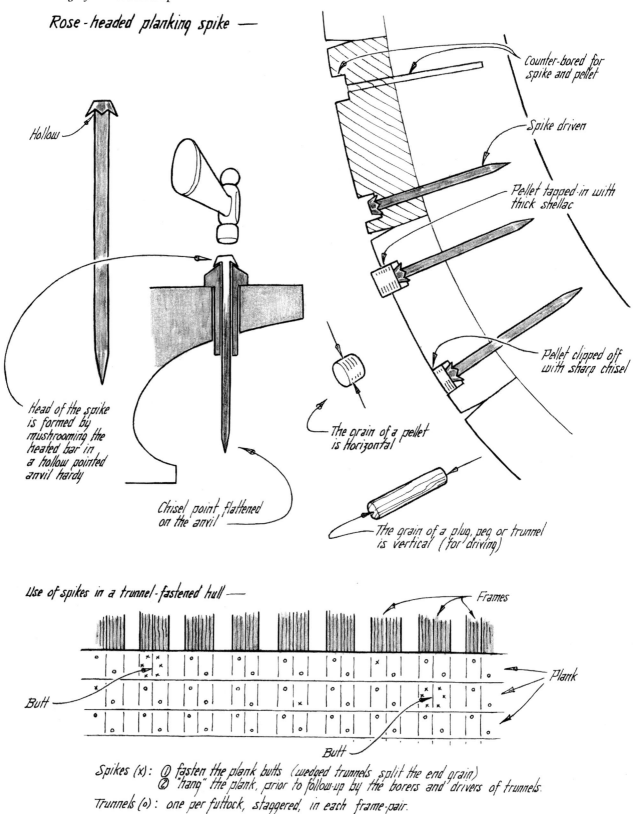

Hollow

Head of the spike is formed by mushrooming the heated bar in a hollow pointed anvil hardy

Chisel point flattened on the anvil

Counter-bored for spike and pellet

Spike driven

Pellet tapped-in with thick shellac

Pellet clipped off with sharp chisel

The grain of a pellet is Horizontal

The grain of a plug, peg or trunnel is vertical (for driving)

Use of spikes in a trunnel-fastened hull —

Frames

Plank

Butt

Butt

Spikes (x): ① fasten the plank butts (wedged trunnels split the end grain)
② "hang" the plank, prior to follow-up by the borers and drivers of trunnels.
Trunnels (o): one per futtock, staggered, in each frame-pair.

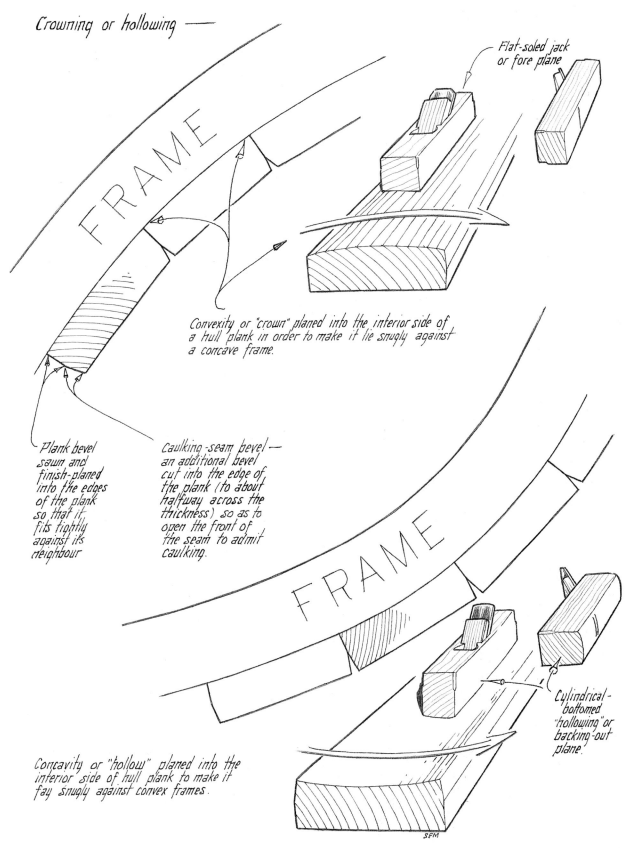

Crowning or hollowing —

FRAME

Flat-soled jack or fore plane

Convexity or "crown" planed into the interior side of a hull plank in order to make it lie snugly against a concave frame.

Plank bevel sawn and finish-planed into the edges of the plank so that it fits tightly against its neighbour

Caulking-seam bevel — an additional bevel cut into the edge of the plank (to about halfway across the thickness) so as to open the front of the seam to admit caulking.

FRAME

Cylindrical-bottomed "hollowing" or backing-out plane.

Concavity or "hollow" planed into the interior side of hull plank to make it fay snugly against convex frames.

SFM

141

Taking off plank widths and bevels —

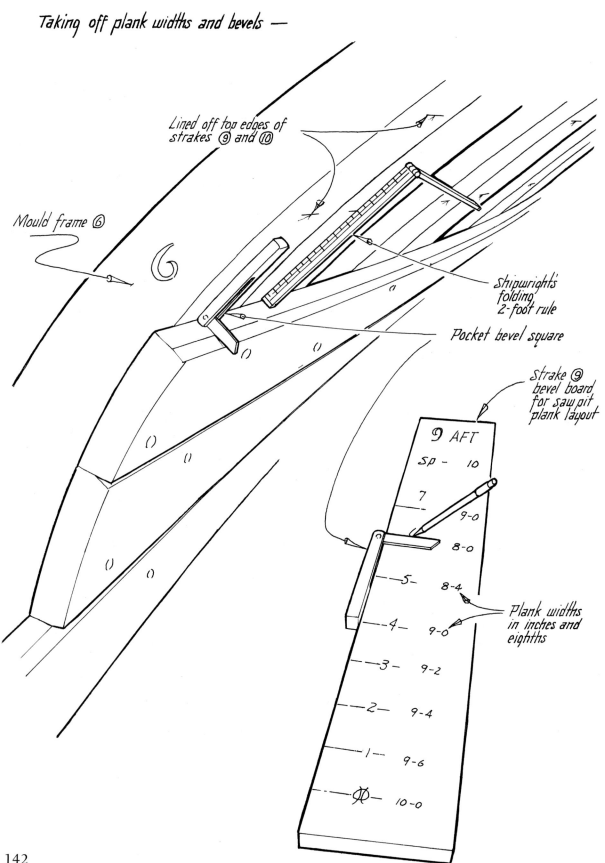

Lined off top edges of
strakes ⑨ and ⑩

Mould frame ⑥

Shipwright's
folding
2-foot rule

Pocket bevel square

Strake ⑨
bevel board
for saw pit
plank layout

9 AFT

Sp — 10

7
9-0

8-0

5 —   8-4

4 —   9-0

Plank widths
in inches and
eighths

3 —   9-2

2 —   9-4

1 —   9-6

∅ —   10-0

Marking out plank taper; pitsawing to bevel. —

Planing plank edges to finished bevel

144

Treenail, trenel, or trunnel — shaped with a hatchet and driven through a die —

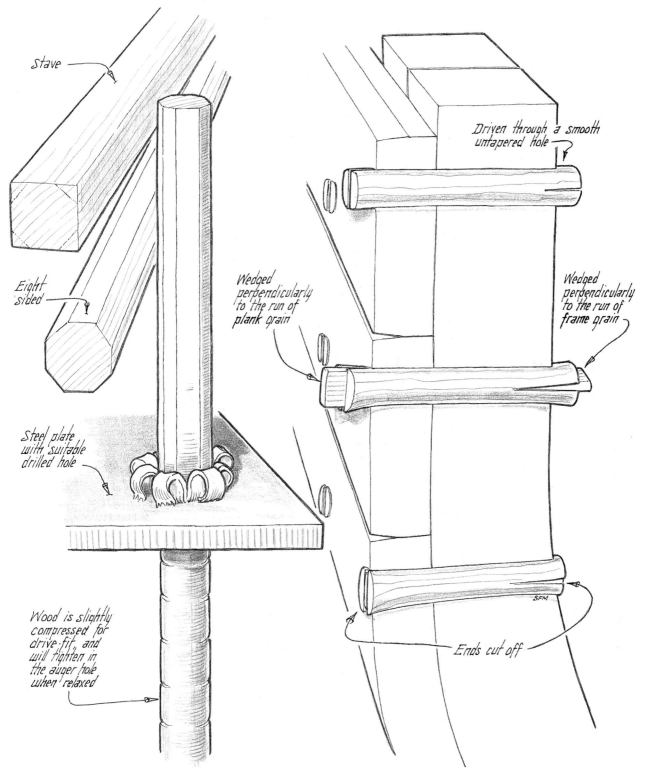

stave

Eight sided

Steel plate with suitable drilled hole

Wood is slightly compressed for drive-fit, and will tighten in the auger hole when relaxed

Driven through a smooth untapered hole

Wedged perpendicularly to the run of plank grain

Wedged perpendicularly to the run of frame grain

Ends cut off

SFM

145

the fit and lay. Usually 20–22 boards would suffice and 'Master' knew to an inch the requirements. The pattern now evolved, wide to the turn of bilge and on the difficult turn of bilge reduce to usual practice and try to even up to widths, bearing in mind a straight line is better than a curve in economy of timber.

When the frames had been divided, and planking begun from the garboards [the planks next to the keel and the only straight planks in the schooner], a curve adequate to reduce shape forward and aft appeared on the plank edges. The edges of the planks were also bevelled one-eighth of an inch to the centre line of thickness of all fairing faces to allow the oakum thread to be driven in to ensure a watertight hull – this was the caulking. Planking up continued with a fuller thickness planking to the turn of bilge and sheer planks to reinforce for the grounding and rubbing experienced in these areas. The overall thickness at these two places amounted to half an inch more than the rest of the hull.

Below the waterline was English elm, and above pitch pine. Fastenings to the planking were blacksmiths' galvanized, rose-headed, chisel-pointed nails, and, in the wetted load area of the waterline, treenails [wooden pins] of English oak, cross-wedged to increase holding power. Above the waterline wrought iron nails were often used with a galvanized coating, but 'Master' frowned on this practice and drove in galvanized fastenings, the same as below the waterline.

Fastenings for planking were driven on every frame [that is, a double frame], two per frame section. The fastenings were staggered alternately to prevent a split in the line of grain. Boring preceeded the nailing, and, when driven, the nail head would be stopped and pelleted with a wood pellet".

The shaping of the planks was an exceedingly skilled business, since they were not only tapered but they were also, though not necessarily throughout their length and certainly not to the same extent, hollowed in the inside to take the curve of the frames. They were also bevelled at their edges because they had to lie snugly together on the inside for the first half-inch or so of their inch-and-a-half or two inches of thickness, and then present an open seam on the outside into which the caulking could be driven. Each plank was shaped in turn, first on the sawpit and then with adze and plane. They were fitted and if necessary refitted until they were right. Most of them had to be steamed in the steam chest before they were finally fastened in position.

With larger vessels, where it was impossible to scan the hull entirely to line in the planking by eye and experience, a plan would be drawn to scale showing the shape and disposition of the planks as they would appear if flattened out. This was also a job requiring great skill and experience. It was not done mathematically, but by eye.

Through and blind trunnels —

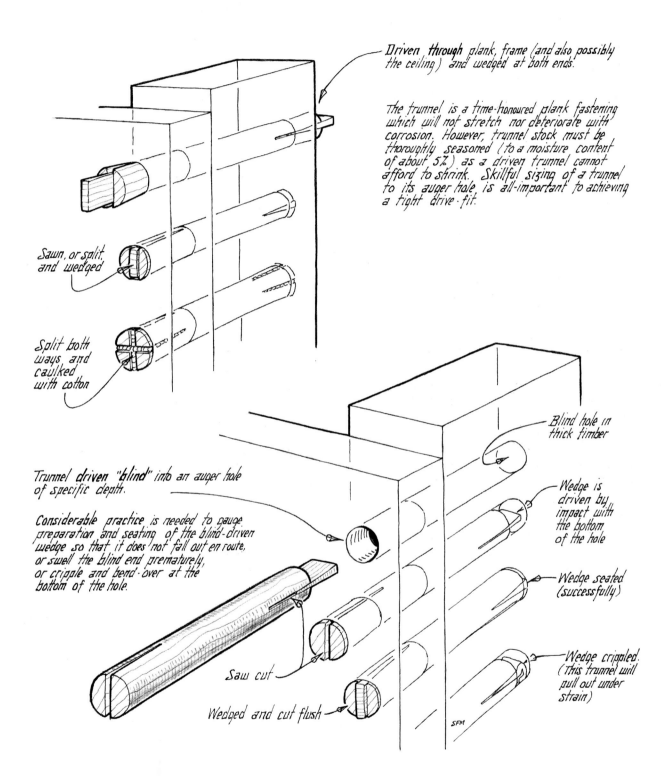

Driven **through** plank, frame (and also possibly the ceiling) and wedged at both ends.

The trunnel is a time-honoured plank fastening which will not stretch nor deteriorate with corrosion. However, trunnel stock must be thoroughly seasoned (to a moisture content of about 5%) as a driven trunnel cannot afford to shrink. Skillful sizing of a trunnel to its auger hole is all-important to achieving a tight drive-fit.

Sawn, or split, and wedged

Split both ways and caulked with cotton

Blind hole in thick timber

Wedge is driven by impact with the bottom of the hole

Wedge seated (successfully)

Wedge crippled. (This trunnel will pull out under strain)

Trunnel **driven** "blind" into an auger hole of specific depth.

Considerable practice is needed to gauge preparation and seating of the blind-driven wedge so that it does not fall out en route, or swell the blind end prematurely, or cripple and bend-over at the bottom of the hole.

Saw cut

Wedged and cut flush

SFM

Devices to hold plank in place while fitting and fastening —

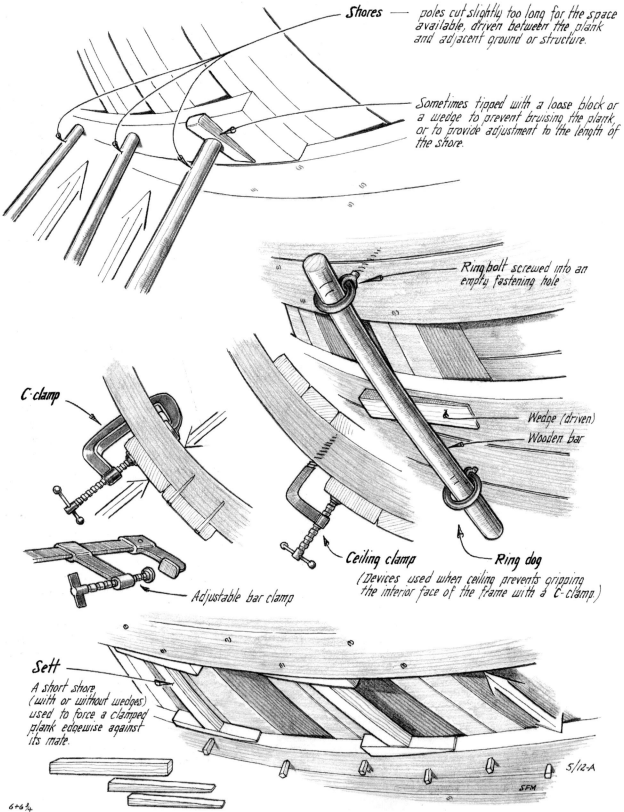

Shores — poles cut slightly too long for the space available, driven between the plank and adjacent ground or structure.

Sometimes tipped with a loose block or a wedge to prevent bruising the plank, or to provide adjustment to the length of the shore.

Ringbolt screwed into an empty fastening hole

Wedge (driven)

Wooden bar

C-clamp

Ring dog

Ceiling clamp

(Devices used when ceiling prevents gripping the interior face of the frame with a 'C-clamp.')

Adjustable bar clamp

Sett —
A short shore (with or without wedges) used to force a clamped plank edgewise against its mate.

5/12-A

SFM

6+6¾

If the vessel was to be classed under Lloyds' Rules for insurance purposes, the butts of the planks in any one strake were not allowed to be nearer than 5 feet to the butts of the adjacent planks. With a strake between them, a distance of 4 feet was allowed. No butts were permitted to fall on the same frame of timbers unless there were three strakes between them. These requirements were designed to ensure a strong and durable vessel.

When the schooner was fully planked-up outside the ceiling would have been put in place. The ceiling was the inner lining of planks, nearly as thick as, and of comparable quality to, those outside. These provided a lot of the strength of the finished vessel. Again, great skill was required for fitting the ceiling – though perhaps this process was simpler than the fitting of the outside planking, because on the whole the frame shapes on the inner side were less complex. It was still, however, a great challenge to the shipwright to complete the ceiling of vessel as economically and tidily as possible. This was a wet weather job, and pitch pine was usually used.

The next stages in building the vessel are described by Tom Perkins:

Around the edge of the sheer, shipwrights would be ready to lay in the waterway of English elm boards 2 inches thick, and usually 20 feet in length, which would receive the deck plank ends with a traditional housing that would line the decking fore and aft. Bulwark stanchions would be dropped and secured ready for the waterway to get around them as it was fastened; fore and aft caulking would be at deck level here around the stanchions to ensure water tightness.

Amidships, in the cargo hold, the wrought-iron knees would be brought from the blacksmith's shop and set to shape with a joggle for the beam shelf, where it stands proud. These would carry the side decking, port and starboard on the carling beams [that is, the short beams on each side of the hatchway]. The wrought-iron knees would be bolted through the ceiling and frame to the outside planking. They were roughly a yard apart when in place.

In the shipwright's shed, the deck main-hatch framings had been made up. They rested on the cargo hatches' main transverse beams and were supported fore and aft on the now completed carling beams and their wrought-iron knee supports. The frames were dovetail-jointed at the corners and rebated along the top edges, internally, with an overall depth of 3 inches and receiving width of 3 inches. The transverse fore and aft frames had their top and bottom edges cambered to suit the camber of the cargo-hatch beams. Drop-in beams usually sub-divided the length of the main hatch into three sections and carried fore and aft beams to give usually nine compartments to the main cargo hatch, requiring metal shoes or wooden cleats on the inside frame face to hold the drop-in beam ends. Each section of the nine divisions housed the wooden hatch boards, which, when in position, were covered by two tarpaulin sheets fitted completely over the hatch and secured to its coamings with battens and wedges, held in the metal hatch cleats bolted on the outside faces.

Coamings for the crew's hatch forward, the access to their accommodation which was below deck in the bows of the schooner, were dovetailed together, along with a coaming for access to the Captain's cabin aft that would be longer, and eventually take a deckhouse perhaps glazed on the fore end port and starboard sides with three-eighth inch plate clear glass, protected by removable wooden shutters or a grid of brass rods. Then both coamings would be rebated to take the hatches fore and aft on their top faces.

The crew's hatch would have a sliding cover combined with a hood, looking aft to be more watertight when and if the vessel put her bows under. The captain's deckhouse had a sliding hatch to the after end, and so ready access was available

Ceiling —

Waterway and bulwark —

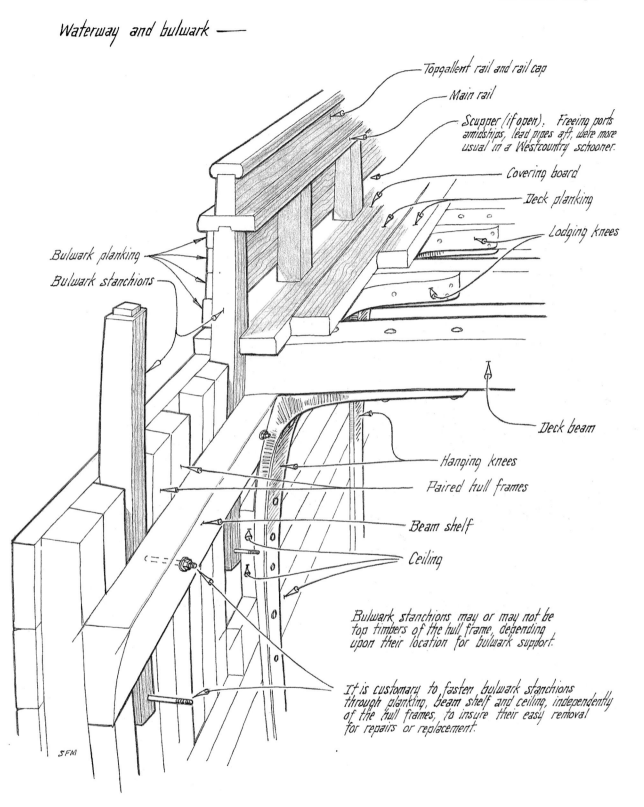

Topgallent rail and rail cap

Main rail

Scupper (if open). Freeing ports amidships, lead pipes aft, were more usual in a Westcountry schooner.

Covering board

Deck planking

Lodging knees

Bulwark planking

Bulwark stanchions

Deck beam

Hanging knees

Paired hull frames

Beam shelf

Ceiling

Bulwark stanchions may or may not be top timbers of the hull frame, depending upon their location for bulwark support.

It is customary to fasten bulwark stanchions through planking, beam shelf and ceiling, independently of the hull frames, to insure their easy removal for repairs or replacement.

SFM

151

Deck plank —

to the tiller. Teak was the usual hatch timber, being excellent for long lasting, in a wet and dry state at sea or in harbour.

Then the deck planking was started at the middle line with a wide board of 'King Plank', the first to be laid. Deck planking of pitch pine was planed and faired with a bevel on the top half of the plank's thickness to allow a caulking iron, and oakum, to make the final watertight seal.

Now our new schooner would at last start looking like a vessel. Her decks would be planed off to a smooth cambered surface, and the planking finished on the outside with planes and adzes. Then she would be ready for caulking, that is, sealing the seams between the planks (still spoken of as 'seams' a thousand years after they had ceased to be sewn) with oakum – hemp fibre held in position with tar on the outside. Caulking was an extremely important process, not only because it rendered the vessel reasonably watertight, but because by squeezing the planks together tightly and holding them in tension once it was wet and had expanded it added to the rigidity and strength of the vessel. During caulking it was very important to allow for expansion of the planks when wetted. If you did not, serious damage could occur. Tom Perkins pictures the caulking process vividly:

Outside, the planking was faired by hand planing to give a smooth finish to the seams, and caulking would begin. Caulking was a task of monotonous repetition. Shipwrights could always caulk, everyone had the gear necessary, but some yards employed wood-caulkers as a gang, something like a sub-contract, and this led to a special breed of worker, with plenty of stamina and an ability to overcome such a mundane task. Before work began, the pitch in block form was broken up by hammering and put into a cast metal pot of traditional shape with a large bow handle. Standing on a grid with a wood-and-shavings fire underneath, the pots would be dotted down the slipway local to each caulker's workplace; ladles would be cleaned of the melting tar, the residue from the previous day's work. Around the fires, squatting on box stools (which housed their mallet and irons) caulkers would be unpackaging oakum in long skeins from the hundredweight bales. Quickly and adeptly, the skein would be teased across the thigh (covered by canvas or a leather patch) and rolled into a thread of uniform thickness forming a ball of manageable size. Stockholm tar [pinewood tar, obtained traditionally from Finland and shipped through Stockholm until 1765, by which time the name had become attached to it for ever] was the preservative used in oakum and it permeated even the skin with a dark brown staining.

As soon as sufficient oakum for a morning was rolled, the caulker would start laying a thread into the garboard seam, and so on up to the turn of bilge, usually working a shift of about seven or eight planks (widthwise) so as to prevent the plank next to the first to be caulked tightening by undue final caulking pressure. The seam, it will be remembered, had deliberately been made wedge-shaped, an ideal shape to effect transverse tension, if the caulking was not gradual in its advance up the hull. Caulking the oakum was the job of the making-iron or caulking-iron; driving it was the job of the mallet, and what a tool that was! Most mallets were handmade, starting with a 4 inch by 4 inch block of African oak or equivalent timber, such as best English oak or box wood, or even *lignum vitae*, about 15 inches long. The block was divided into three parts: two cylindrical striking-blocks or pods and a head that carried a handle 18 inches long and about $1\frac{1}{4}$ inches in diameter. The cylindrical striking-face was bound in an iron ring of external size about 2 inches; the head that took the handle was traditionally shaped; slots in the cylindrical striking-blocks were to give a muscial swish to the mallet when used, and become resilient to a blow rather than dead, when striking

Caulking —

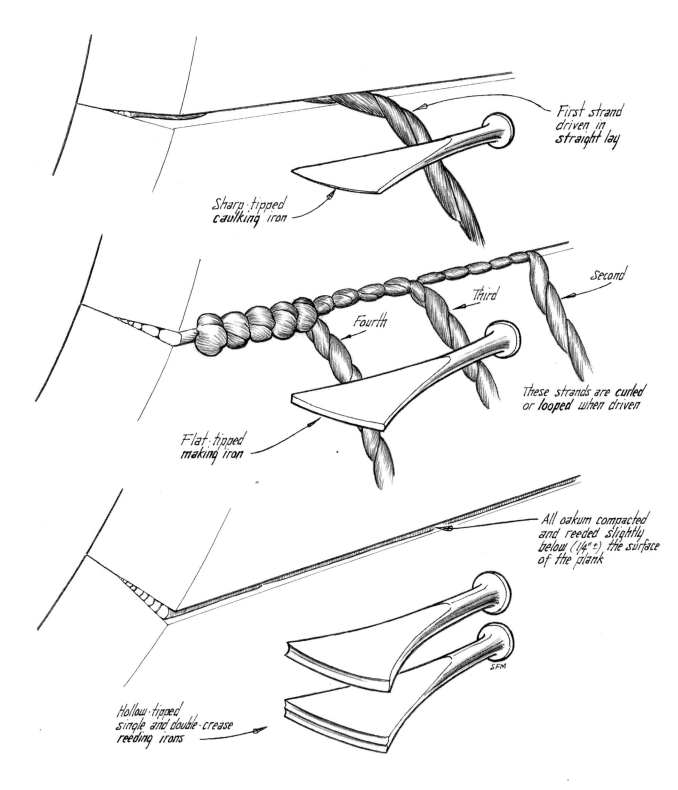

First strand
driven in
straight lay

Sharp·tipped
caulking iron

Second

Third

Fourth

These strands are **curled**
or **looped** when driven

Flat·tipped
making iron

All oakum compacted
and reeded slightly
below (1/4"±) the surface
of the plank

Hollow·tipped
single and double·crease
reeding irons

SFM

154

Caulking —

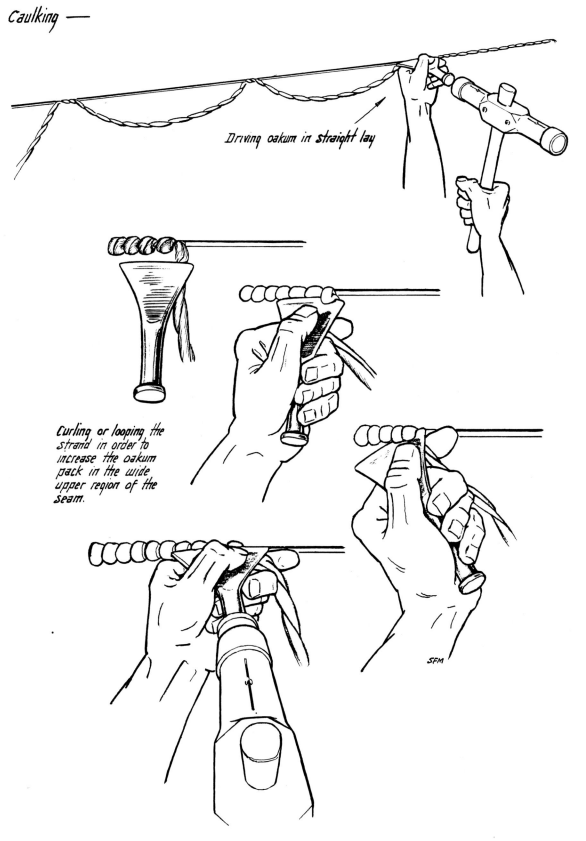

Driving oakum in **straight lay**

Curling or looping the strand in order to increase the oakum pack in the wide upper region of the seam.

SFM

Tarring hull —

the caulking iron. The metal rings on the cylindrical parts were wrapped around with oakum to hold fast when driven on. Two clenched copper nails each side of the handle in the head prevented overall cleavage or splitting. Handles were tapered to allow knocking-up through the head, to be stowed at the day's end in the caulkers' boxes.

The caulking continued up the hull, oakum driven home with mallet and irons, a spike iron gauging the density by being driven into the seam, then the dressing iron to compact, and reeding iron to give a parallel appearance of dressed reeds. The bottom thread would be only a straight lay in the bottom of the seam, number two and three or four would be looped in by the forefinger and iron to widen the lay of the thread to fill the seam wholly. Caulking was finished at the outside of the seam after 'reeding', and molten pitch was 'rolled on' by mops or brushes to fill the seam proud, scraped off when hardened, leaving a watertight joint.

'Paying up' was the operation with the mops, and it was a messy job since 'rolling in', the art of putting pitch up 'under', covered the slipway and the caulker with pitch, especially in a hot summer. Pitch that fell across the back of the hand could be dissolved by benzene, but not before a gigantic blister, yellow in colour, had formed. Many caulkers had surface burns to the face and neck especially when the regular 'payers up' were sick or away from work. Boots stuck to the floor; smoke was in abundance from the fires and boiling pitch; Hades was more acceptable.

All the caulking mallets used at our Master's yard had slots cut in each head, producing a clear ringing note when the mallet was used. There were two reasons for this, one aesthetic and one practical. Since each mallet was cut a little differently, each produced an individual note and thus a whole succession of notes and combinations came from the slipway when caulking was going forward. The practical reason for the slots was that the dull thud of the mallet on the iron very close to the head for hour after hour would have been quite intolerable, indeed perhaps even dangerous, to the men employed in this work. So the mallet was cut to produce a pleasant sound in use and one which did not damage the ears of its user, even though he might swing the mallet for twelve hours a day for days on end. Nevertheless, many caulkers became deaf in their later years.

Tom Perkins describes the final stages of the hull-building process:

From working chaos we return to the upper deck, now planked and ready for the caulkers. The planks had been made from pitch pine, and the centre 'King Plank' was about 7 or 8 inches in width, while the remainder were 6 inches or so, in width. Laying began from the centre line 'King Plank', butts on the beams and from the waterway port and starboard, until one plank's width was left. Into this was hammered a 'shutter plank', to spring the decking tightly together. It was then fastened, with galvanized cut nails, on to the beams.

Caulking would proceed as before with the decking – a span of seven or eight planks' widths – to ensure against undue lateral spread, as the caulking forced the thread tightly into the seams.

'Paying up' was done by pot and ladle, a more sophisticated method than 'rolling in' (as below the waterline). Pouring was fast work. Bearing in mind the deck sheer and the slipway inclination, the ladle 'hand' needed to be able to pour clearly, in a straight line, which was difficult work in rainy weather when the pitch would blow and spit bubbles, forming a potential leak in the decking. Surplus pitch was scraped off the seams.

The deck hatches forward and aft were finished, and the two ladders for access to the quarters. Below deck the bulkhead aft that housed the Captain's quarters was built along the lines of beams. Forward in the deck, a Samson post had been fitted, to carry the pawl gear for the windlass, and double as anchor post for the bowsprit. Also the windlass pawl boards had been anchored below deck level to allow the windlass to be housed in a horizontal lay across the fore deck. The yoke and pawl bits had to be built up to allow independent anchor raising or lowering. The drum ends had been made with alternative slots to house the hand spikes that would wind the drum to raise anchor or warp.

Pawl rings and yokes were made by several West Country firms, casting as required.

Below the forecastle, the cable locker was built, forward of the crews' quarters, with an independent bulkhead of tongue-and-grooved boards in which would be built a drop-in door, for access to the compartment. The cable was not washed as it came inboard, and a perforated tray of galvanized iron would serve as a resting place for the stowed cable, forming entry through a naval pipe, usually to port of the centre line.

Drainage of salt water was to the bilge, and it was pumped out after draining aft to the main bilge pump position. The rest of building consisted of siting the main pump aft of the cargo hatch, and fitting the bulwarks on to the stanchions topped with a capping and wash-boards. Towing bollards and cleats for deck-work were bolted through deck and bulwarks positions.

157

Deck furniture —

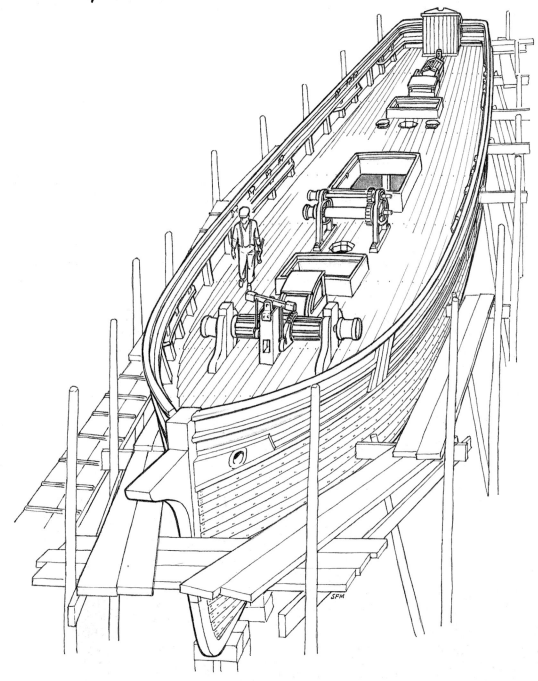

6 fitting out and Launching

Now that the basic structure of the hull of the schooner was complete, our Master had to mast and rig her, fit the crews' living accommodation–and launch her.

Already the schooner as she lay on the slipway would have absorbed perhaps 50 or 60 tons of timber and metal fastenings. It will be remembered that the kind of timber used to construct a vessel depended largely on what was available at a price which her future owner could afford. There would be enough good timber in her, however, fastened with galvanized iron and wooden treenails, to give her a reasonable working life during which she might be expected to recover her costs several times over and make a living for her master and her mate, as well as some money for her successive shareholders.

By the 1890s her quality of construction would have been guaranteed to a degree by certain legal requirements. Under the successive Merchant

This schooner, shown discharging bricks into carts, closely resembles the Master's vessel. She has been damaged in collision and her name is not known. (Royal Institution of Cornwall)

Mast and spar timber —

Shipping Acts she had to be registered as a British vessel at a Custom House; she could not have been so registered until she had been awarded an official loadline – that is, marks on her side to show the depth to which she could be loaded. To sink her deeper in the water, by taking on more cargo, and then putting her to sea, was an illegal act. She would not be awarded a loadline unless the local Board of Trade Surveyor was satisfied that she was constructed of reasonably good materials, to a reasonable standard of workmanship, and that she complied with such other regulations as might be in force under the Acts, or imposed by Custom House administration. The loadline, clearly marked upon her side and never to be submerged by overloading, was her licence to earn her living at sea.

A vessel with a loadline could earn her living in the open sea by carrying cargo upon which freight was paid; she was allowed to make passages from port to port around the coasts or across the oceans as long as she maintained this loadline. If she worked entirely in the river and estuary creeks, as some small sailing vessels did, the loadline was not legally required, so the quality of her construction was limited solely of what the owners could afford and what the builder could bring himself to build.

If the owners were going to use the schooner as a general carrier of cargo, seeking work in competition with other vessels, it was in their interests to have the vessel surveyed and classed by one of the organizations which published data about vessels surveyed by them for the benefit of the insurers of ships and their cargoes (especially cargoes, since they were often more valuable than the ships which carried them). In Britain the chief organization of this kind was Lloyds' Register, and if a Lloyds' classification was asked for while the vessel was being built she was liable to receive visits from the local Lloyds' surveyor all the time that she was on the slip – and he, in theory at least, condemned bad timber and bad workmanship. The consequent published classification of the vessel was a guide to merchants considering employing her to carry their cargoes. Thus the requirements of Lloyds' Register of Shipping imposed a second quality control on the construction of a seagoing vessel.

Lloyd's Register of Shipping classed very few American vessels. The late Dr John Lyman noted in *Log Chips*, March 1950:

> Until the late 1880s, Lloyds' Register ignored vessels not classed with the Society ..... The finding of American-built vessels in Lloyd's before 1880 therefore depends on how easy it was for them to obtain a class. In the early 19th century it was not too difficult; but later there appears some evidence in support of the contention that Lloyd's Register discriminated against wooden vessels in favour of British iron-built vessels. Probably the climax was reached in 1870–6, when the rules required each foreign-built wooden vessel to undergo an annual survey in drydock; it is stated that at the end of this period only one American-owned wooden ship was still classed by Lloyd's Register.

Commencing in 1857, the first American classification society was the New York Maritime Register, not to be confused with the weekly publication of the same name which was established in 1869 to record the movements of vessels and casualties. The first N.Y.M.R. became American Lloyd's in 1860, and this was merged after 1869 into the American Shipmasters' Association, publishers of the register book known as the *Record of American and Foreign Shipping*. In 1898 the American Shipmasters' Association became

Quick layout of eight and sixteen sides with spirit level and pencil compass —

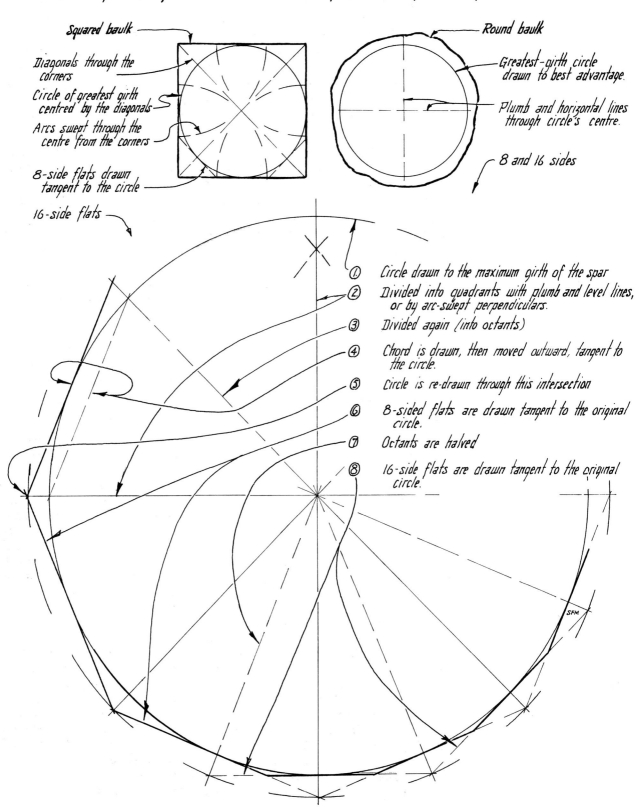

Squared baulk

Diagonals through the corners

Circle of greatest girth centred by the diagonals

Arcs swept through the centre from the corners

8-side flats drawn tangent to the circle

16-side flats

Round baulk

Greatest-girth circle drawn to best advantage

Plumb and horizontal lines through circle's centre.

8 and 16 sides

① Circle drawn to the maximum girth of the spar

② Divided into quadrants with plumb and level lines, or by arc-swept perpendiculars.

③ Divided again (into octants)

④ Chord is drawn, then moved outward, tangent to the circle.

⑤ Circle is re-drawn through this intersection

⑥ 8-sided flats are drawn tangent to the original circle.

⑦ Octants are halved

⑧ 16-side flats are drawn tangent to the original circle.

SFM

the American Bureau of Shipping, and under this name they still continue to publish the *Record*. Bureau Veritas, the French classification organization, classed a good many American vessels in the 1860s and 1870s; they had a good deal of business in Canada until after World War I.

In fact, in the nineteenth century these quality controls did not always operate quite as they were supposed to, especially in rural areas. Surveyors were at times susceptible to pressures of various kinds, which could effect the construction of a vessel. A shipbuilder could be harassed almost to the point of bankruptcy if he did not please a surveyor. On the other hand, a surveyor, a local man perhaps, was subject to local social pressures of various complex kinds. There were cases where new vessels proceeded to sea which were not of the quality of construction indicated on their Lloyd's survey reports (which are nearly all preserved in the National Maritime Museum today).

Today, despite all the surveys and all Master's craftsmanship, our schooner would not be allowed to earn her living at sea without extensive modifications to meet numerous new safety requirements. There has even been talk recently in the United States of banning the commercial use of wooden hulls altogether – the complex structure of organic materials is deemed far too vulnerable for the modern world. Big wooden ships have been called, with *some* aptness, 'great wooden baskets'. They flex, bend and creak like wooden baskets, both at sea and when they take the ground on the ebb tide in harbour–and they leak like baskets, all too often, as well.

Our schooner's main mast was composed of a massive piece of pitch pine, 60 feet long from the heel, where it would be stepped on top of the keelson, to the cap at its top. It began life as a 16-inch square-sided timber baulk floated up the tidal river from the seaport town at its mouth. To quote Tom Perkins again:

> The 60-foot length was examined for shakes [splits] and any end-grain defects, since the mast would vary from 14-inch square at one end to 6-inch at the cap [the iron band on top of the lower mast].
>
> When 'Master' was satisfied that all was well, and that the required measurements could hold up to the sizes, the mast baulk was lifted on to levelled blocks to be set out. The heart of the timber was the focal point of setting out, and lining through, the concentric growth rings would be retained centrally around the heart at each end of the mast. That is what timber selection is all about. Chalk lines were used to centre the mast line throughout its length. At one end the square was set out to its limits, and on the other end, a pair of dividers drew the circular size at the cap; then from the circle a square was drawn around the circle to allow the edge lines to be drawn that were set out from the centre line along the mast's length. Doing this defined the required shape of the mast.
>
> The next operation was to axe the baulk to the chalk lines, on all the four faces, turning as required. Then the yard gang began dubbing with adzes to fair the wood and square it. Long trying planes or fore planes were then used further to fair the mast, to allow eight squaring, the preliminary to 'rounding up'.
>
> The mast was now on trestles at a convenient working height. Eight squaring was done with an adze and a draw-knife; the finish was given by wooden jack-planes. 'Sixteen squaring', the next phase, was aided by the end circles. Trimming was easy since little was left to be removed. Draw-knives were used for this and then the planing would begin to 'round up'. Half-round chocks between mast and trestle allowed easier turning whilst fairing and these were now inserted.
>
> Hollow planes with a curved iron brought the roundness required, and the

Traditional gauge or <u>eight-squaring board</u> *for marking the edges of eight and sixteen facets along the length of a tapered spar.* —

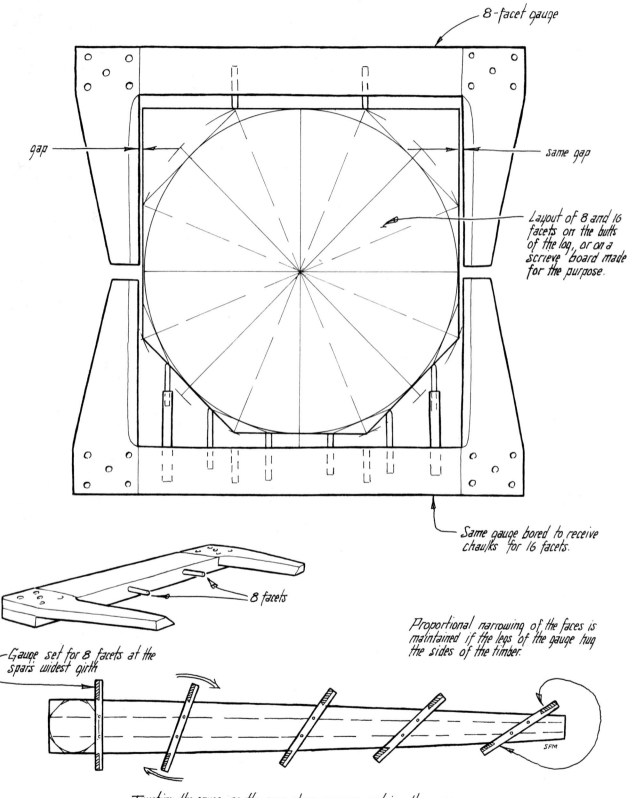

8-facet gauge

gap

same gap

Layout of 8 and 16 facets on the butts of the log, or on a screeve board made for the purpose.

Same gauge bored to receive chaulks for 16 facets.

8 facets

Gauge set for 8 facets at the spar's widest girth

Proportional narrowing of the faces is maintained if the legs of the gauge hug the sides of the timber.

SFM

Twisting the gauge as the spar stave narrows retains the same proportional distance between the scribed edges and the sides.

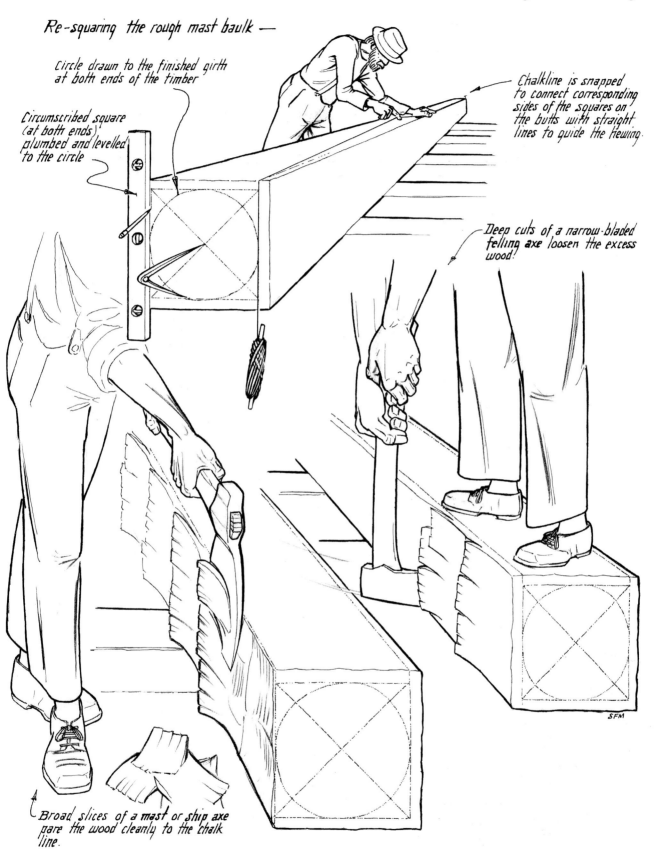

Re-squaring the rough mast baulk —

Circle drawn to the finished girth at both ends of the timber

Circumscribed square (at both ends) plumbed and levelled to the circle

Chalkline is snapped to connect corresponding sides of the squares on the butts with straight lines to guide the hewing.

Deep cuts of a narrow-bladed felling axe loosen the excess wood!

Broad slices of a mast or ship axe pare the wood cleanly to the chalk line.

Hewing the mast timber to eight sides —

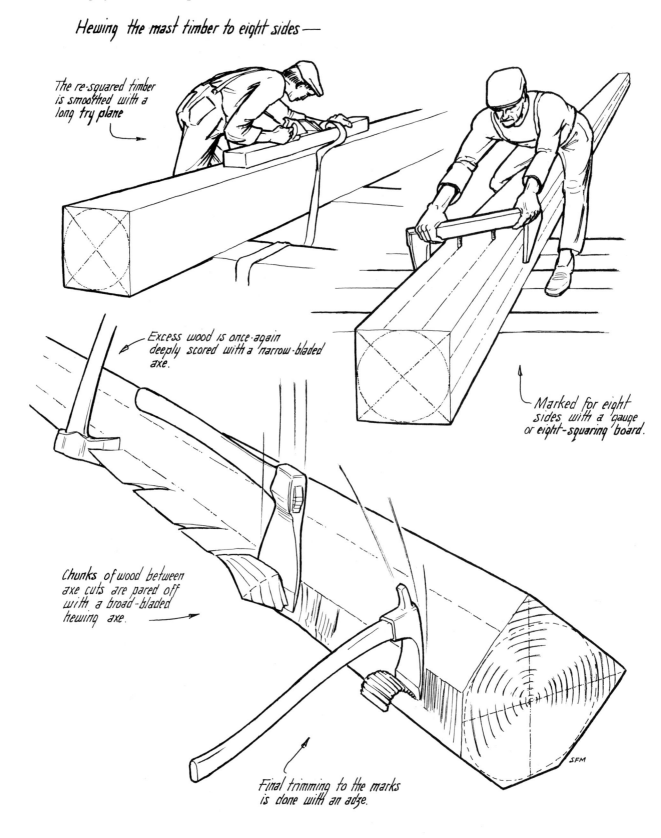

The re-squared timber is smoothed with a long try plane

Excess wood is once-again deeply scored with a 'narrow-bladed axe.

Marked for eight sides with a 'gauge' or 'eight-squaring' board.

Chunks of wood between axe cuts are pared off with a broad-bladed hewing axe. —

Final trimming to the marks is done with an adze.

SFM

166

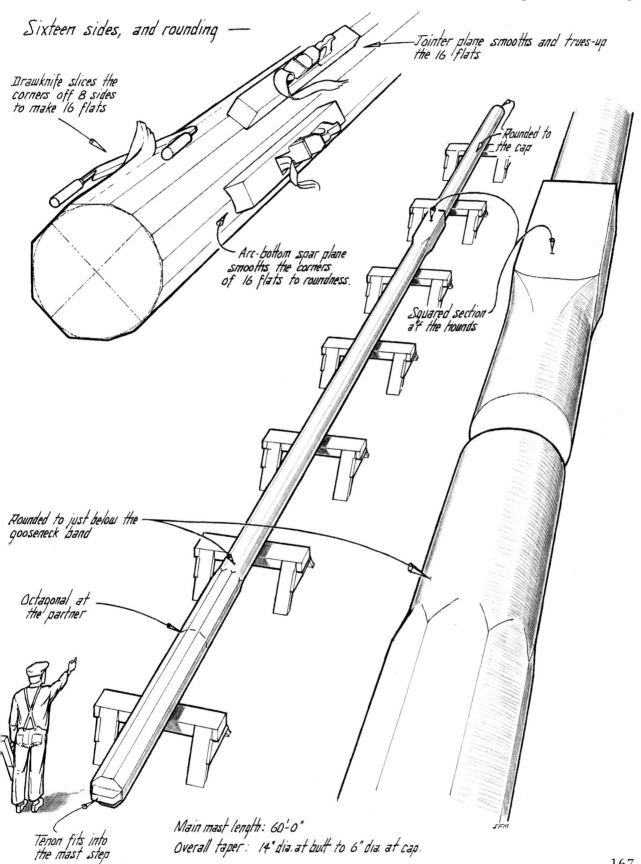

Sixteen sides, and rounding —

Drawknife slices the corners off 8 sides to make 16 flats

Jointer plane smooths and trues-up the 16 flats

Arc-bottom spar plane smooths the corners of 16 flats to roundness.

Rounded to the cap

Squared section at the hounds

Rounded to just below the gooseneck band

Octagonal at the partner

Tenon fits into the mast step

Main mast length: 60'-0"
Overall taper: 14" dia. at butt to 6" dia. at cap.

JFM

Setting the cap iron —

168

squared end was faired to size and neatly chamfered from square to round at the base of the mast. Scrapers and sand papers brought it to a silk-like appearance. Compass-planes were used for the curved work from square to round section. Blocks of pitch pine were fastened through the mast in the hounds position to carry the shroud band, and a back block for the forestay. The top of the mast was iron-banded against 'shaking'.

Eye-bolts for the throat and peak halyards were fashioned by the blacksmith, and positioned by the 'mast-head party'. These were made with curved saddles which fitted the round of the mast and helped to prevent the twisting or wringing of the eye. Sheaves were cut through if required for topsail halyards, etc. Shakes were puttied and the mast painted at its head, given a soaking of linseed, tallow and oil for the lower parts.

The mast would then have been dressed with its standing rigging, comprising the shrouds (which gave sideways support), the backstays (which provided support from aft and sideways, especially when running before the wind) and the forestay (which braced the mast from forward against the strains imposed by sailing and by the weight of the gaff, the boom and the sail set behind it). These were much the same strains as those faced by the rigging of a small yacht today, but they were met in a simpler fashion, without the use of spreaders: iron wire rigging was simply disposed from the hounds of the masthead down to the sides of the vessel and the stemhead.

Raising shears —

Raising mainmast —

The ironwork comprised *the eye-bolts,* to which the blocks were shackled for the throat and peak halyards which hoisted the great gaff sail; *the topping lift-block,* which took the weight of the boom; and *the ring and eye-bolts, truck-bands, sheet-bands* and other items required to secure the standing rigging. This ironwork was usually made up in blacksmith's shop at the yard.

Stepping the masts was a very skilled business. It was done with the aid of sheerlegs. Two suitable spars were selected from the yard's timber stock; they had to be about 35–40 feet in length, and were manhandled on board with blocks and tackles. The spars were placed with their upper ends crossed and lashed together, the ends raised up on a high trestle, placed on the deck facing aft. The fore ends were then placed one each side of the bulwarks, which had now been built on the vessel, secured so that they remained stationary while the spars were hoisted upright. A powerful tackle, made of two treble blocks, was suspended from where the two spars crossed, and the lower treble block was secured to a point near the stemhead of the vessel. Steadying lines were made fast at the tops of the crossed spars, ready to take the fore and aft strain. The fall of the heavy tackle was then led to the winch and the sheerlegs hoisted upright. The two steadying guys were then set tight and made fast, one in the stern of the vessel, the other in the bows. The lower treble block was detached from the stemhead and dropped over the side and secured to the mast at a suitable point, usually about a third of the way down from the cap. The lower part of the mast was then given a heavy steadying line.

Using the winch again, the mast was dragged and manhandled up over the side so that its heel was above the deck. Kept vertical by the steadying line, it was then positioned over the hole left for it in the deck, which was surrounded below the deck by reinforcing chocks secured to the beams. The mast was then steadily lowered through the hole, and its heel manhandled into position in a slot cut on the keelson. A coin was often placed there. It could not be of too great value because everybody concerned with the operation was relatively poor. A half or quarter of a week's wages for an unskilled labourer was a sufficient sacrifice to fortune.

Once the mast was in position the sheerlegs were lowered and dismantled and the rigging, already secured to the upper part of the mast, was set up. Next, the same process was repeated with the foremast and the topmasts, sent up with their own simple standing and running rigging. The running rigging, generally made of three-stranded manilla rope, could be rove off after the gaff, boom and bowsprit (which had already been made) had been fitted in position. The windlass was built, using local castings, and the cargo winch fitted (if it had not already been fixed for use in stepping the mast) just forward and to one side of the mast. These cargo winches were standard products of local foundries and were bought ready made. They stood on timber cleats [bearers] and were secured with bolts which went right through the deck beams, so that they would not pull out under the weight of heavy pieces of cargo.

The principal job remaining was to build the vessel's accommodation. If our Master, like some other shipbuilders, had been producing vessels continuously, so that he needed the slipway to lay his next keel as soon as possible, he would have launched the new schooner at this stage and her accommodation would have been built as she lay alongside the yard. In this

Lowering mainmast —

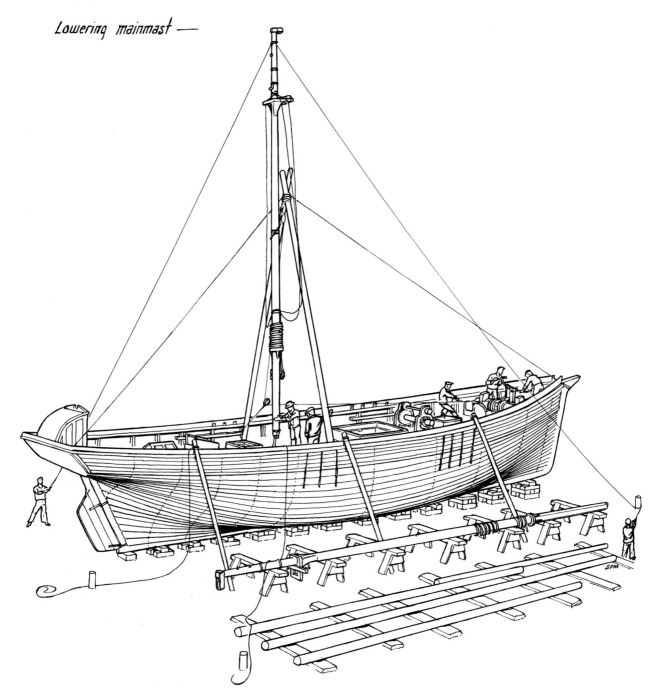

Hoisting foremast —

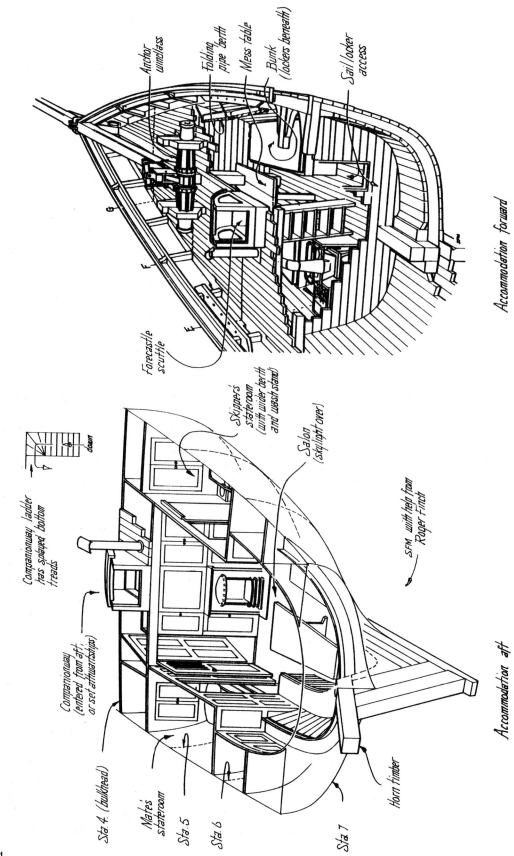

Anchor windlass

Folding pipe berth

Mess table

Bunk (lockers beneath)

Sail locker access

Forecastle scuttle

Accommodation forward

Skipper's stateroom (with wider berth and wash stand)

Salon (skylight over)

SFM with help from Roger Finch

Companionway ladder has splayed bottom treads

Companionway (entered from aft, or set athwartships)

Master's schooner —

Sta. 4. (bulkhead)

Mate's stateroom

Sta. 5

Sta. 6

Sta. 7

Horn timber

Accommodation aft

down

case, however, Master was under no pressure to launch the vessel, as he had plenty of repair work on hand as well as boatbuilding; it would be quicker to complete our vessel as she lay on the slip.

Her accommodation comprised only a very simple 'forecastle', the cabin below deck where the three crew members would sleep, and the master's and mate's quarters aft.

The after cabin of our schooner was typical of the accommodation for master and mate in a trading schooner carrying 100 tons or so of cargo. A twisted companion-way, turning through 90° in the 8 feet of its fall, led down to a space immediately in front of the cabin. This was a panelled, triangular compartment built into the stern of the ship. The two long sides of the triangle were lined with narrow, hard, upholstered seats, backed by panels. Above them was a shelf, margined with a low rail on miniature turned stanchions. This shelf inevitably held all kinds of bric-a-brac. Higher up, panelled lockers sloped back to the deckhead, and aft, above the shelf, was a square mirror set into the panelling. Between the upholstered seats was a small triangular table, shaped to fit the cabin and supported by a single leg rising from the deck amidships. The forward, broader end of this table folded downwards to leave a passage before the fireplace–a readily available standard iron casting of a type also used in cheap houses at this time. The door to the master's cabin was on the starboard side. The cabin was no more than a space just big enough to stand up in to dress and undress, equipped with a tiny washbowl and a shaving mirror, a couple of small lockers, and a locker bunk, built into the side of the vessel so that the greater part of it stretched aft behind the cabin lockers.

The mate's room, on the port side, entered from the porch at the foot of the companion way, was similar. The tall hollow structure of the skylight occupied much of the deck head space of the after cabin, and in it swung the complex brasswork of the great oil lamp; a compass mounted in a gimble was fixed to the after end of the skylight. This latter instrument often served as the binnacle on its reverse side. The whole crew ate together in this little cabin, but in bigger schooners there was usually a mess room forward of the foot of the companion way.

The forecastle furniture consisted simply of four bunks, two of them benches built into the side of the vessel and the other two, above them, bunks of bent gas-pipe covered with canvas which, when not in use, could be folded up against the ceiling. There was also a small table and a coal stove, a couple of lockers and door leading to the sail locker, immediately abaft, between the forecastle and the hold – and nothing else. The forecastle was entered by means of a scuttle and a steeply sloping ladder. This scuttle, as well as the cabin skylight and companion way, lent themselves to relatively elegant craftmanship in contemporary style, but they also had to be well built enough to stand up to the constant working of the vessel and to the potentially devastating force of seas breaking on board her from time to time.

Now our schooner would have been ready for launching. This was a difficult, and sometimes even dangerous, operation. Again, different methods were used in different places. The launch was usually only attempted on a very high tide, when the vessel had the minimum distance to move from the keel blocks to her position afloat in the water. A sort of wooden railway, called 'the ways', consisting of massive baulks of timber, was laid under the

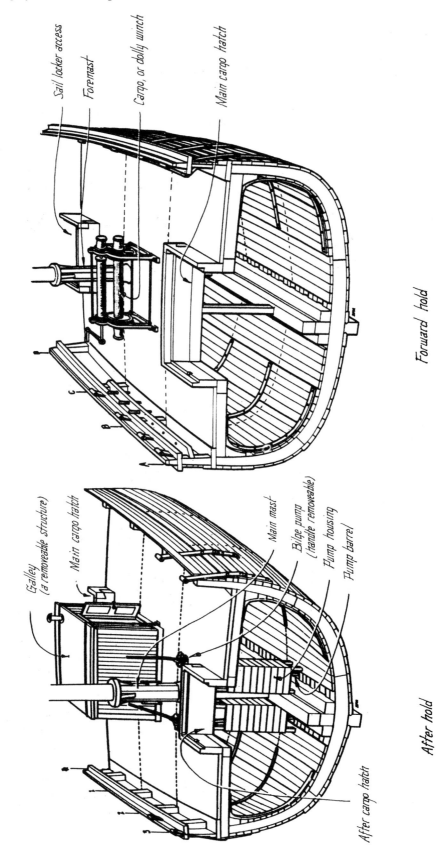

Sail locker access

Foremast

Cargo, or dolly winch

Main cargo hatch

Forward hold

Galley
(a removeable structure)

Main cargo hatch

Main mast

Bilge pump
(handle removeable)

Pump housing

Pump barrel

After hold

After cargo hatch

Masters' schooner —

The launching ways —

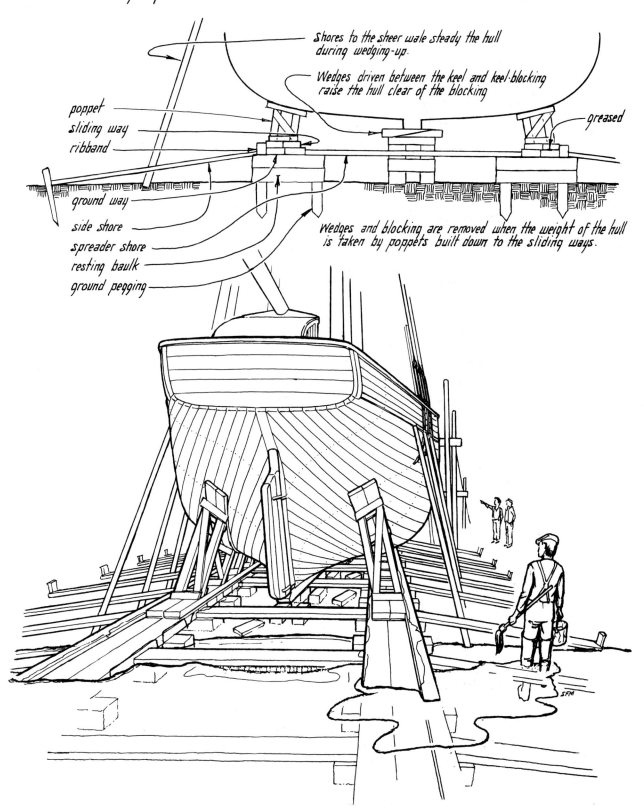

Shores to the sheer wale steady the hull during wedging-up.

Wedges driven between the keel and keel-blocking raise the hull clear of the blocking

poppet

sliding way

ribband

greased

ground way

side shore

spreader shore

resting baulk

ground pegging

Wedges and blocking are removed when the weight of the hull is taken by poppets built down to the sliding ways.

177

vessel, down the yard and just far enough under the high-tide line for her to float off. Two runners were placed on these ways, with massive coats of grease, usually tallow, (the finest kind) applied between the runners and the ways. The runners were nearly as big as the ways themselves and stretched the greater part of the length of the vessel. On the runners was built a cradle and, as this was constructed, the weight of the vessel was gradually eased off half an inch or so off the keel blocks with wedges and jacks and taken onto the cradle structure.

When the cradle was finished, it took the weight of the vessel. In preparation for the launch the ways were again heavily greased, right down their length. The cradle was held in position on the ways by one of a number of devices and at the critical moment whatever secured it was released, whereupon – in theory at least – the cradle and the vessel rapidly slid the short distance necessary for the vessel to come afloat, stern first (as she would have been built with her stern pointing down to the water). To prevent her shooting across the river and damaging her stern against the wharf on the opposite side, check-ropes or chains were used. The cradle itself floated off in a tangle of timber which was salvaged for future use. In the later years of wood shipbuilding, as she started down the ways a bottle of some kind would have been broken on the vessel's stern by a woman connected with the vessel's principal shareholders. this custom was a product of the nineteenth century.

Tom Perkins describes the process of launching the schooner in detail:

When completed, the Master's schooner, although a little smaller, would have looked very much like this vessel. (Amos & Amos)

At the launch the rudder was off, or locked amidships, to prevent damage to steerage. Work proceeded with the bringing up of the sliding-ways port and starboard. The ways were narrow, and had sufficient length to go from the bow to the water's edge, or even into it if the conditions for launching were low for the tide, or perhaps as a precaution against delays. Danger of grounding must be understood. 'Master' knew the amount of water required, knowing his waterline position to an inch. Soundings would always be taken from the mooring boat and dolphins put up, or poles to mark the limits required, usually painted red or white, a visual guide to depth and line of launch.

The schooner was lifted by inserting wedges between the keel and the building blocks, and sufficient height gained by simultaneous driving of the wedges by some forty men in the launching party, most of whom were hired specially for the job. Then the ways were slid in under, and built up to take the weight of the schooner off the keel blocks by making a cradle from the sliding-ways up to the outer bottom of the schooner local to amidships. Top shores secured the ways against movement. Ribband keys of blocks were inserted to scotch the ways by being slightly housed into them to prevent movement as well. Being already tallowed or oiled, the launch proceeded, removing the keel blocks except for a few forward to reduce drag; these tipped when the keel moved, when slipped. So now all was ready to remove the way-shores port and starboard. Sometimes the ways were sloped upwards to a gentle curve in the centre point to slow the first movement and accelerate the final one into the water. Drag chains were used to slow final movement down the slipway and into the water, acting as a shore-line or anchor, preventing a launch from one bank of a narrow river, over and up on to the other.

The men of a west of England shipbuilding yard in the early 1900s. A planked-up vessel is behind the group. (Ian Merry)

Porthmadog harbour, 1890's
(from a photograph)

7 four other building traditions

The description of the building of the simple wooden schooner in the four preceding chapters explains the fundamentals of a complex craft. As we have already said, there were very many variations in detail from yard to yard and from country to country, and the process of building bigger vessels was more complicated. This chapter will illustrate some of the differences in wood shipbuilding in other traditions by describing in turn some aspects of the construction of four actual vessels, each one bigger than the last.

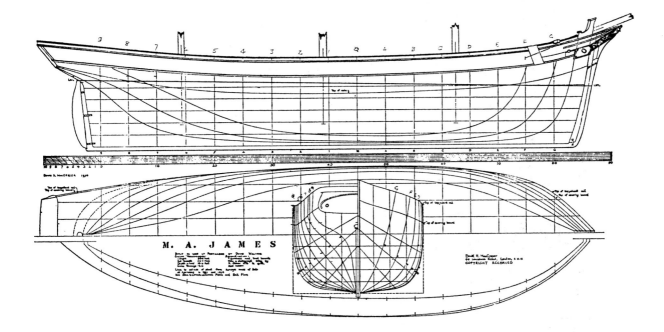

Lines of the M.A. James as drafted by David R. MacGregor following survey of her hull in 1947.

1   Wales: small three-masted schooner

The harbour and the town of Porthmadog, in the county of Gwynedd in north Wales, were creations of the nineteenth century. An artificial harbour grew in prosperity with the great expansion of the slate quarries in the mountains of its hinterland. These quarries developed to meet an ever growing demand for roofing materials for the houses of the rapidly increasing populations of both Britain and north Germany – where the north Wales slate merchants had a well established market. Here the efforts of local promoters and industrialists led to the growth of shipbuilding and ship-owning, and in due course to local involvement in world trade.

The establishment of locally-based insurance facilities for covering vessels, cargoes and freight money in the 1840s was a great fillip for the industry. In the later nineteenth century Porthmadog ships were trading all over the world and the local shipowners had come to specialize in the carrying of dried and salted codfish from Newfoundland to Iberian and Mediterranean ports and to Northern Europe, one of the hardest sailing-vessels trades which ever existed. For this a remarkable type of three-masted schooner was developed in Porthmadog, representing the finest development of the small

The M.A. James *as a motor schooner, but still with long topmasts, moored in Appledore in the 1930s.* (H. Oliver Hill)

The crew of the Gracie of Porthmadog; the ship was built at Porthmadog in 1907 for the Newfoundland trade and is almost identical to the M.A. James *in size and details of construction and rig.* (Aled Eames)

When the M.A. James *was fully rigged and laden she would have looked like her sister ship from Porthmadog, the* William Pritchard, *here seen lying in Cumberland basin in Bristol, having just arrived with a cargo of salted cod from Labrador.* (Bristol Museum)

wooden merchant sailing ship in Britain. The *M.A. James* was one of these schooners. She was the seventh of a series of 15 similar vessels built by David Williams, Master Shipbuilder, of Porthmadog, between 1891 and 1913. Thirty-three of these schooners were built altogether, 18 of them by other builders.

The contract to build the *M.A. James* was a simple document which tells us a good deal about the way wood shipbuilders' yards conducted their business:

AGREEMENT

MEMORANDUM of an Agreement made and entered into this Twenty Seventh day of April in the year One thousand eight hundred and ninety nine, between *David Williams* Shipbuilder, Portmadoc of the first part and *Captain John Jones* Borth-y-gest of the second part.

The said David Williams agrees to build a new vessel (now on blocks), same rig, model, and class as the schooner 'Ellen James'. The masts to be two feet longer than those of the 'Ellen James'.

The said new vessel is to measure under one hundred tons net register, and to be launched in January, One thousand nine hundred, by and on his responsibility, from his yard at Portmadoc. The said vessel to be completed and fully equipped according to the requirements of the Board of Trade, and the regulations of the Portmadoc Mutual Ship Insurance Society.

The sails are to be in accordance with a specification supplied by Messrs. Richards & Jones, Sailmakers, Portmadoc. The vessel to be metalled with the best yellow metal, *and all and everything shall be of the best materials*, executed in a workmanlike manner and to the entire satisfaction of the said John Jones.

The said builder agrees to supply the said vessel, with all and every article necessary on board ship, and which are customarily supplied to new ships built at Portmadoc.

John Jones on his part hereby covenants to pay for the said new vessel, the sum of two thousand pounds, of which six hundred pounds is to be paid by instalments before launching and the remainder after the vessel is complete.

In Witness whereof the said parties have hereunder subscribed their names the day and year first above written

As Witness	Signatures
Hugh Carry	David Williams
Ship Broker, Portmadoc.	John Jones

P.S. Dimension, keel same as now on blocks
  Depth from 10 feet 6 inches to 10 feet 9 inches
  Breadth   22 feet 8.   David Williams
                              John Jones.

Although he ran a larger business than the Master of the yard where our schooner was built, David Williams also worked as hard as anyone in his yard. Born in 1860, he was trained as a shipwright, went to sea as a carpenter and then returned to Porthmadog to help in his uncle's shipyard, which he eventually took over. His yard employed 12 men, but it was David Williams himself who went out into the woods of the Maentwrog area to select the oak for building the new schooner. The pitch pine, yellow pine and greenheart were all imported through Liverpool and delivered direct to the yard in coasting vessels.

Bracket, or hawksnest model —

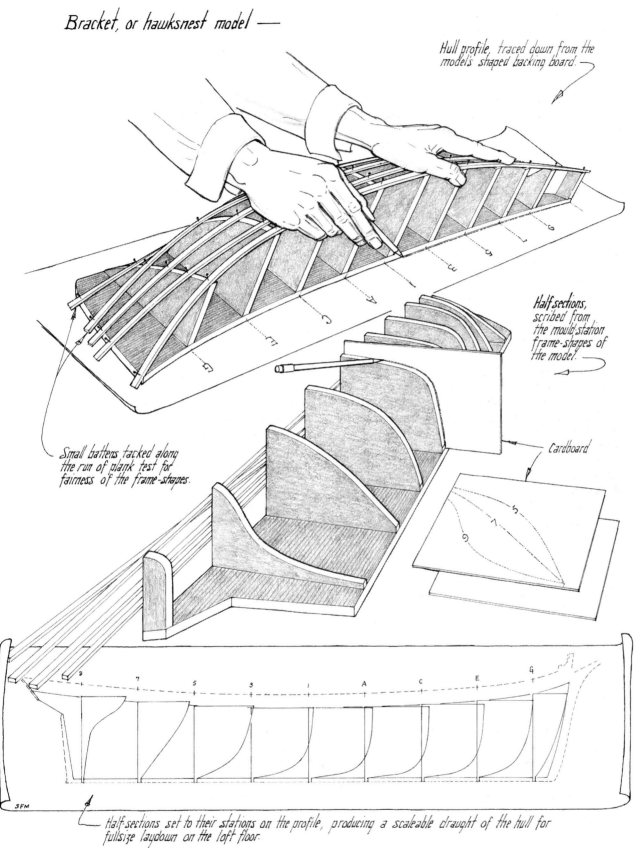

Hull profile, traced down from the model's shaped backing board.

Half sections, scribed from the mould-station frame-shapes of the model.

Cardboard

Small battens tacked along the run of plank test for fairness of the frame-shapes.

Half-sections set to their stations on the profile, producing a scaleable draught of the hull for fullsize laydown on the loft floor.

SFM

David Williams used a different kind of half model from that used by our Master in the south-west of England. He employed what was contemporarily described as a 'bracket model', known in North America as a 'hawk's nest' or 'crow's nest' model. A plank back-board was sawn out to form a profile of the hull, on which plank sections were mounted to represent frame shapes. These were fastened to the back-board with nails, hammered through from the back. The mould sections were usually placed at alternate frames; the sheer, deck sheer, deck lines and the shape of the model at different points between the deck line and the keel were indicated by battens bent round like planks and tacked to the sections. This was a very old form of half model, quite widely used in Britain and North America (in Britain even in the late nineteenth century). The lines were taken off by simply removing the battens, once everybody concerned was satisfied with the shape, and then tracing the outline of each frame section onto paper and scaling up from the paper drawings onto the mould-loft floor. The disadvantage of this type of model was that it was more difficult to alter it in discussion than the layered type and more difficult to test its imperfections by means of drawing the fingers down the shape of the hull. These models were more fragile than the layered block type and consequently far fewer of them have survived.

The Lloyd's Surveyor's Report made on the *M.A. James* when she was completed, now preserved in the National Maritime Museum, shows that the framing, deck beams and the heavy timbers at bow and stern of the vessel were made of English oak, her keel of American elm, her keelson of greenheart (which was an almost everlasting wood), her lower planking of American elm, English elm and pitch pine, her upper planking of greenheart and English oak, and her topsides and sheer strakes of English oak, greenheart and pitch pine. The decks were of New England white pine, called 'yellow pine' in the British timber trade; the beam shelf and clamp were of greenheart and English oak. She was largely fastened, not with galvanized or pitch-dipped iron but with 'yellow metal'–a brass alloy, which, like the greenheart of which she was so largely constructed, was almost indestructible.

There is a piece of this vessel's planking, from below the load line, in the room in which this book is being written. It is still $2\frac{1}{2}$ inches thick and attached to it are fragments of the yellow metal sheathing which covered the whole of her underwater body, protecting it from the attacks of the marine wood-boring organisms which thrived in the warm waters of the West Indies and in some of the Canadian ports (notably Prince Edward Island) into which the *M.A. James* traded. These could attack a wooden vessel so seriously that very expensive repair work was necessary after only a few weeks of exposure to them.

The planking below the waterline was fastened to the frames almost entirely with wooden treenails and with some copper bolts. These treenails were hardwood pins, 15 inches long and $1\frac{1}{2}$ inches in diameter, made up by the boys of the yard like masts, first in an octagonal shape and then planed off with a rotating, circular hand-plane into smooth cylinders. These were driven into pre-drilled holes only a little smaller than themselves; they also had slots cut in their heads into which small hardwood wedges were driven. With the swelling of the treenails and the plank when the vessel was launched the whole became bonded together in an enormously strong fastening.

It was essential to use treenails and copper bolts for fastening the planks

Frame bevels taken directly from a bracket model —

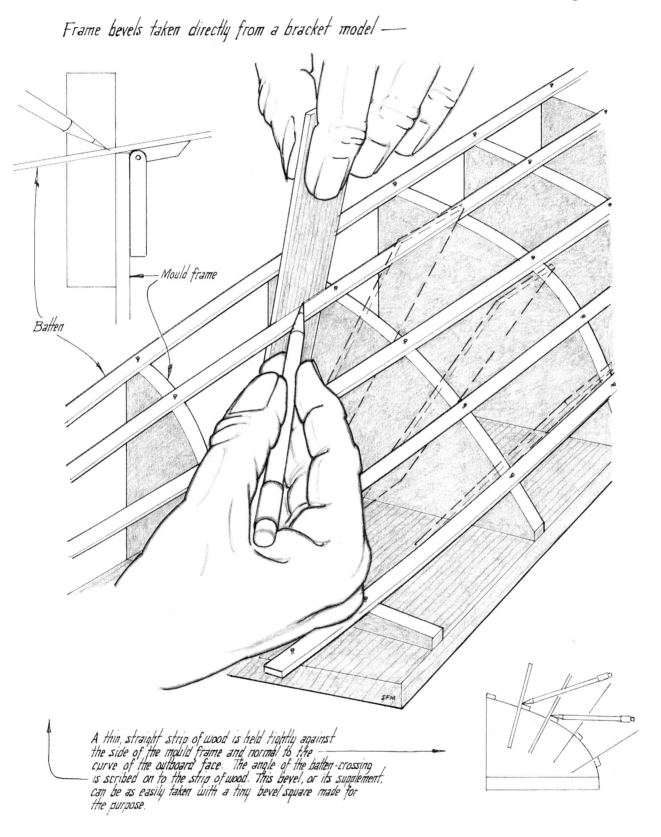

Batten

Mould frame

A thin, straight strip of wood is held tightly against
the side of the mould frame and normal to the
curve of the outboard face. The angle of the batten-crossing
is scribed on to the strip of wood. This bevel, or its supplement,
can be as easily taken with a tiny bevel square made for
the purpose.

Trunnels — *shaped and headed in a moot* —

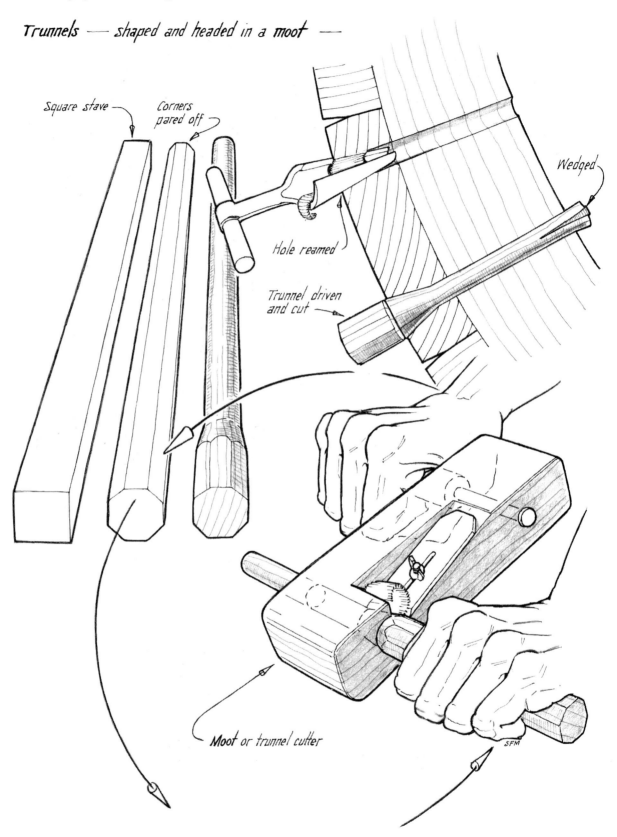

Square stave

Corners pared off

Hole reamed

Trunnel driven and cut

Wedged

Moot or trunnel cutter

SFM

Dubbing off

Here's the look of trimming double-sawn frames to final fairness of bevel on a vessel being planked simultaneously inside and out.

The schooner in-frame here is about the size of the M.A. James. A tightly-pulled string guides the dubbing through the square body of the hull.

The foreman works ahead of the dubbers, liming-off the lay of plank and cutting channels or "spots" across the faces of various frames in order to make the tightened string lie fair along the hull. His tool is a hollow or "liming" adze. The dubbers remove the wood between the spots with a straight-bladed (English) or lipped (American) adze.

Dubbing is awkward, exhausting, highly skilled work. Frame bevels accurately applied to the frame futtocks at the saw pit save a great deal of labour in dubbing when plank is hung later on.

Shipbuilding in Porthmadog. A vessel very similar to the M.A. James is fully framed up. (Gwynedd County Archives)

to the frames below the waterline because of the yellow metal sheathing. A coating of tar-soaked felt was layered on the hull, on top of which were fixed (with copper nails) plates of brass alloy, yellow metal, to make a complete sheathing.

In the *M.A. James* the floors were about a foot square where they rested on the keel, tapering to 8 inches where they joined the futtocks. The futtocks themselves were reduced in siding from 8 to 5 or 6 inches at deck level.

David Williams built his vessel in a different order from that adopted in south-western England. After she was fully framed up, before the beam shelf and the deck beams and coamings were put in – before even the frame heads were levelled off to make a graceful sheer – the *M.A. James* was planked-up both inside and out. Using this method, some of the holes for the treenails and bolts which fastened both the outer and inner planking could be bored at the same time, and the fastenings driven right through, resulting in a very rigid structure ready to receive the beam shelf and deck beams. Where treenails were used extensively, the practice of fastening the outside plank and ceiling together avoided the weakening of the frame which could result from boring two holes where one would suffice. The rest of the structure was finished afterwards.

To offset the effects of rot, consequent upon the use of green wood, most working sailing vessels were over-timbered in anticipation of the day, after some fifteen or twenty years service, when only one out of three frames might still be reasonably strong. It is remarkable that after extensive alterations, sometimes involving the removal of several parts of the main structure, many

190

Aft-accommodation in a Porthmadog schooner —

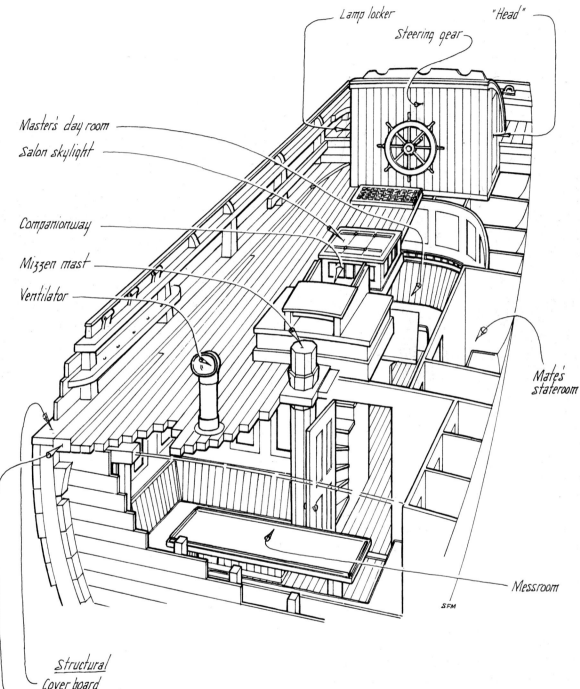

Lamp locker

"Head"

Steering gear

Master's day room

Salon skylight

Companionway

Mizzen mast

Ventilator

Mate's stateroom

Messroom

SFM

Structural
Cover board
Waterway timber

(*Deckbeams are omitted here*)

wooden working hulls have remained strong enough to stay afloat for many years, albeit as yachts or houseboats. The *M.A. James* survived for 45 years of hard work, 40 of them carrying cargoes at sea. This may partly have been because she was salted. To help to preserve wooden vessels for as long as possible it was sometimes common to fill all the spaces between the frames, from the light-load line to under the beam shelf, with coarse salt, to preserve the timbers within the hull. Sometimes, perforated salt-boxes were used, from which brine constantly trickled into the bilges. Provided that the timber of which the vessel was built was well seasoned and mainly fastened with treenails and copper or yellow-metal bolts (iron-fastened vessels were not normally salted), salting certainly prolonged the life of a vessel. This was recognized by Lloyds' and the other classification organizations. The *M.A. James* was salted according to Lloyds' rules and the practice was reflected in the high classification recommended for her by the surveyor at her completion.

The accommodation for the master, mate and crew built into the *M.A. James* was very similar to that already described for our small schooner. The *M.A. James* was a larger vessel, with a net registered tonnage of 97 and a cargo capacity of over 200 tons; she measured 90 feet long by 22 feet in the beam, so there was room for a messroom forward of the master's and mate's cabins, and the crew, with the master and mate, ate there and not in the master's day room in the extreme stern of the ship. The food was cooked in the galley on deck. This was a portable wooden cabin, rather like a garden shed except that it was built of vertical planks with a cambered roof covered with waterproof canvas. It was secured to the deck temporarily with metal straps hooked to ring-bolts, tightened with turnbuckles, partly so that it could be removed when the vessel was carrying deck cargo and partly to make it possible to get at the deck underneath for repairs.

2   Finland: large three-masted schooner

Today the Åland Islands are a Swedish-speaking, quasi-autonomus province of Finland and the 20,000 inhabitants own between them nearly a third of Finland's modern merchant shipping. But for a century before 1917 they were a Russian occupied territory, as was Finland itself. After the Crimean War a merchant shipping industry began to develop in Åland. Capital generation was slow and it was not until 1927 that the Ålanders began continuous investment in steam tonnage. Until then Åland was a sailing community, the last in Europe to own big sailing ships in relatively large numbers.

When Eric Söderström built the three-masted schooner *Ingrid* in 1906 at Knutnäs, Olofsnäs (on the Kalfjärd in the administrative area of Geta on the north western tip of the main island of Åland) he cut the timber, even for *Ingrid*'s masts, from the local woods on each side of the fjärd, using soft woods – pines, spruces and birch of various kinds. The origins of the *Ingrid* are interesting. It was then the custom in Åland, as it still is from time to time in the winter months, for neighbouring farmers to assemble for a party in the big parlour of one of the farms, which would be heated with its great wood-burning stove, lit for the occasion. In the winter of 1905–6 such a

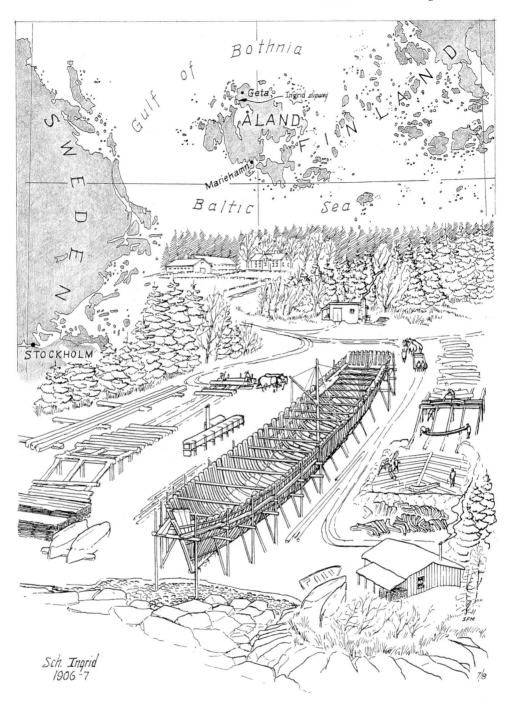

Sch. *Ingrid*
1906 -7

party was held in Geta parish, with the women sitting on one side talking and sewing and the men around the table talking and drinking, with everyone bewailing the hardness of the times. The men and the women separated on social occasions for the same reasons that they did in south-west Britain. Eventually someone said, 'Well, if we cannot sell our wood, let us use it to build a ship like our grandfathers did and let it carry other people's timber.' The men all agreed. There had been a good deal of drinking, but in the morning they stood by their commitment.

The proposed vessel as a property was divided into 200 shares and, as Eric Söderström's grandson told this author, 'everyone in Geta owned some of the *Ingrid*'. A list of the original shareholders still survives in Eric Söderström's notebook, preserved in the Åland Maritime Museum: there were 30 of them, the great majority local farmers, and by 1916 their number had increased to 37. The original shares were bought with cash, with timber cut on the farmer's wood-lots and hauled to the building site, or with labour provided in the course of building by farmers and their sons. About twenty of these men built the *Ingrid* between them. She was the common venture of a highly democratic and relatively prosperous agricultural community with a strong seafaring tradition. Small ships – schooners, ketches and smacks – had been built in Åland at the turn of the century, and had been launched at an average rate of one per year for the preceding ten years in Geta itself. However, no large vessel had been built in Åland since the early 1890s and very few since the early 1880s. This was the 'period of secondhand tonnage' in Åland's history, when the shipowning community depended on old sailing ships bought cheaply from overseas, mostly from Canada, Britain and Sweden. The building of the *Ingrid* in 1906 was a reversion to earlier practices.

Eric Söderström's family had lived on the site of their farm since the seventeenth century. They are living there still. Born in 1835, Eric Söderström had never been to sea, but he had been building ships since 1877 and launched 12 vessels in the intervening 29 years. The largest of them, the barque *Helmi*, was launched in 1892. (Her forecastle is preserved intact in the Åland Maritime Museum.)

Nevertheless, when Söderström was asked by the group of farmers to supervise the building of a big schooner for ocean trading in early 1906, he had no recent model to build from. He therefore took the half model of a successful two-masted schooner, the 64 ton *Emilia*, which he had built in 1889, and he developed it by scaling it up, lengthening it by adding to the body amidships to give a model of a much bigger vessel. This half model was not carved from a block made by pinning planks together, as was the model used by our Master in south-western Britain, but was a solid block of fine pinewood. After he had shaped the model to the satisfaction of all those concerned, Söderström transferred its shape to a two-dimensional drawing by tracing the profile of the model onto paper and then taking off the frame shapes, probably using soft lead bars about an eighth of an inch square bent round the sections. Tracing the shape of these on the paper, he then refined the drawing on squared paper, producing the classic sheer plan, body plan and half breadth plan. Söderström may have used thin cardboard placed with its edge against the model and cut again and again with scissors until it fitted, forming a negative image of the frame shape at that particular point. (This method was used at Hink's Yard at Appledore in the building of sailing barges early in the present century.)

*Hull lines of **Ingrid** as developed by Eric Söderström from a solid block model —*

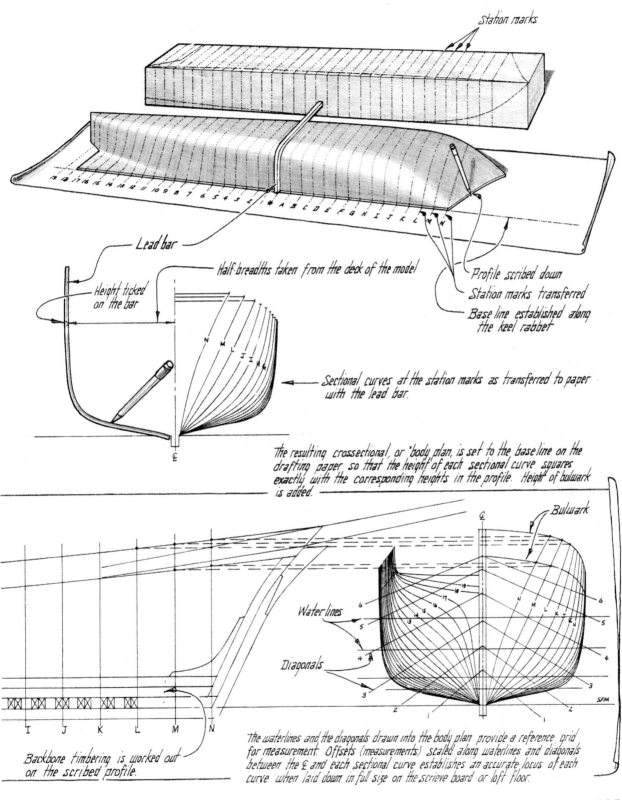

Station marks

Lead bar

Height ticked on the bar

Half-breadths taken from the deck of the model

Profile scribed down

Station marks transferred

Base line established along the keel rabbet

Sectional curves at the station marks as transferred to paper with the lead bar.

The resulting crossectional, or "body plan, is set to the base line on the drafting paper so that the height of each sectional curve squares exactly with the corresponding heights in the profile. Height of bulwark is added. —

Bulwark

Water lines

Diagonals

Backbone timbering is worked out on the scribed profile.

The waterlines and the diagonals drawn into the body plan provide a reference grid for measurement. Offsets (measurements) scaled along waterlines and diagonals between the ₵ and each sectional curve establishes an accurate locus of each curve when laid down in full size on the scrieve board or loft floor.

Top left: *The half model on the right is that of the* galeas Emelia. *Using this, Eric Söderström developed the half model on the left, which, in turn, became the basis for the* Ingrid. (Author's collection)

Pit-sawing plank —

Sch. *Ingrid*
1906-7

Below Left: *The* Ingrid *was built by 20 farmers and farmers' sons working under Söderström as master shipwright.* (Mrs Karlsson)

Eric Söderström's rough but thoroughly workmanlike naval architect's drawing is preserved in the Åland Maritime Museum. He used the oldest form of half model to execute it: the solid block method is known to have been employed in the seventeenth century. This he combined in his design process with a quite sophisticated naval architect's drawing from which the dimensions were then taken for scaling up on the board floor, for the making of the frame moulds.

Although 291 wooden ships were built in Åland between 1838 and 1965, few of them were launched from established shipyards. It was usual to employ a master shipwright, who was often a farmer and perhaps, like Eric Söderström, a blacksmith as well, to supervise the building of a vessel at one of the recognized building sites – places where the granite shore sloped down gently into deep water. At these sites temporary huts were erected and a group of men gathered together, some of whom would have worked at shipbuilding before and some of whom would simply act as labourers and learners. The vessel would then be built.

Eric Söderström chose Knutnäs as his building site, a place where he had constructed vessels before. Here an open stretch of grass leads down between trees to the edge of the fjärd; there is deep water immediately off the narrow beach. In this beautiful place Söderström laid his keel blocks, set up a sawing stage and blacksmith's shop and, with his twenty farmers and their sons, began work on building the 140-foot schooner.

Söderström appears to have been a skilled blacksmith. Indeed it is believed that blacksmithing is the first of many skills that this Åland polymath had acquired. He bought scrap iron and secondhand fittings from Stockholm which were brought over in a small local schooner. From this material he made up the ironwork for the *Ingrid* in a temporary forge built on the edge of the woods. The sawing stage was also at the forest's edge (the pink granite of Åland is far too hard for a pit to be dug in it). The farmers and their sons sawed, usually six at a time, three below and three above (though sometimes with only one above) on the staging, holding long cross-bars attached to the saw, and sawing to marked lines on the timber both above and below. It was the centre-man's responsibility, both above and below, to follow the line.

In Åland, when a vessel was to be completed in the spring, when there was ice still in the water, she was often built with her bows facing the water, instead of the stern, as was the usual practice in Britain. This was so that the rudder was not damaged during the launching. The description which follows is of a launching in Åland in the spring:

> From all parts crowds in their best clothes streamed to the wharf quite early in the morning. As the clock approached eleven the builder, Appelo-Henriksson, began to give orders to his carpenters; greasing and soft-soaping were carried out, the latter with German soft soap; the beams on which the keel rested had earlier had their fill of soap.
>
> Then began the wedging. Hammer blows against a score of wedges took place, tensions showed in the debates of experts and the enthusiasms of youth. After an hour's tense expectation, the craft began to move, increased speed, its fore-end entered the water, the stern made the water and proudly rested, accompanied by thunderous cheers. With good speed the craft moved and stopped in the area where the ice on both sides was broken. At the same time as the craft took to the water, the weak wind unfolded the flag with the name, and she was duly christened the *Neptun*.

Sch. Ingrid - 1906-7

Cradle launching —

Stocks cribwork

Cradle

Wedge

Sliding way
(greased beneath)

Ground way

Ways and cradle are built beneath the hull as it rests elevated on the building stocks. Cross members
of the cradle are run through, tight to the keel, between the stacks of stocks-cribwork.
Then the whole vessel is raised an inch or two by wedges driven simultaneously, both sides,
the length of the cradle, between the cradle runners and the sliding ways. This takes the
weight of the vessel off the stocks so that the blocking can be removed. When locking or
"trigger" timbers are knocked out at the moment of launching, the hull, cradle, wedges and
sliding ways move together down the greased ground ways.

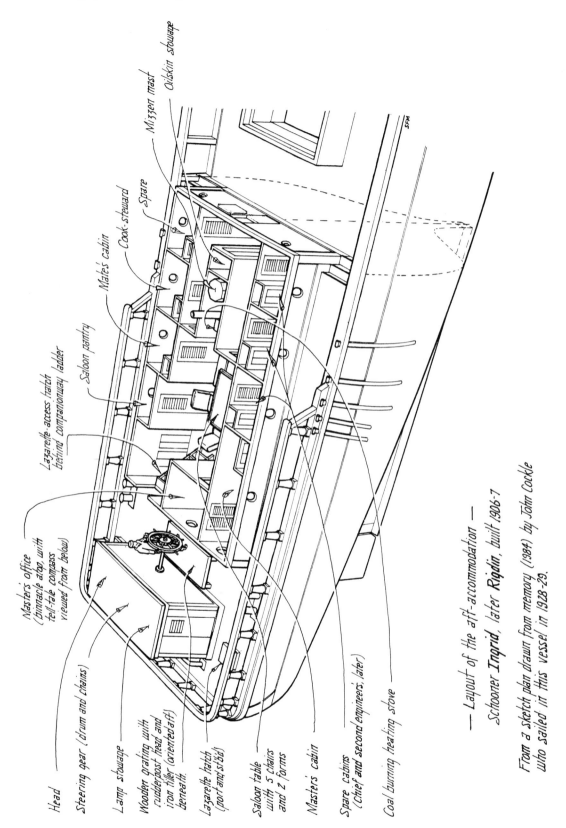

Oilskin stowage

Mizzen mast

Spare

Cook-steward

Mates' cabin

Saloon pantry

Lazarette-access hatch (behind companionway ladder)

Master's office (binnacle atop, with tell-tale compass viewed from below)

Head

Steering gear (drum and chains)

Lamp stowage

Wooden grating with rudderpost head and iron tiller (orientated aft) beneath.

Lazarette hatch (port and st'bd)

Saloon table with 5 chairs and 2 forms

Master's cabin

Spare cabins (Chief and second engineers, later)

Coal burning heating stove

— Layout of the aft-accommodation —
Schooner **Ingrid**, later **Rigdin**, built 1906-7

From a sketch plan drawn from memory (1984) by John Cockle who sailed in this vessel in 1928-29.

200

Layout of the port-side cabins, as suggested by John Cockle's plan of the after accommodation.
*Schooner **Ingrid** – built 1906-7.*

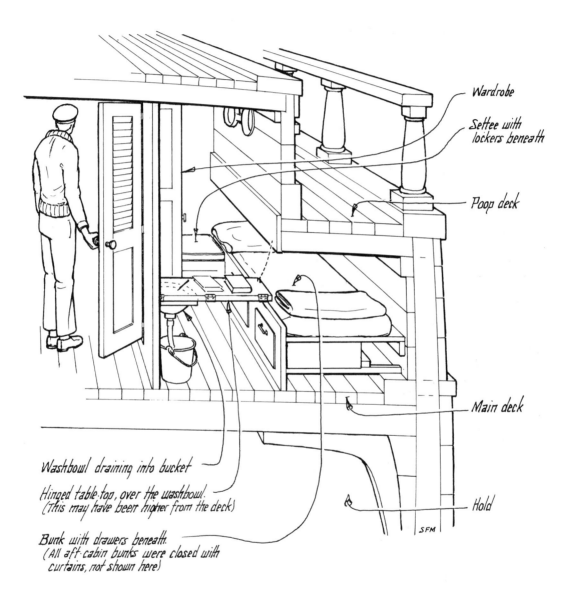

Wardrobe

Settee with
lockers beneath

Poop deck

Main deck

Hold

SFM

Washbowl draining into bucket

Hinged table-top, over the washbowl.
(This may have been higher from the deck)

Bunk with drawers beneath.
(All aft-cabin bunks were closed with
curtains, not shown here)

201

The Ingrid *on arrival at Littlehampton, 8 October 1910.* (Ruben Jansson)

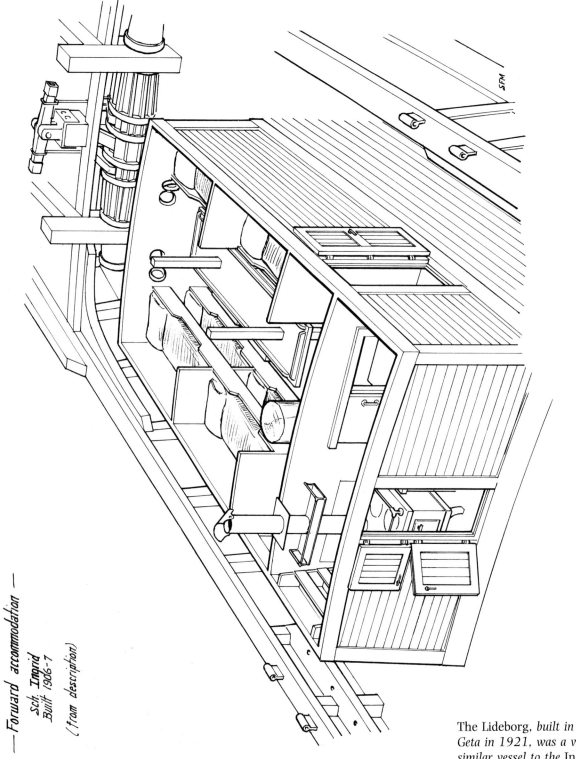

— Forward accommodation —
Sch. Ingrid
Built 1906-7
(from description)

The Lideborg, *built in Geta in 1921, was a very similar vessel to the* Ingrid. (Ålands Sjöfarmuseum)

The celebrations continued with the taking by the crowds of large quantities of coffee and schnapps, while others regaled themselves with toddy. After two or three hours drinking people began to make their way home; but before they did so they foregathered for a communal lunch.

In 1976 Eric Söderström's grandson could still remember that as a small child he was permitted to be present at the launch of the *Ingrid*. He was not allowed on board, but his elder brother was. He remembers the growing tension as everybody waited for his grandfather to give the order to begin the launch. She went down the ways with great speed. Young Söderström hoped that she would go right across the fjärd, and she certainly looked as if she would, but the check ropes stopped her. There was only just enough water to float her light with the minimum of fittings on board her and so she was towed down the fjärd to deeper water, where she was fitted out.

The *Ingrid* was over 130 feet long and 27 feet in the beam; her net registered tonnage was 291 and she could carry 600 tons of cargo. She was a much bigger vessel in terms of volume that our Master's schooner or the *M.A. James*. Her accommodation was also arranged quite differently. The master and mate lived in a deck house built in the after part of the vessel immediately forward of the wheel. Around the deck house was a low poop deck on which the helmsman stood at the wheel. Access to the deck house was either through a scuttle immediately in front of the helmsman or through a door leading straight in from the deck; inside were cabins for the master and the two mates, as well as a comfortable saloon and a steward's pantry used by the cook. The seamen lived in another deckhouse, forward, with the foremast coming straight up through it – as the mizzen mast came up through the master and mates' accommodation aft. The seamens' deckhouse forecastle had six wooden bunks, several lockers and a big table at which the seamen ate. The galley was in the same deckhouse and the hot food was served straight through a hatch on to the forecastle table from the galley stove. The cook had to carry the cooked food along the open deck to the poop house, where it was kept hot on a small stove in the steward's pantry and served to the master and mates on the big dark polished table in the saloon. They sat on heavy, wooden, leather-padded chairs and a big sofa, very like the furniture in the best rooms of the farmhouses ashore.

3   Canada: three-masted square-rigged

Ships built in eastern Canada (of which many were British-owned), like Åland-built vessels, were constructed of local wood. The timber specifications over the years show the gradual changes in the wood used as the natural lumber resources of the Canadian eastern seaboard slowly became exhausted. In the great shipbuilding days of the mid-nineteenth century, larch, oak, yellow pine, birch, beech, ash and maple were used for framing, and white pine (the yellow pine of the English timber trade) was widely used for planking. By the end of the large-scale shipbuilding industry in the 1880s and 90s, even large vessels of many hundred tons were constructed almost entirely of spruce. This softwood was used even for the keels and the decking.

In Canada small vessels were often built some distance from the water and

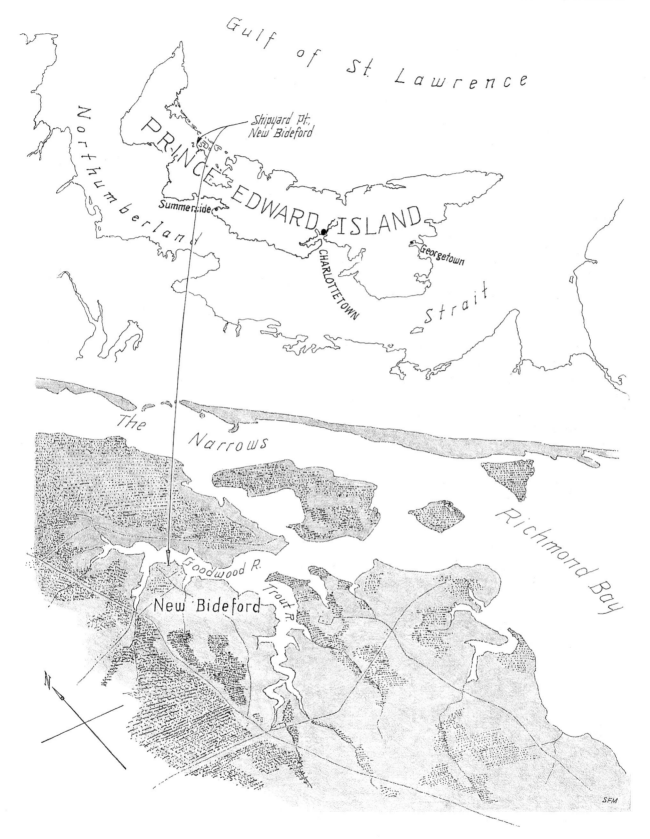

Shipbuilding on Prince Edward Island. The vessel is the three-masted schooner Victory Chimes, *built at Cardigan in 1918.* (Public Archives of Prince Edward Island)

then dragged by teams of horses over the frozen ground of winter to be launched among the ice floes in the spring. There are stories of as many as two hundred horses being collected to help in moving a small ship to the water.

The barque *Victoria*, three-masted, square-rigged, of over 700 tons net register, 170 feet long and 35 in the beam, able to carry over 1000 tons of cargo, was built between May 1873 and July 1874 at one of the oldest established shipbuilding sites in Canada. This was at New Bideford, on the Goodwood River in Prince County, at the western end of Prince Edward Island in the Gulf of St Lawrence. The first vessel, the full-rigged *Mars*, had been launched from this site in 1819, and the last, the barquentine *Meteor*, was to be built there in 1892. The building site is still clearly visible at the edge of a lonely creek and you can till trace the slope of the slipways and kick the red sand of the beach to find rusted iron bolts and other fittings underneath–the debris of 73 years of wood shipbuilding.

J. V. Richards was the registered builder of the *Victoria*. He was the wealthy son of William Richards, one of Prince Edward Island's most prosperous shipbuilders of the period and also a shipowner, farmer, merchant and banker. The *Victoria* was totally financed by the Richards family and managed by them for the greater part of her working life at sea. The master shipwright who actually built the *Victoria* was George Ellis, grandson of William Ellis, a master from Bideford, England, who had built the *Mars* with the aid of a handful of pioneer settlers in the winter of 1818–19. George Ellis constructed the new ship from a laminated half model, in the West-of-England tradition, and employed very similar methods to those used by our Master in building his schooner, although, of course, the *Victoria* was a very much larger vessel.

The *Victoria's* lumber specification shows the depletion of the Canadian island's timber resources. Her keel was made of birch and maple, her keelsons of imported pitch pine and native spruce, her stem and stern-post, her beams, the upper parts of her frames and nearly all her deadwood and other heavy timbers of spruce. She was planked entirely with spruce; her wooden knees

Barque *Victoria* — 170' x 35' —
Built at New Bideford, P.E.I.
1872-73

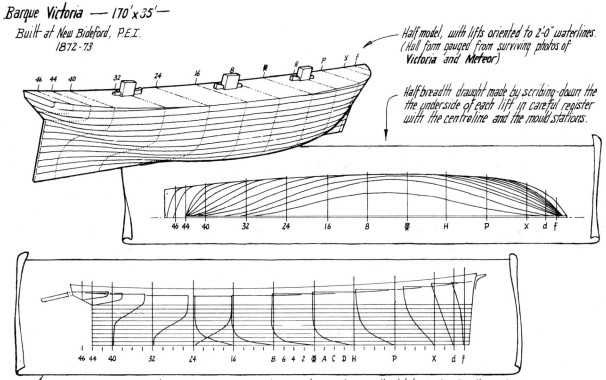

Half model, with lifts oriented to 2'-0" waterlines.
(Hull form gauged from surviving photos of
Victoria and ***Meteor***)

Halfbreadth draught made by scribing-down the
the underside of each lift in careful register
with the centreline and the mould stations.

Profile, or sheer draught made by scribing-down the perimeter of the model's flat backside atop the grid of
mould stations and waterlines. Half-sections at the mould stations are derived by measurements ("offsets")
taken outward from the hull's centreline to the edge of each lift or waterline shown on the halfbreadth
draught. This is a working drawing, easily scaled upward to full size on the scrieve board or mould
loft floor.

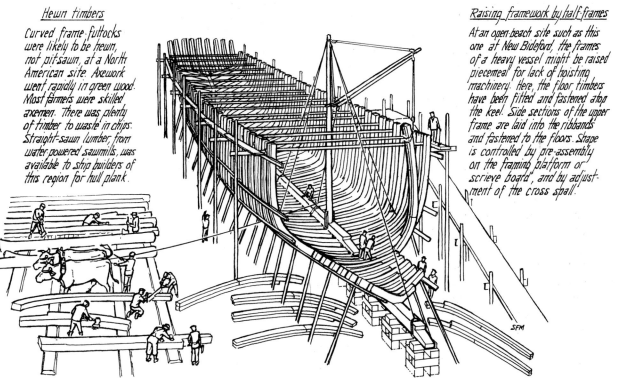

Hewn timbers

Curved frame-futtocks
were likely to be hewn,
not pit-sawn, at a North
American site. Axework
went rapidly in green wood.
Most farmers were skilled
axemen. There was plenty
of timber to waste in chips.
Straight-sawn lumber, from
water-powered sawmills, was
available to ship builders of
this region for hull plank.

Raising framework by half frames

At an open-beach site such as this
one at New Bideford, the frames
of a heavy vessel might be raised
piecemeal for lack of hoisting
machinery. Here, the floor timbers
have been fitted and fastened atop
the keel. Side sections of the upper
frame are laid into the ribbands
and fastened to the floors. Shape
is controlled by pre-assembly
on the framing platform or
'scrieve board', and by adjustment of the cross spall.

SFM

and her ceiling were of spruce, although she had iron knees as well. Even the treenails with which she was partially fastened were made of spruce, larch, and some 'Australian hard wood'. Canadian spruce was considered poor material by British shipbuilders, yet the *Victoria* served out over thirty years of hard, profitable work, sailing all over the world carrying cargo, and many times round Cape Horn.

In Canada people flowed in and out of the shipbuilding industry in the nineteenth century, as the demand for new ships rose and fell. In boom conditions farmers left their farms and went into the shipyards to make more – and more regular – money as labourers and semi-skilled workers, and the shipwrights returned from building wooden houses, turning their highly developed skills back to use in the trade they had first learned. They would then go back to building on land again when the boom period was over. Often working in the shipyards for the merchant who financed the shipbuilding and was the principal supplier and banker of the neighbourhood was a means of working off debt to him, for all too often the settlers were obliged to the merchants. One of the reasons that the wood shipbuilding industry was extremely successful in Canada was simply that labour costs, like timber costs, were low, because the use of a farmer's labour was a way in which a merchant could recover debts he had no hope of otherwise realising while the farmer gained a brief freedom from the fear of a debt burden that might even lead to the horrors of eviction. This was a very different situation from that endured by the landless, but on the whole debt-free craftsmen who built our Master's schooner and the *M.A. James,* or from that of the independent

Sketch plan for the aft accommodation in the barque **Victoria** *as drawn for her builder by Capt. Robert W. Brisco, the vessel's first master, in 1872. (Re-drawn for publication here)*

His comments (as best as can be read) —

Nº 1   Wash room and closet.

Nº 2   Medicine chest 3 ft. long by 18 in. deep. Glass doors.

Nº 3   Spare room and locker.

Nº 4   Seat across the stern frame.

Nº 5   Master's sleeping room, bed 3 ft. broad to fold
with hinges so as to form a single berth when
required, chest of drawers at fore end, and
against the ship's side a seat, lockers under,
also a door communicating with the water closet.

Nº 6   After or private cabin, 11 ft. long, 12 ft. broad.

Nº 7   After cabin table 4 ft. square, fixed seats,
a fireplace bricked-in or otherwise, after
cabin skylight 5 ft. long by 3 ft. 6 in. broad.

Nº 8   Spare stateroom.

Nº 9   Steward's room with locker.

Nº 10   Fore cabin 12 ft. square.

Nº 11   Fore cabin table 5 ft by 3 ft., fore cabin skylight
5 ft. by 3-6 to be placed right over table.

Nº 12   Second mate's room.

Nº 13   Mate's room, each of these rooms to have a
chest of drawers.

Nº 14   Cabin companion 4 ft. long, 3½ ft. broad.

Nº 15   Steward's pantry storeroom.

Nº 16   Mizen mast, 26 ft. 6 in from fore part of stern post.

Nº 17   Boys place.

Nº 18   Skylight aft of companion best built in with it,
18 inches being skylight & 3½ ft. scuttle,
entrance from forward.

Nº 19   Entrance to cabin from aft.

Nº 20   Sail locker.

P.S.   For cabin stairs I would suggest the following ⟶
rough sketch

Say 3 steps down on to a platform, then say
3 or 4 steps down on each side, underneath
the lamps & could be kept.

I venture to suggest this as the long perpendicular ladders are so very awkward and dangerous.

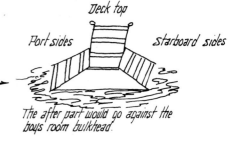

Deck top

Port sides   *Starboard sides*

The after part would go against the
boys room bulkhead.

RWB

(I think that the good captain labelled this stairs sketch backwards
or he's drawn it from underneath. It relates to item 14 above. —S.F.M.)

farmers of Åland who joined together to invest their labour and resources in the *Ingrid*.

The *Victoria's* first master, Robert W. Brisco, planned her accommodation himself. He made a detailed drawing and specification which have survived and are reproduced here, redrawn because the original is somewhat damaged and the writing in places difficult to read. In this we see the master's, mate's and cabin passengers' accommodation on board a first-class, wooden, square-rigged sailing vessel built for trading all over the world during the last great boom in the building of such vessels.

Captain Brisco's specification is very carefully drawn up and from this and from the original plan, it would be perfectly possible to build the accommodation again, or to make a model of it, bearing in mind the style in which it was fitted out – which was that of the prosperous Canadian home of the Victorian era. The woodwork was dark, the panelling beautifully finished and polished, relieved with gleaming brass-work; there were carpets, heavy chairs and tables and sofas in the style of similar accommodation ashore, with basket chairs, an organ perhaps, or a piano, and the judicious use of mirrors. Life under these conditions could be very pleasant indeed, and often, particularly in American and Canadian vessels, the master's wife accompanied him on passages and even lived on board with a growing family for years on end. Sometimes the ship was the family's only home.

The men who fitted out the *Victoria* were capable of turning their hands to any kind of high-grade construction work in wood. The men who made the comfortable cabins of the *Victoria* also built the local church at New Bideford out of local timber, as well as many other buildings. Thus, although only two complete examples remain in the world of the master's and mate's accommodation in wooden square-rigged merchant sailing ships of the late nineteenth century (the cabins of the barque *Sigyn* at Åbo in Finland and the after accommodation of the full-rigged ship *Benjamin F. Packard* stripped from the wreck of the vessel and rebuilt at Mystic Seaport in Connecticut) it is possible today to learn something of the methods employed and the standards achieved by those who fitted out such quarters. For this we must study contemporary buildings and the workmanship that went into them, in some areas of Prince Edward Island and elsewhere in maritime Canada.

The crew of the *Victoria* lived in a deckhouse forecastle which was an enlarged version of that on board the *Ingrid*. These deckhouse forecastles, increasingly in use from the 1870s onwards, could at their best provide relatively comfortable accommodation. Often, as in the *Ingrid*, the galley was continued in the same deckhouse and the hot food could be served straight through the hatch from the galley stove. Two of these deckhouse forecastles have been preserved and can be seen today in museums in Europe. The forecastle of the three-masted *Hoppet* is preserved in the Swedish National Maritime Museum in Stockholm along with all its equipment – and the stains left by bed-bugs! Particularly evocative of living conditions at sea in wooden sailing ships is the forecastle of the barque *Helmi*, built by Eric Söderström in the parish of Jomala in the Åland Islands in 1892 and now preserved intact in the Åland Maritime Museum. The barque *Sigyn's* forecastle is also open to the visitor.

4   United States: four-masted schooner

In 1879, in response to the increasing demand for coal carried from loading ports on Chesapeake Bay to developing, industrial New England, the first four-masted schooner was launched on the East Coast of the United States. The economics of the operation of this big sailing vessel depended on the steam hoisting-engine – deck machinery which made the handling of the huge gaff sails possible with a small crew. She was to be followed by hundreds of similar vessels, the best of which with their speed, handiness, economy of operation, and indeed their beauty, were probably the best all-round merchant sailing vessels ever built. One of the finest of them, in terms of the quality of her construction, and probably the longest lived of them all–she was still carrying cargo under the German flag in 1947 as a fully rigged sailing vessel without an engine – was the *Bertha L. Downs*, later renamed *Atlas*.

Our Master's schooner was built by a small group of craftsmen centred round a family of shipwrights and dominated by the head of that family. The *M.A. James* was built in a bigger yard, staffed principally with hired men. The *Ingrid* was built by free farmers working together in an effort to construct a jointly-owned vessel under the leadership of a farmer/shipbuilder. The *Victoria* was built by farmers obliged to the shipbuilder/merchant/landowner, in part working off their debts at the cost of their farms and farmwork, and led by skilled shipwrights who worked in construction ashore when there were no ships to be built. All these vessels were built in yards which were really little more than building sites – in the case of the *Ingrid* literally that – without machinery, without equipment other than a few huts and the stocks of timber and ironwork needed to build the vessel. The same men worked with their own tools throughout the construction of all these ships. They laid the keel, they framed up and planked up, they did the inside joinery, they stepped the masts and in due course some of them helped to rig her. Except in the case of the *Ingrid*, they were men who for the time being at least were employed by the yard and took their instructions from the yard management. These four vessels were constructed in their different ways at rural yards in what were practically pre-Industrial Revolution conditions. There was precious little difference between the building of ships in the eighteenth century and the building of Master's schooner or the *Victoria*. Indeed, the circumstances of the *Ingrid's* construction were reminiscent of the building of a sixteenth-century vessel. But to build on the scale of the *Bertha L. Downs* quite different methods were needed, not simply because she was big – the *Victoria* was much the same size – but because many large ships were being built in the same area at the same time. In the year 1900, for instance, the Percy and Small yard at Bath, in Maine – now splendidly restored and shown in the Maine Maritime Museum very near the yard where the *Bertha L. Downs* was built seven years later–was fitting out five schooners at one time: one huge six-master, four great five-masters, and a four-master.

So, the *Bertha L. Downs* was the product of an approach to shipbuilding quite different from anything described so far in this book. She was a child of the first Industrial Revolution; she and her sister four- and five-masters from New England were the only large, wooden, merchant sailing ships in history built in relatively highly capitalized, well equipped and well organized big yards.

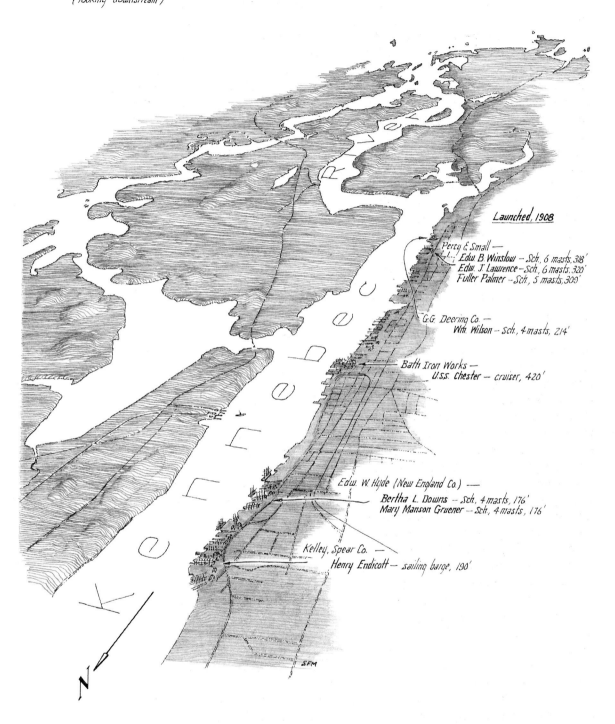

Bath, Maine, 1908
(looking downstream)

Launched, 1908

Percy & Small —
  Edw. B. Winslow — Sch., 6 masts, 318'
  Edw. J. Lawrence — Sch., 6 masts, 320'
  Fuller Palmer — Sch., 5 masts, 309'

G.G. Deering Co. —
  Wm. Wilson — Sch., 4 masts, 214'

Bath Iron Works —
  U.S.S. Chester — cruiser, 420'

Edw. W. Hyde (New England Co.) —
  Bertha L. Downs — Sch., 4 masts, 176'
  Mary Manson Gruener — Sch., 4 masts, 176'

Kelley, Spear Co. —
  Henry Endicott — sailing barge, 190'

N

SFM

Working on assembling the keelson of the four-masted schooner, Rachel W. Stevens, *built in the same yard as the* Bertha L. Downs.
(W.J. Lewis Parker)

Erecting a frame during the building of a schooner at Camden, Maine, in 1894. The two vessels are the J. Holmes Birdsall *and the* Mary Manning. (W.J. Lewis Parker)

Captain W.J. Lewis Parker U.S.G.G. (retired) and Ralph L. Snow very kindly provided the information about the building of the *Bertha L. Downs* summarized briefly in the following paragraphs:

The New England Company yard at Bath, near the mouth of the Kennebeck River, where the *Bertha L. Downs* was built, was not as well equipped as some yards, such as nearby Percy and Small's, but it had extensive machinery, driven by shafting and belting from several electric motors totalling 150 horsepower. These big yards had covered saw-mills with both circular and jig-saws and powered planers. The planing-table of the Percy and Small yard was 43 feet long and the planer-bed 93 feet long. It was used for all big heavy finishing work, planing the huge timbers for keel and keelsons, stern posts and knees. It could plane a 2 feet by 2 feet by 45 feet baulk of timber easily.

There were separate tree-nail-making shops with power driven lathes which could turn out the 20,000 tree nails required for a big schooner quite quickly. There were large blacksmith shops capable, with the use of some power drills, of handling the three or four hundred tons of iron and steel which were needed for the building of a big schooner. This iron came from dealers in Bath – Allens – who kept large stocks of it. Iron and steel came ultimately from Pittsburgh, transported in small schooners from New York and Boston and in horse-drawn wagons to the yard. Iron was needed for bolts, nails, chain plates and mast ironwork among other things, and for the massive steel reinforcing straps which, let into the frame faces before planking, strengthened the long narrow hulls against the huge stresses set up in them not only when sailing but when simply lying afloat, especially when not laden with cargo. The straps were often nearly an inch thick and four inches wide and several thousand holes had to be drilled in them. These straps were vital to some of the later, very large, five- and six-masters. Less sizeable vesels like the *Bertha L. Downs* did not have them, but similar strapping was built into much smaller British vessels – even schooners the size of that described in the preceding chapters, in at least one yard in south-western England. As the historian of Bath's shipbuilding industry, William A. Baker, put it in *A Maritime History of Bath, Maine*:

> For all their massive appearance, the great schooners [here he refers to the large five and six masters and specifically not to vessels of the quality of the *Bertha L. Downs*] were very flexible assemblages of relatively short pieces of timber, iron straps, bolts, spikes and treenails. Age did nothing to improve the tightness of these assemblages and frequently recaulking, particularly of deck and topside butts, was a growing expense. As steam made sail and anchor handling simple on these schooners it also made the vessels themselves feasible; they leaked so badly that they could not have been kept afloat without steam driven pumps.

In some yards there were separate oakum shops. Here the caulkers could spin their raw materials in wet weather. A big four-master had about six miles of seaming to be caulked. On a basis of four threads to each seam, each thread divided into loops, about 48 miles of oakum had to be spun and driven – work for 12 to 15 men labouring six days a week for approximately three months. Near the oakum shop would be a pitch oven; pitch was used almost exclusively for caulking decks in these big schooners (and as a substitute for chewing gum). On the exterior of the hull the bottom seams were finished off with Portland cement; about the waterline they were finished

215

Establishing hull shape — Bath, Maine — turn-of-century —

Half-model, draft of lines made from the half-model, and full-size patterns for mould frames and backbone timbering (not shown here) — all delivered to the shipyard, under subcontract by a local modeller and loftsman.

Shown here are the lines of the 4-masted schooner **Addie M. Anderson** taken from her builder's model by the late Wm A. Baker, N.A. This vessel was built by the New England Company **eighteen years** earlier than the **Bertha L. Downs**. She was 24' longer than the **Downs**, proportionally broader and deeper, but essentially of the same hull model.

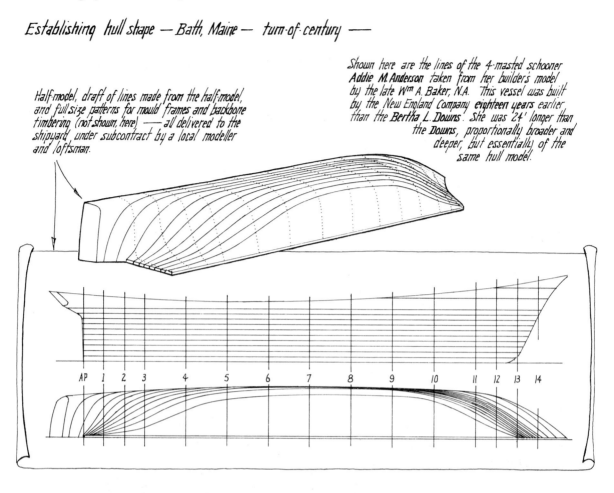

The **Addie M. Anderson** was 200' from stem-head to taffrail. It was important that her mould frames be closely patterned from from an accurate, full-scale, and comprehensive lines-laydown, or a great deal of timber and labour would be lost to dubbing.

Here the modeller has scaled the lifts of the half-model to lay out (and fair) the profile and waterlines in full size on his loft floor. He has worked out the crossectional curves of the body plan by measurements taken from the faired, full-size waterlines rather than simply scaling the lifts for sectional curves. Error in scaling-up can be considerable. The width of a pencil line on this model scales-up to nearly a foot in width on the 200' hull.

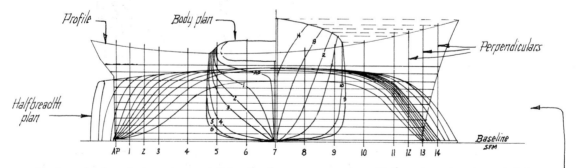

How do you lay down the lines of a 200 ft hull within the confines of a shipyard loft? This is the look of a loft drawing with profile, halfbreadth plan and body plan overlaid on the same baseline. Length is contracted to save floor space. It is the 200' **Addie M. Anderson** shrunk to 50% of her real length by halving the spacing of perpendiculars. Heights and halfbreadths remain in full dimension. The lengthwise curves of sheer and waterlines can be faired and proven accurately in this array. From them is created (by projection) the body plan for patterning mould frames. Bow and stern (distorted) must be re-drawn in profile to normal spacing of perpendiculars before accurate patterning of stem and stern timbering can be done.

Sch. Bertha L. Downs, 1908 —

Frame timber, pre-cut to the loftsman's moulds, was delivered to the shipyard wharf by a timber contractor.

Keel blocking was set up and the keel laid, fastened together, aligned and carefully shored in-place by (sometimes) a third subcontractor.

Framing of the hull (a fourth subcontractor) was begun with erection of sternpost and fashion timber, then progressed forward to the bow.

Cants and square frames were assembled on a framing platform at the elevated bow-end of the keel and were slid to their positions along a set of rails established for the purpose. The hull was normally ribbanded and ready for dubbing at the completion of this contract.

The head saw (shown in separate foreground projection) with cable-drawn carriage and top blade, took the labour out of straight siding of keel timber, posts, wales and plank.

217

Rigging the six-master Eleanor A. Percy *at Percy and Small's yard at Bath, Maine in 1900. All the lower masts have been stepped, and work has begun on setting up the shrouds on the spanker and driver masts.* (W.J. Lewis Parker)

with white-lead putty. The caulking of hulls with cement would have been unthinkable in Britain (and probably in Scandinavia) at the time, and yet it worked perfectly well for many years in these huge American schooners.

Prodigious quantities of timber were needed to build the five- and six-masted schooners. They were constructed with a high sheer, yet still their ends dropped – they 'hogged' in the shipbuilders' terms. To attempt to counteract this the keels were laid curved, the centre 12 inches below the ends. The masts were about 120 feet long and over 2 feet and 6 inches in diameter at the step. The topmasts alone were as big as the foremast of Master's schooner. The stepping of these huge masts involved the use of sheerlegs, or of the vessels own gear, as illustrated. Stepping such masts was a heroic business, involving the greatest possible skill, and this was usually carried out without the use of power or with the schooner's own steam hoisting engine, since it would have been uneconomic for the yard to install power winches on the scale necessary for this one job.

The planking of the *Bertha L. Downs* was all of pitch pine and no length in it was of less than 40 feet. Her ceiling was of 14-inch square pitch pine and the keelson was built up of 24-inch square Oregon pine baulks, bolted

Sch. Bertha L. Downs —1908—

Steam-powered ship saw, or tilt-head bandsaw relieved the hewing to-bevel of the moulded faces of frame futtocks. Such timber was too heavy to be handled easily through a tilt-table 119.

Here, the man at the handwheel is adjusting the tilt of the saw in accordance with directions shouted by the sawyer whose hands guide the baulk nearest the blade.

Sch. Bertha L. Downs — 1908 —

Slab sides, flat floors, sharp ends, great length, and great depth of hold were characteristic of successful American deep water carriers in the late nineteenth century. The resulting box-like structure lacked the pipe-wall strength of the more cylindrical models.

Lack of lengthwise stiffness caused a long hull to sag at the ends, or "hog" early in its working life. An old or strained vessel exhibited "lumpy sheer, or straightening of the sheer, due to hogging.

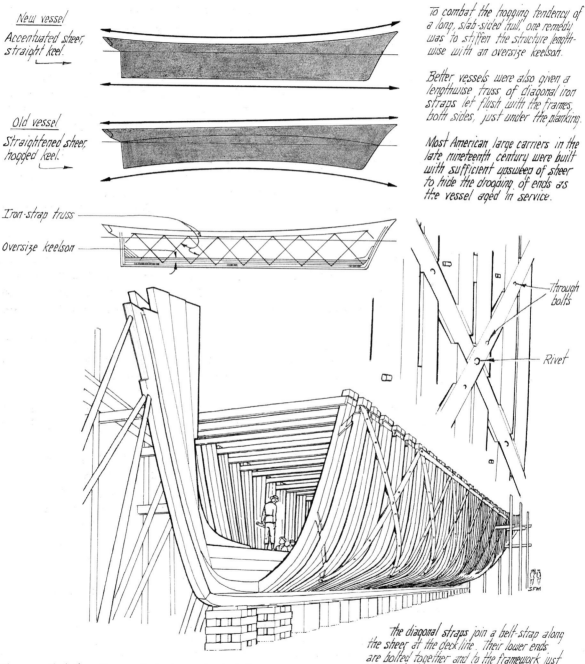

New vessel
Accentuated sheer, straight keel.

Old vessel
Straightened sheer, hogged keel.

Iron-strap truss

Oversize keelson

To combat the hogging tendency of a long, slab-sided hull, one remedy was to stiffen the structure lengthwise with an oversize keelson.

Better vessels were also given a lengthwise truss of diagonal iron straps let flush with the frames, both sides, just under the planking.

Most American large carriers in the late nineteenth century were built with sufficient upsweep of sheer to hide the drooping of ends as the vessel aged in service.

Through bolts

Rivet

The diagonal straps join a belt-strap along the sheer at the deck line. Their lower ends are bolted together and to the framework just under the turn of the bilge.

Strapping the hull would normally be done after the hull was fully in frame and faired for plank. This drawing is a schematic view intended to show also the forward end of the keelson.

right through to the keel and built up 6 feet high. Her pin rails, bulwarks and fittings were correspondingly massive, and although she had a gasoline hoisting engine of 12 horsepower on deck it was hardly ever needed for the pumps since the vessel leaked very little, even late in her life.

The lumber for the ship came from all over the eastern states and further afield. Hackmatack was cut up in Aroostook County of Maine, in Nova Scotia and Prince Edward Island, and in Michigan, and sent by rail to the shipyards. As with the *Bertha L. Downs*, many schooners frames were made up of oak bottoms and hackmatack tops. The oak was most resistant to rot when kept wet with salt water through normal leakage. Hackamatack was strong, lighter than oak and much more resistant to rot in a vessel's topsides. Timber contractors wherever they were working were supplied with moulds from the scrieve board by the builders. The moulds were taken in schooners down to the southern states and individual frames were roughed out in the woods with axes from newly felled oak trees. In the south they were cut in the derelict plantations of Virginia along the Pamunkey, Mettaponi and James Rivers, and in eastern Delaware. Some schooners were engaged almost entirely in taking down lumber gangs from Maine for this work, bringing back the semi-completed frames, some already roughly bevelled in the woods, to the shipyards. Hard pine came from Georgia and South Carolina, where sawmill towns had been founded before the Civil War by families sent down from Maine.

The *Bertha L. Downs* was built from a laminated half model carved out by an established modeller–not the master builder, but a man well known for his excellent schooner models. He might have been a gifted pattern-maker from a foundry. The final form of the model was agreed upon by the principal sponsor of the vessel, the master, who was a shareholder, and the master builder.

In the early days, masts were built up from many pieces of timber bolted together. The durability of these white pine-built masts depended on caulking, since if fresh water got inside them they rotted very quickly. Most schooners built in the 1870s and 1880s had built masts but by the time the *Bertha L. Downs* was fitted out pine-masts came on flat railway cars from Oregon, carried right across the continent from the west coast and delivered by a branch-line along the street to the yard door.

There were plenty of suppliers of equipment in Bath. J.S. Jackson & Son manufactured blocks until their block-shop was destroyed by fire in 1902. The Hyde Windlass Company and two other local manufacturers offered boilers and engines, windlasses, pumps and tanks, and were general iron-founders as well. Five sail-makers were in business in Bath at the turn of the century and the sails for the *Bertha L. Downs* and other Bath vessels were made in local lofts. There was no local manufacturer of rope however. The rope-walk had long gone out of business and the rope factory which succeeded it had been shipped – lock, stock and barrel – south to Massachusetts by the late 1890s.

The rigging, like most of the work on these vessels, was done by sub-contractors; the riggers, when they moved in to do a job, were much admired locally for their feats of skill and daring. They never used safety nets; they worked 150 feet above the deck with a coolness demonstrated by their habit

Sch. Bertha L. Downs — 1908 —

The steam-powered thickness planer smoothed rough-sawn timber or plank to accurate scantlings (dimensions). A heavy shipyard machine could wipe off up to a quarter-inch of oak surface in a single pass.

The two-side planer gave uniform thickness in one operation, leaving rough edges for shaping to curved or beveled shapes.

The four-side planer insured machine-squared edges and parallel opposite faces in straight-cut stock.

Knives extend to the full length of the drum

<u>Planers</u>

One side

Two sides

Four sides

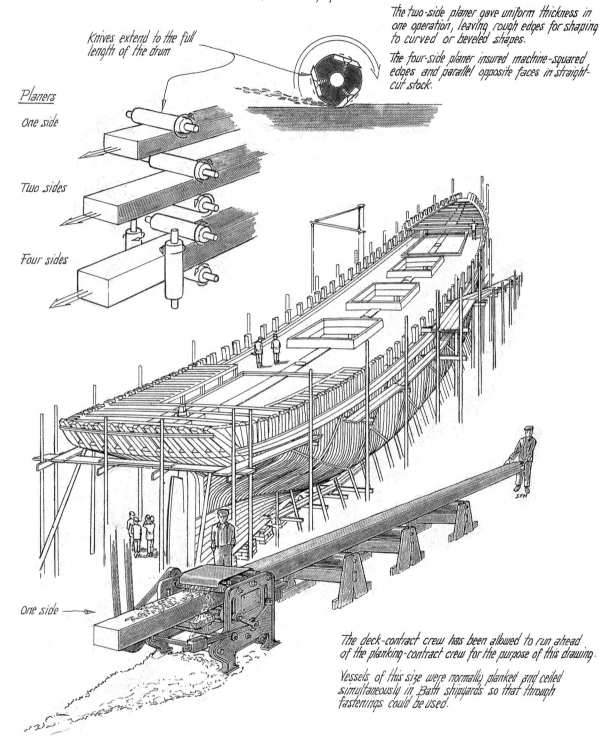

One side →

The deck-contract crew has been allowed to run ahead of the planking-contract crew for the purpose of this drawing.

Vessels of this size were normally planked and ceiled simultaneously in Bath shipyards so that through fastenings could be used.

Sch. Bertha L. Downs, 1908 —

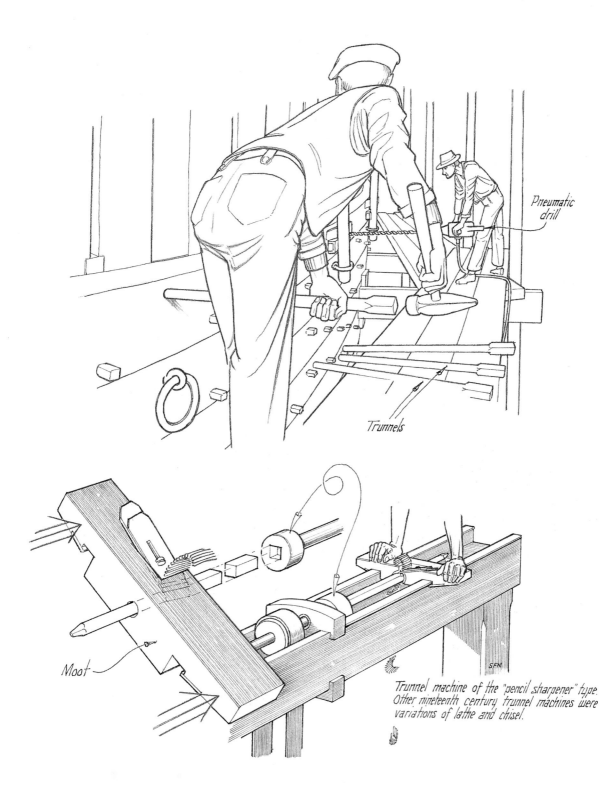

Pneumatic
drill

Trunnels

Moot

Trunnel machine of the "pencil sharpener" type.
Other nineteenth century trunnel machines were
variations of lathe and chisel.

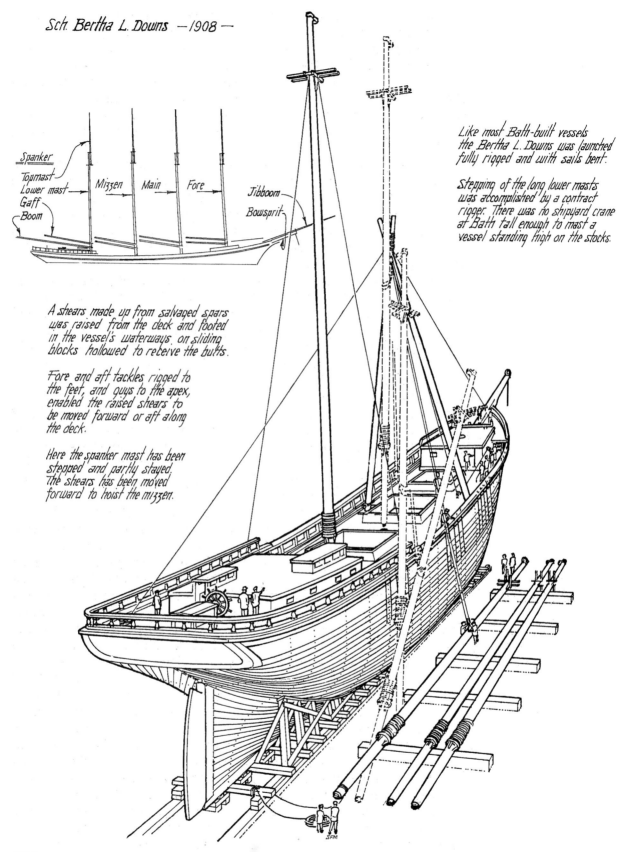

Sch. *Bertha L. Downs* —1908—

Spanker
Topmast
Lower mast
Gaff
Boom

Mizzen Main Fore

Jibboom
Bowsprit

Like most Bath-built vessels
the Bertha L. Downs was launched
fully rigged and with sails bent.

Stepping of the long lower masts
was accomplished by a contract
rigger. There was no shipyard crane
at Bath tall enough to mast a
vessel standing high on the stocks.

A shears made up from salvaged spars
was raised from the deck and footed
in the vessel's waterways, on sliding
blocks hollowed to receive the butts.

Fore and aft tackles rigged to
the feet, and guys to the apex,
enabled the raised shears to
be moved forward or aft along
the deck.

Here the spanker mast has been
stepped and partly stayed.
The shears has been moved
forward to hoist the mizzen.

of getting from mast to mast by going hand over hand along the spring stay, the horizontal wire stay which linked the heads of the huge lower masts.

Launching such large schooners was a great test of organization. The launches were publicized with handbills; there were special fares on the electric street-cars carrying people to see the launch—and you could travel miles by electric street car in those days in Maine. Special lunches were laid on; bands played all day. The handbills advertised: 'Ever seen a launch?'; 'Ever visit Bath?'; 'Come to Bath and see the launch of the largest sailing vessel in the world'.

The huge hull of the vessel was cradled and the cradle wedged up; the cradle-bolts, which held the cradle, were then knocked out, whereupon the monster would slide, stern first, into the water – at least in theory. The launch, like all the other work on the vessel, was in general charge of the master builder. His job involved the supervision of many sub-contractors and he had to develop cost estimates for future work; sometimes he was the only permanent employee at a yard.

To build the *Elisha Atkins*, a four-masted schooner slightly larger than the *Bertha L. Downs*, at Bath cost G.G. Deering $71,533.76, of which the largest single element was $12,833 for the hard pine for planking, ceiling and keelsons. To the Hyde Windlass Company went $3416 for the steam engine and gear essential for the operation of these big schooners. H. & S. Lord, sail-makers, charged $629 for labour and $1577 for cotton duck for the sails; J.S. Jackman, block-maker, charged $821 for a complete suit of blocks. The chain, which was brought up from Chester, Pennsylvania, cost $1471; the crockery for the cabins and forecastle $258, the spar-maker charged $782 and the caulkers $1138. The riggers' bill was only $711, but the masts cost $1070. Willie Southworth, carver, made the very simple billet-head and carved the official number for $35, and the launching party cost another $64. The vessel was sold in 1916 after ten years of profitable work for $100,000 with five per cent brokerage fees.

The bills for the *Elisha Atkins* underline another aspect of the building of the big American schooners which has already been touched upon and which has no very close parallel in any of the other shipbuilding operations described in this book. Most of the workforce answered not to the yard management but to sub-contractors. The sub-contractors used the yard facilities, but built up, paid and controlled their own workforces; and they themselves were not employees of the yard but contractors to it. The greater part of the labour force of the yard, therefore, did not regard themselves as yard workers but as skilled craftsmen who might, like the earlier itinerant shipbuilders of Britain and Europe, work anywhere where employment was available. Sub-contracting was often necessary to obtain the services of the most skilled workers in shipbuilding—the caulkers, blacksmiths and riggers. Frank A. Palmer was the leading rigging contractor in Bath at the time of the building of the *Bertha L. Downs*. The painters and dubbers, with shipbuilding on the scale with which it was being conducted in the early years of this century in Maine, were able to make a good living out of simply finishing the bevelling of the frames. Such men could command wages of as much as $4.00 a day (about six times the wage of their British contemporaries) for their labour, and the boss of the gang who negotiated the contract with the shipyards paid them out of his overall sum, which was based on the gross tonnage of the vessel under construction. The boss himself made ten per cent or more of the

Sch. Bertha L. Downs —1908—

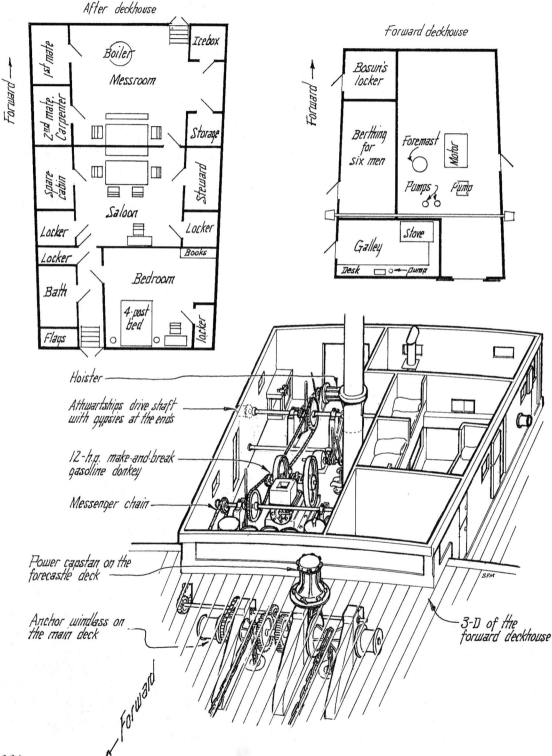

Plan of the deckhouse accommodations of the schooner *Atlas*, ex-*Bertha L. Downs* as remembered and sketched by Capt. Karl V. Karlsen.

After deckhouse

- 1st mate
- Icebox
- Boiler
- Messroom
- 2nd mate. Carpenter
- Storage
- Spare cabin
- Steward
- Saloon
- Locker
- Locker
- Locker
- Books
- Bath
- Bedroom
- Flags
- 4-post bed
- locker

Forward deckhouse

- Bosun's locker
- Berthing for six men
- Foremast
- Motor
- Pumps
- Pump
- Galley
- Stove
- Desk
- Pump

Hoister

Athwartships drive shaft with gypsies at the ends

12-h.p. make-and-break gasoline donkey

Messenger chain

Power capstan on the forecastle deck

Anchor windlass on the main deck

3-D of the forward deckhouse

Forward

total wages to cover his costs—and give himself a reasonable living. Frequently, with a bit of luck, he did more than that. He did not take his gang around with him from shipyard to shipyard; some men who were used to working with him might be re-employed by him again and again, but usually many new men were employed each time.

Some workers, especially those who handled timber, followed the demand for labour from shipyard to shipyard. In winter they might move south; in slack periods they went away to wherever there was work, travelling hundreds, and perhaps thousands, of miles between jobs. In this, as in almost every other respect, the life based around the building of the *Bertha L. Downs* and her sisters—although the basic skills required were the same—bore little resemblance to the life of the workforce in Master's yard, or the lives of the farmers who built the *Ingrid* on the granite shores of the Kalfjärd in Åland.

The *Bertha L. Downs* crew lived in a deckhouse forecastle very much like that of the *Ingrid*, but larger, with the galley in the same deckhouse. This galley was exceptionally large and has been described by those who knew the vessel as three times the normal size. Her accommodation aft for the master and mates was very well fitted out, with oak and larch panelling in

The launch of the Bertha L. Downs. (Maine Maritime Museum)

Sch. Bertha L. Downs — 1908 —

the big rooms. The *Bertha L. Downs*, in common with some of her sister big American schooners, also had central heating in her after accommodation.

Perhaps the best way to depict the *Bertha L. Downs*, and something of the atmosphere surrounding her building and launch in Bath, Maine, is to quote in full an account which appeared in the *Bath Anvil* for 18 January, 1908.

The first in Bath in 1908 and the first vessel to be launched from the yard of the New England Co. for two years went down the ways Thursday (Jan. 16) morning, a veritable triumph of the modern shipbuilders' skill.

The schooner was the Bertha L. Downs, built by Hon. E.W. Hyde for the Benedict-Manson Co. of New Haven, Conn., to be added to their large fleet of coastwise vessels.

In spite of the lowering skies and the slight rain of the morning, a large crowd gathered at this famous yard to see the schooner take her maiden dip into the blue waters of the Kennebac.

The launching was scheduled for 10.30 and it was just five minutes past the allotted time when the cry went up, 'she moves', and the craft slipped easily and gracefully down the ways. As the vessel went into the Kennebac, Miss Bertha L. Downs of New Haven, Conn., the sponsor of the craft and the young lady for whom she is named, christened her with a magnificent boquet of roses and gracefully waved the United States flag. The whistles along the waterfront tooted and signalled to the waiting city that another maritime triumph had been added to Bath's long list.

On board the craft with Miss Downs as members of the launching party were Capt. and Mrs. E.H. Weaver, J.W. Haskell and Miss Villa Haskell, Miss Corey and M.B. Hemmingway of New Haven, Capt. Robert F. Wells of Stony Brook, L.I., who is to command the Downs, Capt. F.C. Crosseley of New Haven, who is to go in command of the duplicate of the Downs which Mr. Hyde is building at the New England yard, and Rev. and Mrs. Culbert McGay of this city. Many prominent Bath citizens and mariners of note witnessed the launching of the craft from points of vantage on shore.

The Downs swung easily into the stream where she was anchored and then brought back to the wharf and the launching party disembarked, going to Mr. Hyde's home on High Street where a very enjoyable buffet luncheon was served in honour of this event.

The party here were joined by Senator Harold M. Sewall, Treas. and Mrs. I.S. Coombs of the New England Co., Mrs W.S. Glidden, Sheriff John W. Ballou, N. Gratz Jackson, Capt. J.W. Hawley and others. A tempting menu of lobster salad, sandwiches, coffee and ices was served and many impromptu speeches were made in honour of the event.

Both Capt. Weaver who is a director of the Benedict-Manson Co. and Capt. Wells, who is the commander of the new craft, expressed themselves in unmistakable terms as to their satisfaction with the new vessel. Capt. Wells is very proud of her and says that he never saw a better built or finer equipped craft.

The Downs is a duplicate of the William J. Quillin, built by the New England Co. in 1905, which has made one of the best records for speed and carrying. She is 716 gross tons, 175.4 feet long, 37.1 feet breadth, 14.2 feet deep, and will have a carrying capacity of 1200 tons of coal and 600,000 feet of lumber. The frame is hard wood, bottom, oak, and top Michigan hackmatack. The decks are of white pine with composition fastening and in every particular the best of material is used throughout in her construction. She is single-decked and is intended for the general carrying trade. She has all the modern conveniences for handling a cargo, including a 12-horsepower gasolene hoisting engine, a Hyde windlass and patent riding stoppers. The masts are of Oregon pine, 92 feet long, the fore being 26 inches in diameter and the others being 25 inches. The rigging is wire set up with turnbuckles, and she will spread 5000 yards of canvas. She carries two small boats, the larger being 22 feet long and equipped with a 4 H.P. gasolene engine, one of the first launches ever provided for a vessel in this city. The other is 16 feet in length. Both boats were built by the Bath Auto and Gas Engine Co. of this city.

All the iron work about the decks is galvanized and the Downs carries two Baldt stockless anchors of the most improved style, weighing 4070 and 4090 pounds and attached to 1 7/8 chains.

The cabins of the craft are finished in quartered oak and are fitted with every convenience of latter day shipbuilding. They are heated by the hot water system and are ornaments to the splendid craft.

The Downs is rated A1 for 15 years and launched ready for sea. She is expected to leave this port today for Philadelphia to load for New Haven and has shipped a crew of eight men.

Capt. Robert F. Wells, her commander, although one of the youngest captains in the coastwise service, is considered one of the best and is one of the best appearing young men that Bath has seen for a long time. He has been here for some time getting his craft ready for the launching and while here has made a host of friends who extend to him congratulations on his good fortune in getting so fine a craft and their best wishes for his success with her. His former commands have been the schrs. Clifford N. Carver and George W. Wells.

The men who are directly responsible for the building of the craft, by that we mean the men who actually worked with their hands upon her construction and who in the past have helped to make Bath's name famous as the finest shipbuilding city in the world, are Horatio N. Douglass, master workman in charge of construction; master joiner, Frank N. Haggett; master fastener, George Lightbody; master blacksmith, Hiram Pattee; master painter, James Wheeler; rigger, Capt. Robert H. Goodman; sailmaker, A.M. Cutler; planker, H.E. Worrey; caulker, Tibbetts and Oliver; sparmaker, Frank Parris.

The members of the launching party from New Haven returned to their homes on the afternoon train, greatly pleased with their visit to Bath. They all say that they will be sure to come down to the launching of schooner No. 2 for the Benedict-Manson Co. which will be a duplicate of the Downs and which is expected to be ready for launching about the first of April.

The Downs presented a pretty picture in the stream Thursday, gaily bedecked with signal flags. She is almost a yacht in her graceful lines and splendid construction, and well may her captain feel proud of being the commander of such a vessel.

This is Hon. E.W. Hyde's first venture into the wooden shipbuilding field, although as president of the Iron Works he has a long list of steel vessels to his credit. The approximate cost of the Downs is $55,000 and as one of the sailors in the crew said yesterday after a tour of inspection, 'she's worth every cent of it and some more'.

Captain Karl V. Karlsson, who was master and part owner of the vessel for four years after she had been sold to Åland islanders in the 1920s, made a plan of the aft accommodation of this magnificent schooner, from which Sam Manning has made the drawing on page 226, showing the comparative luxury in which the commander of a vessel of this quality lived in the last days of the commercial operation of wooden sailing vessels.

The Bertha L. Downs under sail in the 1920s. She is 'light'—that is, without cargo. At the time the photograph was taken she was owned by an Anglo-Finnish syndicate and employed in the timber trade from the Baltic to London. (Ålands Sjöfarsmuseum)

tailpiece

by Basil Greenhill

I said in the foreword to this book that it began with talks in 1946 and '47 with Fred Harris, then Managing Director of P.K. Harris & Sons Ltd., the shipbuilders at Appledore. In fact the germ of it really arrived much earlier, when, instead of playing games in the afternoons at school, I slipped down to the docks in Bristol and visited my friends, the masters of the Appledore ketches which were still trading regularly into the port in the 1930s.

Way back in 1935 or '36 I spoke with Captain William Lamey of the coasting ketch Hobah, *a vessel of just about the dimensions and cargo capacity of our Master's schooner. On board the vessel, in her little wedge-shaped after cabin, I told him of the determination I had formed to be involved one day with the preservation of one of the little sailing vessels in which he and his father before him had spent their whole working lives. At that time he was still master and owner of the* Hobah *and was earning his living with her in the trade around the small ports of the Bristol Channel. He replied in his broad north Devon accent: 'Now don't you do that. Don't you ever try to preserve a wooden vessel. You'll find you have a load of trouble that will never leave you. If you've got to preserve one of these things, you go for a steel vessel. If you keep her painted, she won't fall to pieces beneath your feet. These vessels are falling to pieces around you all the time. It takes me all my time to keep her afloat.'*

We live in a world now in which the preservation, or, often, the attempted preservation, of wooden ships in one way or another is becoming commonplace. But what has been preserved is a series of isolated examples of a material artefact, divorced completely from its real purpose. That purpose was to earn money by carrying cargoes at sea, and nothing else, in a society in which this was a normal activity which could be carried out profitably, and in which the industrial conditions and the skills involved were all commonplace. This social, technical and economic environment has totally and irretrievably vanished – and in many ways this is no bad thing either. You cannot preserve or replicate a whole society.

A preserved ship and especially a preserved wooden ship, is a most unnatural object. She was never meant to lie static in still water without natural ventilation, perpetually exposed to the climate, no longer providing a fierce economic incentive to those responsible for her preservation as a working vessel on which they depended for their very livelihood.

Moreover, new techniques, materials and economic conditions have completely overtaken the traditional ways of building wooden ships. As Tom Perkins puts it:

Wood has many enemies, built-in, distressed framing often has understood end results. In wooden ships, fastenings and bearing surfaces, called 'faying surfaces' were often weaknesses; butts could have been bolted to prevent springing of planks, and preservatives introduced to prevent nail sickness. Movement in hulls set up its own stresses. The restoration of old ships is beset by problems. History has obscured the dates of changes from iron wire to flexible steel rope, from deadeyes to bottle screws, of the adoption of screw shackles and fore lock shackles.

233

It is extremely difficult even to make an accurate model of a vessel of the past. Apart from the Pommern, preserved at Mariehamn in Finland, there is probably only one latter day four-masted barque, a type of vessel still trading in the 1930s, of which sufficient detailed information exists to make a really accurate model possible. When it comes to restoring old ships the problem is all the greater for the absence of traditional materials – and the skills necessary for handling traditional tools and doing things in the old way. The result, far too often, is a compromise. There are very few restored ships in the world (or replicas) which represent in every detail the working vessels of the past. Tom Perkins' Shamrock is one of these very few examples, thoroughly researched and restored entirely using old equipment and original materials and methods.

One danger is that vessels restored with a high degree of compromise, or replicas inadequately researched and built with the use of much modern technology in another generation, are going to be taken to represent the real thing, rather than what they really are–late twentieth-century man's idea of what the vessels of the past should have been like.

How different the world was in the days when the last wooden ships were working is illustrated by the further careers of the vessels described in this book.

The M.A. James had a long and successful life. She was employed at first in the trade to Newfoundland and Labrador, returning across the North Atlantic with cargoes of dried and salted cod-fish for western Europe. For this trade she had a crew of five, handling the eighty-foot vessel, with no power on board of any kind. They had no navigational aids, no communication with the shore or other vessels, no metereological information, no preserved food and no waterproof clothing, even though they sailed the North Atlantic in winter. In due course her main business was in the slate trade to the Elbe from Porthmadog. She was sold in the 1920s to the Plymouth Co-operative Society and principally employed by them in bringing coal from the Mersey area to Plymouth. In this trade she was the last schooner to discharge a cargo at Halton Quay on the River Tamar. The cargo was discharged by hand, the baskets of coal carried ashore and thrown into the coalstore by men who were paid one penny a ton for the work – less than £1 each for moving 150 tons of coal. In 1928 she was sold to W.J. Slade of Bideford and employed profitably in the home trade until the Second World War. She was then commandeered by the Navy for employment as a mother ship for a barrage balloon. Grossly neglected during her war service, she returned to her owners unfit for further employment at sea. After prolonged negotiation the Slade family were adequately compensated and the hulk saw service as a barge for P.K. Harris's shipbuilding yard. She was eventually put out on the mud, and her remains still lie in the River Torridge.

The Ingrid was also a successful vessel. She sailed far and wide, to the White Sea, to Canada and the Gulf of Mexico, and very extensively between the Gulf of Bothnia and Britain in the timber trade. Her crew was made up of the seafaring farmers of Åland, who had grown up on the 60th Parallel–with all that this implies in terms of immunity to rigorous conditions of life. In 1919 she put into Falmouth in distress, partly dismasted on a passage towards Martinique. She was bought by British shipowners, renamed Rigdin and employed in trade to the West Indies (which probably included rum-running to the coastal waters of the United States during Prohibition). In 1929 she was sold to Annie Stephens, a member of a famous shipowning family from Fowey in Cornwall, and employed in the home trade. She was broken up in 1939.

The Victoria, for the first 16 years of her life, was owned by her builders, the

Richards family of New Bideford, Prince Edward Island. She was employed in trade all over the world, principally carrying coal out from South Wales ports and returning to the United Kingdom with bulk cargoes. Her crews comprised the drifting professionals described so brilliantly in Joseph Conrad's The Nigger of the Narcissus *– a type of human being almost extinct by the end of the last century. In 1890 she was sold to Norwegian owners in Drammen and continued to be employed principally in the timber trade. She was broken up in 1908.*

The Bertha L. Downs *was to have a remarkable career. She was registered first at New Haven, Connecticut as owned by the Benedict-Manson Marine Company; she then sailed principally in the lumber and coal trades from the southern ports to New England. She offered much better working and living conditions on board than any of the other vessels described here, but even then there were few native-born Americans in her crews. Some of her contemporaries had no American crew members at all, but were manned (from the mates downwards) entirely by Scandinavians and Finns who hoped thereby to acquire American citizenship. In 1916 she was bought by her master, Captain Bob Wells, in the guise of the 'Bertha L. Downs Shipping Corporation of New York' and in turn sold at the height of the First World War shipping boom in December 1917 to Danish owners who renamed her* Atlas. *She was employed in the timber trade from the eastern Baltic to west European ports until 1923, when she was sold to an Anglo-Finnish shareholding group based in the Åland Islands. There she was employed in the same trade, making regular voyages to London, where she discharged timber at the Regent's Canal Dock. In 1931 she was sold to Estonian owners and continued in the same trade until she was taken over by the Russians when the Baltic States were overrun. She is said to have been sunk near Riga in 1942–and to have been raised by the Germans in 1943. She ended her life at Kiel where she was broken up in 1948 at the age of 40 – the longest lived of all the big American schooners and the last to carry cargo purely as a sailing vessel.*

Our Master's schooner may be imagined to have had a typical life for a vessel of her class. Built for the home trade she would nevertheless on a number of occasions have been taken up to load salt cod in Labrador, for discharge in western Europe. By the First World War she would probably have changed hands twice, and have been employed entirely in the general home trade. Sold to owners in Appledore in 1914, we can imagine that she was immediately rerigged as a handsome ketch, which meant one hand less in her crew. Having survived the war, making considerable sums for her owners taking coal to north French ports during the conflict, in 1924 our schooner was fitted with a Swedish-made, hot-bulb, semi-diesel auxiliary engine of thirty horse power. She continued working mainly in the trade to southern Irish ports from the Bristol Channel until the Second World War, during which time she was employed entirely inside the Bristol Channel, mostly with coal from Lydney in Gloucestershire to north Devon. In 1948 she was fitted with a new engine of forty horse power; at the same time her topmast was sent down and her mainmast lengthened with a piece scarphed on to it and poled off. By 1958 she could no longer be kept in the condition necessary for her to be given a load-line by the Board of Trade Surveyor. She was sold for conversion to a yacht, but her purchaser had neither the resources nor the knowledge to complete the work and she was in fact far beyond conversion short of a complete rebuild. After several changes of ownership we can imagine that she was abandoned in a Devon creek. Her floor timbers and keelson could still be seen in 1988, weed and shellfish encrusted, at low water.

Glossary

The technical terms used in this book are all explained in either the text itself or the drawings. As with rigging and sailing terms, many basic expressions are widely used, but there is no standard technical terminology. The brief notes which follow are not, therefore, definitive, but a short supplement to the text.

Batten Length of square-edged flexible wood used for fairing (*q.v.*).

Bevel A surface of timber which has been shaped at an angle so that it can fit another timber.

Bilge The part of a vessel which lies below the upward turn of the floors or first futtocks. 'Turn of the bilge' is the general area in both the inside and the outside of the vessel where the change in shape from near horizontal to near vertical takes place.

Blind fastening A fastening which does not break through to the surface at the far end from which it is driven. The common nail is a blind fastening.

Boat The many common definitions of boat and ship clearly illustrate the wide differences in usage which have existed. A boat has been succinctly described by the late Eric McKee and Professor Séan McGrail.: 'A boat being smaller than a ship is unable to support the life of those on board for long periods. Boats tend to be owned by their users, while those in ships are paid to be there.'

Body plan A drawing (usually one part of a three-part drawing of a boat or vessel which is referred to as a draft or the lines) showing the half breadths or transverse vertical sections.

Butt To place a piece of timber squarely against another.

Caulk To insert stopping in a seam, after the adjoining components have been fastened, in order to make it watertight.

Cleat A short, shaped length of wood or metal used for turning up ropes.

Counter The integral part of the hull which projects aft of the stern post out over the water. This may be flat or slightly curved – a transom counter – or strongly curved and shaped – an eliptical counter.

Deadrise The angle the bottom of a vessel makes with the horizontal athwartships.

Deadwood The inner timbers which give additional strength to the junction of stem and sternpost with keel and keelson.

Draft *See* **Body plan.**

Drag The amount the after end of the keel of a vessel is lower than the forward end when the vessel is afloat and in normal laden trim.

Entry The underwater forebody of a vessel.

Fair A line is fair when it passes through its guide marks in a continuous curve without abrupt changes.

Fairing The act of checking that such lines can be drawn in full size on the scrieve board.

Fay To fit closely.

Faying surfaces Two surfaces which fit closely.

Floor *See* **Frame.**

Frame An athwartships assembly of timber providing a rib-like unit of the skeleton of the vessel. Its component parts are named floor, futtocks and top timber.

Full ended A vessel which has a full, burdensome hull with ample buoyancy in the entry and run.

Futtocks *See* **Frame.** The term is also used (as futtock shrouds) to describe that part of the topmast and topgallantmast shrouds of a square-rigged mast which lie between the top or the crosstrees and the spiderband on the lower mast or topmast.

Garboard The strake next to the keel.

Hanging knee A vertical timber or iron knee.

Hood end The end of a strake which butts into a rabbet; the hooded or hidden end.

Joggle To cut out a notch. Covering boards at the deck edges are joggled to take the shaped ends of the deck planks.

Landing A surface available for making a plank joint.

Laying off Drawing out the lines of a vessel full size on a loft floor or scrieve board.

Lines *See* **Body plan.**

Line off To work out the shape of the strakes and how they are to be run.

Lodging knee A horizontal timber or iron knee.

Mast step A wooden or metal fitting or shaping of the keelson used to locate and secure the heel of a mast.

Mould Wooden pattern used to convey frame shapes from the loft floor to the sawyers.

Plank A component of a strake (*q.v.*). Planking refers to the whole outer skin of a vessel.

Rabbet, Rabbit, Rebate A groove or channel worked into a timber to accept the sides or end of another.

Rivet To beat the end of a metal fastening so as to form it into a head.

Run The underwater afterbody of a vessel.

Scarf, Scarph, Scarve A tapered joint between two pieces of timber of similar section at the joint.

Seam The junction of two members required to be watertight.

Sheer The curve of the upper edge of the hull.

Ship *See* **Boat.**

Sided The dimension of a timber which remains constant and indicates the thickness of the material from which it may be converted.

Station Position on the keel or a mould or frame.

Strake A combination of planks running from one end of the vessel to the other.

Through fastening A fastening which passes through all the parts being joined.

Topside The part of the side of a vessel which is above water at any time.

Transom An assembly of boards, often curved in shape, which comprises the afterend of a transom counter.

Treenail, Trenail, Trunnel Wooden peg through fastening.

Tumblehome A vessel is said to have tumblehome when her beam narrows as the topsides rise. Obvious examples which can be seen today are the steamship *The Great Britain* at Bristol and H.M.S. *Victory* at Portsmouth.

Vessel A ship of moderate size.

Wale A thick strake.

index

9776